THE WOMEN OF COURTWATCH

UNIVERSITY OF TEXAS PRESS 🐂 AUSTIN

THE WOMEN OF
COURTWATCH

Reforming a
Corrupt Family Court System

CAROLE BELL FORD

First edition, 2005

Requests for permission to reproduce
material from this work should be sent to:

PERMISSIONS
University of Texas Press
P.O. Box 7819
Austin, TX 78713-7819

⊗ The paper used in this book meets
the minimum requirements of
ANSI / NISO Z39.48-1992 (R1997)
(Permanence of Paper).

Library of Congress Cataloging-in-Publication Data

Ford, Carole Bell, 1934–
    The women of CourtWatch : reforming a corrupt family court system /
Carole Bell Ford.— 1st ed.
        p.   cm.
    Includes bibliographical references and index.
    ISBN 0-292-70682-0 (hardcover : alk. paper) —
    ISBN 0-292-70958-7 (pbk. : alk. paper)
    1. Kusnetz, Florence.   2. Lawyers—Texas—Biography.   3. Judical corruption—
Texas—Harris County.   4. Domestic relations courts—Texas—Harris County.
I. Title.
    KF373.K827F67   2005
    346.764′141015′0269—dc22

                                                            2004025535

To my beloved daughter, Julie.

Always, her reply is,
"Yes, I can. Yes, I can!"

If you will tell me why the fen
appears impassable, I then
will tell you why I think that I
can get across it if I try.

—MARIANNE MOORE (1887–1972)

Contents

Acknowledgments

In addition to Florence Kusnetz, who is first and foremost, there are many Houstonians who need to be thanked for their help with this project. They shared hours of their time in the midst of pressing professional schedules: Melanie Harrell; Diana Compton; Family Court Judges Bonnie Hellums, Mary Sean O'Reilly, and Linda Motheral; attorneys Maureen Peltier and Kay Kreck. Randy Burton, founder and director of Justice for Children, was extraordinarily generous with his time and sent valuable material from his personal files. Howard Kusnetz was helpful many, many times in many ways since the outset of this work. These people *are* the story of CourtWatch; it couldn't possibly have been told without them.

Thanks also to two accomplished writers and biographers who are good friends as well. Gerald Sorin and Robert Polito read early drafts of the manuscript and gave sound advice as well as much-appreciated encouragement. Ellen James, a retired attorney and former teacher of legal writing who, I'm happy to say, is a new friend, read drafts and offered important corrections as well as suggestions. My lifelong friend Marjorie Osman, a gifted writer and storyteller, helped me solve a particularly vexing structural problem. And I want to thank my son, Gregg Isaacson, for helping in so many ways with photos and data and fixing dozens of annoying computer glitches.

Myra Sorin read and edited the first draft of the manuscript with enthusiasm and unfailing sensitivity to nuance. Most times she sits on my shoulder when I'm writing, pointing out sentence fragments. Or worse—"Jargon!" Or asks for clarity—"Huh?" But in the end, when I've been complacent since I know she will fix it, she spots every misplaced semicolon.

William Bishel, sponsoring editor at the University of Texas Press, thought this was a book worth publishing, even before it was completed. When I did finish the final draft he passed me on to his capable Editorial Fellow Alex Barron, who quickly responded to my concerns and questions with good advice and an infectious energy. She was wonderful to work with.

Finally, my sincerest thanks to my husband Steve Ford, who likes to pass himself off as an anti-intellectual. Nevertheless, he is my first reader and most important, discriminating, and honest critic.

THE WOMEN OF COURTWATCH

Introduction

"After you talk to my wife, you just might want to write a book about her."
— HOWARD KUSNETZ

One day in the spring of 1993, the phone rang at the home of Florence Kusnetz, a recently retired family law attorney in Houston, Texas. Florence was surprised to hear that the caller was FBI Special Agent Kathy Loedler; after a brief conversation, the two women agreed to meet for lunch the next day. The consequence of that meeting was CourtWatch, a political action committee of about two hundred volunteers, all but one of whom were women.

The women of CourtWatch did what they were told couldn't be done. They drove a group of powerful and entrenched family court judges off the bench—someone called CourtWatch "the babes who slew the Goliath" (Rodriguez). It was quite a victory. In the election of November 1994, newcomers to the Houston family courts replaced all but two incumbents. Now that more than a decade has passed, it's possible to look back upon the spectrum of events which began with a phone call, led to the formation of CourtWatch, and ultimately resulted in the major reform of a large, urban, and very seriously troubled family court system.

Over that 1993 lunch at an Italian restaurant, Agent Loedler disclosed some confidential information to Florence Kusnetz. During the previous three years, the Bureau had been investigating allegations of corruption involving some judges on the family court bench of Harris County, in which Houston is located. Florence wasn't surprised; the FBI investigation of the bench was only one of several taking place at the time. One statewide task force was looking into questions of judicial appointments, while another was examining allegations of judicial misconduct; a gender bias task force was about to publish its findings; and the results of an informal investigative report in the form of a television documentary called *America Undercover: Women on Trial* had recently been broadcast. The film, produced by the actor and director Lee Grant, focused on several shocking custody cases in which there were allegations of child abuse and in which the alleged abusers had been granted custody of the children. Houston was accustomed to being in the spotlight, but it was shaken by this notoriety.

Agent Loedler had sought Florence out because she'd learned that Florence had been at odds with the family court system for many years. Florence Kusnetz had spent much of her career in family law finding alternatives to what she described as the "bloody domestic battles" acted out in the courts—battles in which children not only were innocent victims but were also used as weapons.[1] Loedler hoped Florence would be able to help the investigation, but Florence had no information "that had solid evidence behind it." However, she told Loedler what was being said: "The talk is that judges play poker with the big money lawyers and that paper bags of cash change hands at these games. Also, I heard that some lawyers gave judges their credit cards to use on trips to Las Vegas. Some claimed that these lawyers had an open line to the judges and often got favorable rulings that were unwarranted by the evidence."

And, according to Florence, there was a lot of socializing between judges and certain attorneys who ended up appointed in special capacities on many cases. The lawyers then took in large fees, which were paid, in addition to their legal fees, by the divorcing parties.

For reasons that remain uncertain—perhaps political pressure, perhaps lack of evidence, perhaps something more insidious—the FBI investigation was subsequently abandoned. But Loedler had urged Florence to contact Melanie Harrell. In a public forum, Melanie had recently confronted some of the family court judges for alleged cronyism. "You are of like mind," Loedler said. Florence remembers:

I called Melanie and we met. We spent two hours finding out that we both felt something needed to be done about reforming the family courts. I told her I had had this idea for several years, of forming a committee to educate the public about the abuses of the courts and the need to shed some light on what was going on. After all, the family courts were the ones most people were likely to have contact with, and they didn't know anything about what was going on there.

I remember telling Melanie that I had a great deal of mental energy but little physical energy and would welcome help from some young people to explore what we could do. She suggested we have a first meeting at her friend Diana Compton's house where the three of us, and those we invite, could talk about the best way of bringing about change.

The three women—Florence, Melanie, and Diana—later thoughtlessly dismissed by a critic as "housewives dabbling in politics," would, on the contrary, prove to be formidable advocates for reform.

CourtWatch was conceived at the meeting in Diana's home, and in Florence the group had found its leader. In the Houston legal community she was known as an innovative family law attorney and a feisty and forceful opponent. The fact that she had retired from her twenty-year practice was thought to be an advantage, since Florence seemed immune to reprisals from the bench. As it turned out, she was not, but that is part of the story to come.

The story of CourtWatch is the record of a successful grassroots reform movement that offers a model for communities struggling against judicial systems originally meant for their protection that have since gone astray. Unfortunately, according to recent studies by the highly respected American Law Institute, American Bar Association, and other groups, there are many such communities throughout the country.

But the history of CourtWatch is more than a case study. Entwined with the tale of CourtWatch is another success story, the story of a woman, a homemaker for almost twenty years, who became an attorney when she was forty-four years old. Photos of Florence Kusnetz taken during her early years as a lawyer show a small trim woman with short dark hair and big dark eyes; she doesn't turn away from the camera. That was in the early 1970s, a time when few women were admitted to law schools and even fewer mature women were entering the profession.

During the succeeding twenty years, Florence had a significant impact upon the practice of family law in Houston. She provided the first alternative to the divorce courts by introducing mediation as a method for resolving family disputes. She helped found an organization of family mediators who advocated and promoted the process. And she established an association of attorneys who were committed to practicing family law in a collaborative, rather than adversarial, manner.

Houston was an unlikely place for Florence to have settled so comfortably

and successfully. It was, in every respect, light years removed from Brownsville, where she was born and raised—not Brownsville, Texas, but a Jewish, immigrant, working-class neighborhood of the same name in Brooklyn,
New York. Yet, because Florence would bring the values and attitudes she
acquired in the Brooklyn community to her work as a Houston family law
attorney, the two communities would become oddly joined.

Florence's decision to direct the CourtWatch reform effort was an expression of her social consciousness. And it was consistent with the deeply held
Jewish values she internalized as she grew up within the shared culture of
Brownsville. Among these is her commitment to the concept of *tikkun olam,*
a Hebrew phrase which translates roughly as the "repair and improvement
of the world"—literally, to fix the universe. *Tikkun olam* is not an option
for Jews but rather one of the most profound and lifelong obligations of the
Jewish faith. It accounts, in good measure, for the disproportionately large
number of Jews of Florence's generation who were involved in radical and
liberal social movements, as well as in the helping professions.

Still, Florence admits that she did try to resist being recruited into the
fledgling reform movement and what was to become CourtWatch. She
was genuinely torn; the timing was very bad. Her husband, Howard, had
recently retired from a successful career of his own with Shell Oil, as an
expert in occupational health and safety. Florence and Howard agreed that
the last thing she needed at that point in her life was another demanding
project; she was just beginning to enjoy her retirement.

Fortunately for Houston, Florence sensed her own importance to the
reform effort. Her decision was not quite so fortunate for Howard, who
knew that for the duration he'd enjoy less of his wife's company. Yet he also
knew that Florence was not able to refuse; she had been fighting the family courts for too many years to turn away. She may have retired from her
professional practice, but she wasn't absolved from her social responsibility, from *tikkun olam.* And, by accepting the commitment to CourtWatch,
Florence was acknowledging yet another obligation, an admonition to all
Jews that can be found in a collection of Biblical commentary known as the
Mishnah: "It is not incumbent upon you to finish the task, yet neither are
you free to give up."

I first learned about Florence Kusnetz and CourtWatch while researching a book, *The Girls,* about women who grew up in Brownsville. Florence
responded to an ad I'd placed in the alumni newspaper of the high school
she'd attended, but she was out when I called back. Howard answered the

phone. When I told him why I was calling, he said, prophetically (actually, I suspect he fixed the idea in my mind): "After you talk to my wife, you just might want to write a book about *her*." He was right.

By the end of this first of many conversations with Florence—a phone call that lasted about three hours—not only was I impressed by the story of CourtWatch but by Florence herself. She was an ideal role model: a woman successful in both her domestic and professional lives. With determina-tion—sometimes sheer stubbornness—she overcame a succession of for-midable barriers. She grew up in a poor, immigrant family. She lived in a community, and at a time, where there were many cultural prohibitions and limited expectations for women. She confronted prejudice related to her age and gender when she returned to school as a mature student, and she chose to enter a profession that was not only male-dominated but was very hostile to women.

Florence and I spoke for the first time in 1996, only two years after CourtWatch's achievements. As soon as I was able, I set about trying to understand the events, as well as the philosophical, historical, and social context that formed the background for CourtWatch. I knew little, but I managed to learn the basics. I had a crash course in "Family Law 101," with Florence as my mentor. Under her guidance, I read countless pages of news-paper accounts, as well as books and other literature dealing with the nature of the law, family law, gender, and issues related to divorce and children in domestic crisis. I found that a fuller understanding of the history of women and the law helped me understand the circumstances surrounding the devel-opment of the reform movement; consequently, there are occasional digres-sions into some of these areas in this book. These will not provide new information for those already informed, but will enrich the story for the lay reader.

My first visit to Houston was not until December 1999. I went through the arrival gate at the Houston airport a bit anxiously, looking for a couple I knew only through photos. But I recognized Howard right away. He had assured me that I would; he said to look for someone wearing a souvenir hat from the Houston Opera's production of *Hansel and Gretel*.

Florence didn't quite look as I had expected from her photographs. Her hair was lighter and, since her retirement, her contours gentler. But I rec-ognized her voice from our many telephone conversations. It has a slight hoarseness, which softens her speech. When she smiles, her eyes sparkle. All of this seduces you into thinking that she is just another mid-seventyish

Florence and Howard Kusnetz were married in 1950. They are seen here in 1994 at a family gathering. Photo courtesy of Florence Kusnetz.

Jewish grandmother and belies her forthright, direct, no-nonsense attitude. Lurking behind the sweetness and roundness is a formidable intellect, firm opinions, and impatience with illogical thinking. And she loathes injustice.

As the story unfolds you will meet other women (and a few supportive men) who initiated reform by exposing the complex problems endemic in the Harris County Family Courts and all too similar to problems elsewhere. Women such as Melanie Harrell and Diana Compton. Women with the unlikely names of Donna Ringoringo and Phrogge (pronounced "Froggy") Simons. Family court judges Bonnie Hellums, Mary Sean O'Reilly, and Linda Motheral. Men such as Randy Burton, founder of Justice for Children. And others like Mary Frances Parker and Sandi Hebert, who are survivors of the system.

The momentum of their protests against alleged abuses in the courts drove the reform movement forward, led to the organization of CourtWatch and ultimately resulted in its success.

PART I

CHAPTER I

Before CourtWatch

A Broken System

"The Mary Frances Parker case got Houston focused on what was happening down there at the Family Law Center; the city erupted."

— DIANA COMPTON

I n October of 1992 Home Box Office broadcast a shocking documentary called *America Undercover: Women on Trial,* one of the events leading to the development of CourtWatch. By that time the family court system of Houston, that is Harris County, had acquired such a notorious reputation that it had attracted the attention of Lee Grant, the actor, director, and social activist who directed the film. *America Undercover: Women on Trial* included disturbing courtroom footage as it documented four particularly difficult domestic disputes. In each of these cases, custody was granted to fathers who had been accused of molesting their children; one was a previously convicted rapist. (This was the Parker-Casterline case that Diana Compton was referring to in the quote above.) For Diana, the case confirmed what she already believed: the family court system in Houston "was broken." Irreparably, she thought.

Of course, the film could have caused an immediate furor and then been forgotten, but that didn't happen. Dean Huckabee, one of the judges shown in the film, decided to sue Lee Grant and HBO for libel, charging that the documentary was biased, and fortunately, the documentary itself and the subsequent notoriety over the libel suit kept the issues alive. A *Houston Chronicle* writer facetiously thanked Judge Huckabee: "Perhaps now a full investigation of the Harris County Family Law Center will take place" (Rafferty).

The publicity surrounding the film also drew attention to a protest that Donna Ringoringo and Rose Abraham had initiated earlier that year outside the courthouse (called the Family Law Center) in downtown Houston. It had turned into a vigil. For over a year, well into the spring of 1994,

One year into the protest at the Houston courthouse, Harris County's Family Law Center.
Photo courtesy of Mary Frances Parker.

the women were joined by scores of additional protesters who took over a
sprawling space on the sidewalk that ultimately contained more than fifty
signs, three beds, a table and chairs, and a filing cabinet. If that spectacle
wasn't sufficient, Ringoringo kept media attention focused on alleged abuses
in the family courts by periodically staging melodramatic episodes such as
chaining herself to the columns of the courthouse when the protestors were
threatened with eviction.

At the same time that these boisterous public events were occurring,
Houston family law attorney Florence Kusnetz was meeting with Melanie
Harrell and Diana Compton. The women formed a small but growing
group of Houston women who quietly developed a strategy to oust the
most powerful and politically entrenched judges on the family court bench.
This was CourtWatch.

For more than a decade, serious charges had been mounting against a
number of Harris County Family Court judges; Huckabee, the judge who
was suing Lee Grant, was one of them. By the early 1990s, the charges added

up to a formidable list: accusations of cronyism in the form of a good old boys network through which certain attorneys who were "in the loop" could count on certain judges for favorable decisions; allegations of flagrant abuses of the political system, particularly regarding contributions by lawyers to judges' election campaigns; sexism and racism; incompetence; and claims of corruption that included bribery and fraud. Yet there had not been an organized effort to unseat those judges until the above series of events occurred, which coalesced the opposition into an explosive critical mass.

No one knows exactly why the Harris County Family Courts were so troubled. Certainly they were overburdened, as they still are today, more than a decade later. In the Harris County Family Court system, nine judges were handling a caseload equivalent to approximately 10 percent of the entire civil trial docket for the state of Texas, or about 27,000 new cases a year. The family courts had jurisdiction over 400,000 children (Barth, 29). The judges dealt with divorce, child support, child custody, paternity, and other suits including a large number of cases involving family violence. Caseload alone, however, doesn't provide an answer for why the Houston courts had so many problems. In that respect, Houston was not unique among major American cities. But Houston was and is unique in other ways, both in its modern history and in its particular urban character.

"Houston has never been like other cities," where people settled because of "beauty or climate or because [they are] in any natural way a place to live," says the *New York Times*. In the nineteenth century, Houston was nothing more than a wet plain "cut through only by a sluggish creek colonized already by flocks of mosquitoes and herds of snakes." However, as the center of Texas's oil industry, it quickly became—and still is—a "mecca for making money" (Patterson, 82).

In the 1970s, when Florence's family moved there from Cincinnati, Houston had many things to recommend it as a place to live, including fine universities and cultural institutions[1]—theaters, a ballet, a symphony orchestra, and an innovative opera company. Unfortunately, a recent barrage of negative publicity is giving the false impression, laments Elyse Lanier (wife of a former mayor), that Houston is still an "unstable frontier town" (Patterson, 82).

When Florence Kusnetz and her family first arrived in Houston, there was so much migration from the north feeding the insatiable growth needs of the city that the saying around town was, "The last one out of Detroit, please shut out the lights." Houston grew to become the fourth-largest U.S. city in population (in the second most populous state). And it is huge in area as well; it covers 617 square miles, "enough space to contain Chicago, Philadelphia, Baltimore and Detroit" (Yardley 2000).

In the 1970s Houston was a place of "freewheeling capitalism" that attracted many entrepreneurs. And for decades the interests of business and government were joined in businessmen who also ran the city. Perhaps "unjoined" is a better characterization; they ran the city with the laissez-faire attitude that "government should stay out of the way of business and development" (ibid.).

In those years, Houston developed its peculiarities and idiosyncrasies, its late twentieth-century personality: a post-modern version of a frontier town with all of the contradictions. Family Court Judge Bonnie Hellums characterizes this personality as "extreme rugged individualism, bravado, independence, a willingness to think divergently, an exuberance for life and freedom—sometimes positive, sometimes not." There is an odd blend of respect for law and order and exceptions to the rules. Houston's desire to accommodate the self-made man carries with it a distrust of government regulation, Hellums thinks, as seen in the issue of gun control, for example, where the dominant value system expects men to behave honorably, as men should, but evokes a laugh, a wink, and a nod when it is clear that "boys will be boys." In recent years, with the slight decline in the domination of the petrochemical industry, Houston's personality has been changing, but the change hasn't been an easy one. "In some respects," Judge Hellums says impatiently, "it hasn't changed at all."

One of the charges against the Harris County Family Court judges was, in fact, that they resisted change. An example of this involves mediation.[2] In 1987 the Texas legislature passed one of the best family mediation bills in the country; Florence Kusnetz was among those who fought for its passage. From that time onward, mediation was not mandatory, but it was state policy to use mediation in cases involving parents and children (with one major exception: for a number of reasons which will be discussed later, mediation is not recommended in cases involving domestic violence). Many issues could be resolved through mediation before a family plunged head-long into the distress and expense of a divorce or custody trial.

In Dallas, Fort Worth, Lubbock, Galveston, Midland, and many other Texas jurisdictions, judges immediately began implementing the practice. Only Harris County judges, Florence says, led by opposition from two prominent members of the family court bench, Allen Daggett and Bill Elliott, refused to consider referrals to mediation. Similarly, a 1989 state law which *required* judges to be trained in issues related to domestic violence had never been implemented in the Harris County courts (Ledgard 1992). Harris County judges were able to disregard the statute because of their entrenched political power.

Houston judicial politics, therefore, are very much a part of the Court-Watch story. Whether judges are appointed or elected, as they are in Houston, politics compromises the judicial system. First, as Family Court Judge Bonnie Hellums explains, just running for election is a time-consuming process: "It's a waste of time. You work your tail off for three years. Then you spend that fourth year shaking hands and fund-raising and doing campaign appearances while the county and the state are paying you, instead of staying on the bench and doing what you're supposed to be doing. You work three years so that you can spend a year getting ready to work another three years."[3]

Judge Mary Sean O'Reilly, who is a visiting judge in Houston, believes politics is "in complete collision with our ethical duty as jurists." Yet it is so taken for granted as the norm that few of us are offended or even surprised by the notion of political intrusion into the judicial process. Naïvely, we continue to believe that judges can achieve a high standard of impartiality in interpreting the law—in spite of politics, in spite of their personal values, philosophies, and political orientation, indeed, in spite of numerous court decisions to the contrary. We only have to look at the historical evidence to be reminded that the judicial system is not above or separate from social and political influences.

For example, the historic case upholding segregation, *Plessy v. Ferguson* (1896), and the *Brown* decision to dismantle institutionalized segregation about sixty years later (1954), were diametrically opposite interpretations of the same legal issues. Both questioned whether forced separation was harmful. "Both Courts observed the same reality . . . Plessy saw it from the standpoint of white supremacy; Brown saw it from the standpoint of the black challenge to white supremacy" (MacKinnon, 612). Would the Plessy decision have been reversed if not for the civil rights movement, which resulted in both a changed social consciousness about race and the newly acquired political power of the black community?

Recently, in decisions affecting the outcome of the 2000 presidential election, we saw evidence of how difficult impartiality is to achieve even by the most esteemed judicial body in the United States, the Supreme Court, to which justices are lifetime appointees.[4] The eminent attorneys Alan M. Dershowitz and Richard A. Posner recently wrote books in which they analyzed the Supreme Court's intervention in the 2000 presidential election. An editor for the *New York Times* wrote in his review: "That two such nimble and serious legal thinkers . . . can arrive at such opposing conclusions speaks to the distressingly subjective nature of the law" (Bronner, 11).

How much more difficult, then, is impartiality for Houston judges who not only have to run for reelection but have to run on party lines? In Houston, judges are formally affiliated with one of the major political parties upon which they depend for fund-raising, advertising, and other forms of electoral support. I believe Judge Hellums when she says that party affiliations are irrelevant to her—"I don't make decisions because I'm an 'R' or a 'D'"—but there is considerable potential for partisan politics to taint the courts. It was, and is, a matter of serious concern. "A regular feature" of elections in Houston and elsewhere in Texas was "public outrage over the outsized role of special interest dollars in judicial campaigns" (Diehl). Hellums agrees with critics. "It's one of the things we still need to change," she says.[5]

Unfortunately, the reality is that support by one of the major political parties, being an "R" or a "D," is essential to election or reelection. Consequently, judges may be tempted to show favoritism toward their backers. In Houston, attorneys made up a large share of the judges' campaign contributors, and some judges were not reticent about soliciting funds. Randy Burton, who was chief prosecutor in the Family Offenses Section of the Harris County District Attorney's Office (and later founded the watchdog and advocacy organization Justice for Children),[6] said that some judges were quite outspoken. They would not hesitate to ask an attorney, even one who was in the midst of trying a case before them, if he or she would be attending an upcoming fund-raiser. Randy said that this happened to him on more than one occasion. Others confirmed his experience. "In interviews with litigants, attorneys, and judges," the *Houston Chronicle* learned that attorneys felt "compelled to donate to the family law judges' campaigns." If they did not contribute they risked "jeopardizing their pending and future cases" (Piller, 25 August 1991).

Another area of abuse in the Houston family courts involved potentially lucrative court appointments in which political or financial favors could be returned, legally if not ethically—so-called "clubhouse control of lucrative

How Do :R You Spell ; Extortion? Ad-Litem

Harris County Family Code Definition :
A RROGANT
D ECEITFUL

L IARS
I NEPT
T HREATENING
E GOISM
M EAN while

A
A

S

Children are HUR

One of the most explicit charges made by the protestors was the existence of an old boys network of favoritism and cronyism, particularly in lucrative ad litem appointments. Photo courtesy of Mary Frances Parker.

courthouse patronage" ("New York's Farcical Judicial Elections").[7] Generous sums for providing expert testimony, such as depositions by psychologists, were paid to some court appointees whom attorneys called "hired guns." Others received large fees to act as guardians ad litem. Literally, ad litem is a Latin term that means "for the litigation." It is used to denote someone, usually an attorney, who represents parties who are not able to represent their own interests, such as children. Ad litem fees, which are paid by the litigants, can involve large sums of money. The amounts are determined by the parties and the ad litem appointees, with the judge's approval, and can amount to many thousands of dollars.

Melanie Harrell, a child advocate and former certified public accountant who was one of the founding members of CourtWatch, presented findings related to ad litem appointments in a report to the Texas Supreme Court Task Force investigating appointments by the judiciary. Harrell's report demonstrated a pattern of favoritism in ad litem appointments in Harris County. It showed that 62 percent of Family Court Judge Allen Daggett's appointments between 1989 and 1991 were given to just two attorneys: Michael Stocker and his former partner, T. Wayne Harris. Family Court Judge Bill Elliott's ad litem appointments were questionable as well—

21 percent were given to state legislators. One of those legislators, Senfronia Thompson, was the chair of the Judicial Affairs Committee, which has control over bills affecting the judiciary (Lenhart).

Judges subject to partisan elections are vulnerable to undue pressure and influence. But in Houston, at least one judge was charged with offenses that were not tied to politics, at least not directly. In 1993, Harris County Family Court Judge Henry G. Schuble was accused of fraud in a federal civil suit, for allegedly scheming with an estranged husband and others to destroy a woman's business, which had been put in receivership. A receiver, under the direction of the court, takes control of family assets such as real estate or businesses and can either operate them or sell them (Pack). Judges appoint receivers when property issues are in dispute—another responsibility that can be corrupted. As Florence Kusnetz explained, posing a hypothetical scenario:

Suppose, just suppose, for a moment that the receiver was a member of the good old boy network that the judge belongs to. And then suppose that the case before the judge has some prime property, which is very valuable. And then suppose that the receiver is told to sell that property to pay part of the costs of the case. The receiver offers the real estate for sale, and then suppose that the buyer is one of the good old boys, or if they are more cautious, an agent working for one of them.

Then the agent bids on the property at a price that is considerably under the market value. And suppose the property is sold at this bargain price, and then suppose that after a subsequent series of transfers, the property ends up in the portfolio of the judge's wife, son, daughter, or best buddy.

Consequently, fraud and collusion were included in the ever-growing list of alleged abuses in Houston, to which gender and racial discrimination were also added.

At the time that CourtWatch was evolving from a small ad hoc group into a coherent organization, finally a woman was appointed as one of the nine judges on the bench. Governor Ann Richards had recently appointed Linda Motheral to fill a vacancy. Motheral had been a family law attorney and, prior to her appointment, an associate judge. In that capacity Motheral initiated some programs new to Houston, including one in which divorcing couples with children were required to participate called "Children Cope with Divorce." (This was a nationwide program to teach parents the impact of divorce on their children.) Another of Motheral's projects was a pilot program administered through Baylor Medical College in which mental health evaluations were conducted in abuse cases to determine appropriate custody and visitation rulings. Motheral's appointment was cheered by Donna Ringoringo, leader of the protest at the Family Law Center, and was "widely praised by her colleagues in the legal community as well as by leaders of citizen organizations" (Harper, 2 January 1993). Susie Alverson, of Justice for Children, said, "We are hoping that this is the beginning to the end of a very bleak situation in our family courts" (quoted in Harper, 2 January 1993).

There was, then, one woman on the bench. But there were no Latinos. And there was one black judge. A proposal had been presented to the state legislature that, it was hoped, would result in more minority representation (Barth). Although the party organizations were ultimately responsible for selecting candidates, the judges played a surreptitious political role. One reason, given by an "insider," for the lack of women on the bench could have applied equally to any challenger: "Many women who practice family law were afraid that if they decided to run, the judge might take it out on their clients" (Kennedy).

Harris County judges were not only being criticized by the public but also by many within the legal profession itself. A poll taken by the Houston Bar Association in September of 1993 asked its members to rate judges as outstanding, average, or poor on six qualities including impartiality, courtesy, and whether they follow the law. The attorneys were asked to rate only those judges they had actually practiced before, to avoid responses based solely on the judges' reputations. More than half the lawyers gave a poor rating to three family court judges: Allen J. Daggett, Henry G. Schuble, and Bill Elliott. In fact, only one of the family court judges, Linda Motheral, Governor Richards's recent appointee, was termed outstanding by a majority of poll participants (but as someone pointed out, she couldn't reform the courts by herself). There was a large gap between Motheral's rating (64 percent outstanding, 6 percent poor) and that of the next highest rated judge, John Montgomery (33 percent outstanding, 30 percent poor).

When questioned about the poll, one family court judge dismissed it by saying that a miscarriage of justice only occurred in 20 to 30 percent of the cases! ("Contempt of Court"). His attitude was especially troubling because the effects of those miscarriages were multiplied many times over—they involved not only individuals but also families. The decisions handed down by family court judges affect hundreds of thousands of people. Florence Kusnetz makes an important point: it is in family court that most Americans find themselves engaged with the legal system, not in criminal or civil courts. And we know that there continues to be an ever-rising number of divorces in this country; more than half of American marriages are likely to end in divorce (Wallerstein).

Incompetence and abuses by family court judges—racism, sexism, fraud, favoritism, and political wheeling and dealing—have far-reaching consequences. And in Houston, decisions made in family courts had an even greater impact than elsewhere, since Houston had an exceptionally high divorce rate. In 1990, shortly before Florence retired from her law practice, the divorce rate in Harris County had already peaked. But it was still 75 percent higher than in Cook County, Chicago and Los Angeles County, and 50 percent higher than in New York City. In boom times Houston was ranked as having the third-highest divorce rate in the *world* (Barth, 29).

Besides the fact that grounds for divorce in Houston were lenient, there were many theories to account for Houston's particularly high divorce rate. It may have been a result of the city's high transient population—people moved there without the support of their extended families. Perhaps it was because there were a lot of rich people living in Houston, among whom divorce tended to be more common than among the less advantaged. One writer suggested that as Houston's economy retreated from boom times, spouses who had become used to the ease of an affluent lifestyle blamed each other when they found themselves "without housekeepers, without beach homes, without ranch homes" (Barth, 31). Whatever the reason, divorce in Houston was rampant, if difficult and very expensive.

Not surprisingly, in too many cases, the outcome of a Harris County divorce dispute favored the rich, the powerful, and the politically connected. They were generally represented by attorneys who were part of a good old boys network (not necessarily male—some females were included). "Many family attorneys and litigants," a journalist reported, "agree that the family courts tend to be a system where people with more money stand a better chance of winning their case, and where it pays to have a lawyer who is friendly with the judge" (Piller, 25 August 1991). Harris County Family Court judges were, many believed, using their power, both decision-making power and discretionary power, to interpret the law in favor of particular clients or attorneys. This point may need some elaboration.

According to Florence Kusnetz, "Family court judges operate under a document, the *Family Code.*" It provides all of what is called the "black-letter law" that judges and lawyers use to bring cases to court. These are the statutes, regulations, and rules of procedure that have been passed by the legislature. Like any legal document, the *Family Code* tries to cover all of the procedures that are necessary to handle a case. The problem is, Florence says, the facts of every legal case are always different in some ways from every other case. And ambiguities in how to apply the code are common.

Deciding which facts to take into consideration in applying the *Family Code*—fact finding—is one area of judicial decision making or judicial discretion. Florence believes it is a judge's most important function—especially family court judges. Marie Munier, a prosecutor who headed the Family Criminal Law Division at the Harris County District Attorney's Office in the early 1990s, pointed out that "things are spelled out a lot closer" in the criminal courts than in family court (quoted in Piller, 25 August 1991). Therefore, family court judges have broader discretionary powers than do criminal court judges.

Other instances of judicial discretion occur in cases in which the facts themselves are disputed. In these cases we look to the judge for an impartial and unbiased interpretation of the disputed evidence. But ultimately, a judge's decision is subjective. What's more, because it is very difficult to have a judge's ruling reversed in the family courts, Houston's family court judges, Florence says, had "virtually unlimited powers to rule as they wished."[8]

It is very difficult to reverse a family court judge's ruling for several reasons. Because the family code is not as "spelled out" as the criminal code, family court judges have much greater latitude in applying their discretionary powers. And it is too expensive for most people to challenge a ruling and take a case to the next level of appeal. "Most people with average incomes," Florence says, "were broke afterwards," even if they had some financial resources at the beginning of a divorce or custody case. "Justice was unavailable for people without legal fees. The judges knew this and became even bolder."

Whether or not there was deliberate bias, women were the chief victims in these situations. Because men usually earn more than their wives and tend to control the family finances during the marriage, it is women who are generally at a financial disadvantage in divorce cases.[9] Family courts throughout the country favor those with money and power, particularly in cases where litigants can be brought back into court numerous times, racking up legal fees as a form of harassment. There is an overabundance of examples, not limited to Houston, that show that money equals justice.

Emotions always run high in divorce cases, but long, drawn-out custody battles make the situation even more complicated and far more expensive—

and Texas was the worst place in the country to have a custody dispute.[10] Texas was and continues to be one of only two states (the other is Alabama) that allows lengthy jury trials in custody and divorce cases. Either party can request a jury trial but women rarely do, and not only because of the expense: in disputed cases women are likely to lose custody of their children.[11] Consequently, women would agree to unreasonable settlements not only "through the threat and fear of loss of their children but also through the prospect of formidable and prohibitive expense" (MacKinnon, 615).

In Houston at the time, the average cost of a custody trial ranged from $25,000 to $100,000 in attorney fees, court fees, and payments for the cost of psychologists, psychiatrists, and ad litems (those attorneys, or others, who are appointed to act as a child's advocate). The outcome of a custody decision was often, too often, a result of who had more money, rather than who was the better parent. Many women decided to settle on the eve of a jury trial, after years of painful negotiation, and often it was because the money had simply run out. One woman, upon giving up a custody struggle, said: "It was turning into a slaughterhouse. It was awful . . . And not one time did anyone discuss what was in the best interest of the kids" (Barth, 31).

Even if the dispute did not reach such an extreme, attorneys' fees ranged from $100 to $400 an hour. Florence often said to clients: "Look, you can send my kids to college or your kids to college, which do you want?" But she was rare. One high-priced lawyer, speaking anonymously, admitted that attorneys took advantage of the emotional vulnerability of the clients; their fees could "empty the litigant's bank accounts and often those of relatives as well" (Piller, 25 August 1991). Nor was it only women who were complaining about the expense of settling domestic disputes. Representatives of FAIR, a national fathers' support group, and Texas Fathers for Equal Rights, expressed the same grievances. Among the most compelling objections of well-intentioned men struggling to support two households was the high cost of attorney services. One father, who had been denied visitation because he fell behind on child-support payments, had to drop his appeal. He was understandably bitter: it seemed obvious, he said, that if he could afford a lawyer he would be able to pay the child support. FAIR's national program director wondered where the logic was in a system that caused fathers "to support their attorneys and not their children" (quoted in Kaplan).

Although Houston was not the setting for his memoir, *Washington Post* journalist Nathan McCall recalled his experience with the family courts at about this very time in his book *It Makes Me Wanna Holler*—his tale is instructive since it's typical. When he was young, McCall had spent some time in prison and was not a stranger to the court system. But "compared to my divorce," he wrote, "doing time . . . was like a day at the beach." If pressed, I imagine he would admit to some exaggeration, although his passion was intense. "Divorce is *hell*, pure and simple," he continued, "a classic example of how screwed-up and backward-thinking the court system is." By the time he and his wife had gone through what seemed to be "an endless series of hearings and postponements that stretched out for more than a year," their original hostilities had had "ample time to simmer and grow." McCall wrote:

More than in any other ordeal in my crazy life, my frustrations with the courts during and after my divorce showed me that the folks running the system don't have a clue. Nothing in that process works as it should. Nobody has figured out a way to make divorce fair to all concerned. Some women get shafted beyond belief, while others abuse the system . . . Some men abandon their parental duties and skip out, certain that the system can't or won't track them down . . . And children get caught in the middle of all that mess.

For McCall, the case was simple. He couldn't afford to pay the support his wife was asking for and have enough money left over for his own needs. She was awarded half of his take-home pay (five hundred dollars a month) plus monthly mortgage payments of nearly seven hundred dollars. He discussed it with his attorney:

"I'm not saying I refuse to pay child support. I'm saying I can't pay that full amount and survive. Isn't there somebody I can talk to, to explain?"
"No."
Then he looked at me and did what lawyers often do. He shrugged his shoulders and said, "That's just the way it is."
In no time, I got caught in that recurring cycle that body-slams lots of men after divorce. Every time I fell behind on support payments, Debbie filed an action to take me to court. Every time I went to court, it forced me to spend money on legal fees. (The judge would order me to pay her lawyer too.) That was money that could have been used to catch up on support payments. It went round and round like that . . . (McCall, 379–383)

Added to the support payments and legal fees was the cost of setting up a separate household. McCall used all of his savings and went deeper and deeper into debt. He borrowed from friends and family, applied for bank loans, and finally exhausted all his resources. It was only because he got his job with the *Washington Post* that he managed to survive the ordeal.[12]

There is no question that much of what was wrong with the Harris County family court system was also wrong with family court systems all over the country. But in Harris County, the problems were exceptional because they were so abundant and so extreme. In the years leading up to the 1994 election, formal and informal charges included all of those discussed earlier: abuse of political power and influence, favoritism and cronyism, discrimination, fraud and bribery. However, the coup de grace—what would finally drive Harris County family court judges from the bench—was the gross abuse of their discretionary powers in cases involving allegations of child abuse.

Attention became focused on the Harris County family courts because of several particularly notorious cases in which there were allegations of child sexual abuse. These were not sex abuse cases involving deranged, lurking strangers; more than half of the accused were male acquaintances and close relatives of the victims, who were usually, although not exclusively, young girls. At that time it was reported that sexual abuse of girls under eighteen was as high as 45 percent; a comparable figure for boys was 10 percent (Baer). Contrary to the perception of several attorneys that when "female clients allege abuse or violence, the judge immediately believes them" (*Gender Bias Task Force of Texas Final Report*, 52), most Harris County family court judges found such allegations very difficult to accept. To be fair, however, denial was not limited to Harris County judges.

Throughout the nation there was (and is) a singular and stubborn resistance to accepting allegations of sexual abuse despite attention drawn to the subject by fiction, nonfiction, television, and films. Randy Burton doesn't find it surprising. He had been chief prosecutor for the Harris County District Attorney's Office in their Family Offenses Section prior to founding the child advocacy organization Justice for Children in 1987. Since then, he has devoted the better part of his legal career to documenting cases of child abuse (although to avoid even the appearance of benefiting from his advocacy work, he does not accept cases involving an abused child for which he would receive a fee.)[13] Burton says that although first-degree child sexual assault is rape, a criminal act which must be treated as such, it is "such a repugnant idea, an instinctive response is to deny or repress it."

Harris County Judge Bill Elliott was one of those in denial. He simply couldn't believe that a father could abuse his own child. "It is beyond me," he said. Then he added what he thought was the greater problem: "Over the years I have seen how repeated interviews with psychologists and medical examinations have done far more damage to the child than maybe one or two actual abuses that might have occurred" (quoted in Gillece, 15).

Unfortunately, there was another reason for Elliott's dismissive attitude. Some attorneys had begun to indiscriminately exploit charges of sexual abuse as a tactic in custody cases. Even if there were only a few, they gave already-skeptical judges another reason to doubt the allegations. This may account for the willingness of Family Court Judge Robert Webb, in one sensational case, to have accepted a psychological report based upon an interview with a child "*in the father's presence*" (ibid.) and to view damaging physical evidence—a rash on the inside of a child's thigh, evidence of rape, and a diagnosis of *trichomoniasis,* a sexually transmitted disease—with skepticism. When the examining physician wrote, in a Child Protective Services intake report, that the child could only have gotten the infection through intercourse, the father's attorney (a woman, incidentally) accused the mother of an elaborate scheme. "I wouldn't put it past that woman to have inoculated the child with the trichomonas herself," she said (ibid.).

It seemed that many sexual abuse charges were presumed at the outset, among some family court judges, to be false. "If a child complains of sexual abuse, especially if the abuse involves the father, the response from the court is to put the parent who believes the child on trial" (Gillece, 12–13). A prosecutor in the Harris County Family Criminal Law Division said that she had spoken to some women whose attorneys had advised them "to keep allegations of child abuse out of the court" (Piller, 26 August 1991). In a diabolical version of *Alice in Wonderland* logic, "the courts will transfer custody to the alleged perpetrator under the rationale that the parent who believes the child's story has actually brainwashed the child into believing these awful things" (Gillece, 13).

In January 1991, Judge Allen Daggett precipitated a crisis when he gave temporary custody of a three-year-old to her father, Robert Casterline. Not only had Casterline been accused of molesting the little girl, but he was a convicted rapist! The case, which received a great deal of publicity, outraged Melanie Harrell and Diana Compton and prompted them to begin scrutinizing ad litem appointments by Harris County Family Court judges. It was also one of the cases that came to the attention of Lee Grant. She had been conducting interviews in and around Harris County for a more general film on divorce and custody issues, but when she learned about the Casterline case and several others, she changed her focus. *America Undercover: Women on Trial* documented actual stories of four women: Sandi, Ivy, Sheri, and Mary Frances.

Sandi lost custody of her five-year-old son when she brought charges of sexual molestation against his father, a Houston police officer. The judge declared that she was mentally unstable. Sandi wasn't allowed a visit with the child for three years, from March 1988 to August 1991. Then, she was forbidden to tell him why she hadn't seen him for all of that time.

Ivy's son and daughter were taken from her when she accused their father of abuse and refused to let him see the children. Despite repeated appeals to the judge from the boy himself to allow him and his sister to live with his mother, the judge would not return custody. It was the father who eventually returned the children to their mother.

Sheri killed her ex-husband when she learned that he had violated a court order by spending time with their son at his parents' home. The grandparents had gained custody of the boy after Sheri accused the father of molesting their son. She was sentenced to life in prison.

Mary Frances, who accused Robert Casterline, the previously convicted rapist, of sexually abusing their child, lost custody of her daughter. Of "all the bad things we see happen in these cases," Susie Alverson of Justice for Children said, Mary Frances "got every one" (Piller, 14 January 1993).

Ironically, *Parker v. Casterline* was not a divorce case. Mary Frances Parker and Bob Casterline had been engaged, but Mary Frances was having second thoughts about the marriage when she learned about the rape; when Casterline was evasive, she became increasingly concerned. Although the couple went for prenuptial counseling when Mary Frances learned that she was pregnant, they never married.

When the child was a year old, the couple came before Judge Allen Daggett to settle a dispute over child support. At that time Daggett gave the father visitation rights, but it wasn't until the child was two years old that Casterline had an extensive five-day visit with her. On the last day of the visit Mary Frances unexpectedly came into the room where Casterline and their daughter were sitting. She saw the child "poke his penis," Mary Frances claimed, "and he's got an erection" (quoted in Barth, 33). She immediately hired an attorney to modify Casterline's visitation rights so that they would be supervised.

Meanwhile Casterline, who had only seen the child a total of six times since her birth, had made plans to take her on a long visit. Mary Frances tried to get a temporary restraining order, but Judge Daggett did not allow her or her live-in babysitter or a consultant, psychologist Laurence Abrams, to testify. "The only things I was permitted to answer were the things the father's attorney was permitted to ask me," Mary Frances is quoted as saying. Her attorney "attempted to bring in the witnesses, but Daggett disallowed it" (quoted in Barth, 71). Instead, Mary Frances was told that she had two hours to get the child ready for a two-week visit with her father. What's more, she was ordered to pay Casterline $688.56 for airfare and $2,500 to one of Daggett's favored ad litem appointees, T. Wayne Harris, who happened to be Casterline's attorney. In addition, Mary Frances had to put $10,000 in escrow in anticipation of additional attorney and ad litem fees. Failure to make these payments, the order read, "would result in all pleadings being stricken from the record." Mary Frances said that when the child returned from the visit with her father she complained that "Bob" hurt her genitals with a machine (Mary Frances guessed it was a vibrator). And the child's behavior was troubling: she became withdrawn, had trouble sleeping, and screamed when her mother turned out the lights (Barth, 32–33, 71).

The accusations, refutations, and counter-accusations by both Mary Frances and Casterline went on and on. At one point, Mary Frances was served with a warrant for her arrest. She was charged with contempt of a court order for refusing to make her child available for an unsupervised visit with her father. In fact, the three-year-old had been hospitalized on the advice of a therapist who was concerned over her severe acting-out behavior—throwing clothes, refusing to stay in bed, expressing anger and fear that Bob, as the child called him, would hurt her. Mary Frances had informed Bob's attorney but didn't disclose the name of the hospital.

As Mary Frances remembers it, she was taken from her office in handcuffs, brought to the courthouse, and handcuffed to a chair. Meanwhile, her house was searched. After being charged, Mary Frances was transferred to the county jail until the hearing. She found herself hooted at by male inmates as she was deposited in a holding cell among drug-addicted women and prostitutes. Many, she says, were "extremely compassionate." She thinks of one woman as her "guardian angel"—a tiny black woman, Mary Frances says, who was ravaged by drugs but fierce. She literally stood watch over Mary Frances, who cried incessantly, during the two days she remained in the jail.

Mary Frances was brought back to the court on a Friday morning and found in contempt for refusing to surrender the child. She was fined $500 and ordered to spend ten more days in jail. She was understandably distraught. When she began to shake Judge Daggett agreed to allow Mary Frances to sign herself into a psychiatric hospital as an alternative to the additional ten-day sentence. She was then taken back to jail until the paperwork was completed. Mary Frances waited all day, but it was only due to the intervention and insistence of her office colleagues that she was released to the hospital late in the day. Otherwise she probably would have spent the weekend in jail.

Mary Frances remained in the hospital for the next nine days. The day before her release from the hospital, she contacted Christi Myers of ABC-TV, who subsequently broadcast the story on Houston's Channel 13. By this time, the child had been placed in a foster home (Barth).

Mary Frances's story, which was broadcast on the news that same evening, provoked an immediate outcry. Marinelle Timmons of the Victim Assistance Center arranged for Mary Frances to meet with an excellent and highly regarded attorney, Rusty Hardin. He had just left his job with the District Attorney's Office; he hadn't even set up his private practice yet. But after they spent six and a half hours going over Mary Frances's case history, he was outraged. Although family law was not his area of expertise, Hardin agreed to represent her.

Finally, Mary Frances requested a jury trial to determine custody.[14] This proved to be a good decision, not because the case was decided in her favor, but because it became impossible to seat a jury. During the jury selection, the story of Casterline's conviction for sexual assault came out. When the first set of sixty potential jurors were asked if they could disregard that information, fifty-six disqualified themselves. Daggett tried again. But the "eighty-four new potential jurors never were brought into the courtroom" since Casterline, apparently seeing the handwriting on the wall, finally withdrew his petition (Piller, 3 July 1991).

Oddly, although the Parker-Casterline trial over which Judge Daggett presided was the most disturbing in the HBO film, it was not Daggett who brought the lawsuit against HBO and Lee Grant. Rather, it was Judge Dean Huckabee, who claimed that the film was edited in such a way that only information supporting the program's point of view was included. This resulted, Huckabee concluded, in allegations of abuses in his court that had not only damaged his reputation but had prompted numerous threats against him (Harper, 14 January 1993). Kay Kreck, a Houston attorney, was the local counsel representing Grant in these suits (for Dallas attorney Julie Ford). In a phone interview, Kreck told me that Grant was not a naïve newcomer to documentaries. She was careful to use testimony, public record, and interviews—and to secure releases. But H B O was cautious; the film was never shown again.

On one of my visits to Houston, I was able to track down a home-taped copy of *America Undercover: Women on Trial*. It was riveting. The compelling courtroom dramas didn't need any embellishment; the spectacle told the story. The film was, as a *Houston Post* reporter wrote, a troubling exposé of "a system that punishes women who bring justified charges of abuse against the fathers of their children, and that gives abusers access to their victims" (Manson, 14 November 1993).

H B O may have decided against rebroadcasting the documentary, but it was already too late for damage control; the film had hit its mark. In the sequence of events that led to the formation of CourtWatch, *America Undercover: Women on Trial* was not merely an anecdotal footnote. The documentary played an important role in the subsequent reform movement. The time was exactly right for such a catalyst; the film was broadcast just as pressure was swelling.

At the time the film was shown in October of 1992, Donna Ringoringo was already picketing the Family Law Center. She had had personal experience with the family court system, representing herself in a bitter custody battle after her attorney advised her to give up custody of her children since she didn't have any money. But Ringoringo did not use this public protest as an attempt to publicize her personal case, which had been settled some years before. In fact, she wouldn't discuss her case, saying that it would draw attention from the purpose of her protest, which was to prod Governor Ann Richards into persuading a state Commission on Judicial Misconduct to hold hearings on the Harris County courts.

Ringoringo's protest steadily intensified. She picketed outside of the Family Law Center every Monday (her day off from work), calling attention to alleged "intimidation of women, poor treatment of children, and cronyism at the court" (Feldstein). In the summer of 1992, Rose Abraham became the first to join Ringoringo in her protest. After a while, others came. When the area in front of the Family Law Center began to resemble a campsite, the protesters were threatened with eviction. Ringoringo then shackled herself to the columns of the building with a rusty chain. She was arrested and jailed for trespassing. Soon after, although the charges were dropped, she began a hunger strike.

All this high drama, naturally, fueled the attention of the media. There were persistent pictures in the papers of Ringoringo chained to the courthouse columns, being hauled away, and wasting away on a hunger strike. Although the protest drew rebukes from some attorneys and judges, it also drew surreptitious but daily encouragement by many attorneys who passed the site, nodding approval at cardboard signs reading, "Stop Campaign Contributions from Attorneys to Judges" and "Harris County Extortion Center" (Gillece, 12). But it was other women from women's groups around the area, and some exceptional men, who developed a support network, the Women's Action Coalition. They eventually set up a twenty-four-hour vigil to watch over Ringoringo and help her as she weakened. In January 1993, after five weeks, the newspaper reported that "Donna Ringoringo's spirit had to give in to her body" (Teachey). She agreed to go to Methodist Hospital on the condition that supporters would continue the protest. At that point, Phrogge (pronounced "Froggy") Simons took over.

Simons, a housewife and the mother of a twenty-one-year-old daughter, had never been divorced, although she had been separated from her husband for many years. She had never sought legal redress because she didn't trust the courts. Now, she was determined to remain at the courthouse for as long as it took. Simons was still there more than a year later (as was Rose Abraham) when the protesters were finally forced to remove their cots. But by then it was March 1994, the primaries were about to be held, and "reform fever" was raging.

After the primaries, Florence Kusnetz told a *Houston Post* reporter that the reform movement had grown out of the determination of the demonstrators, first Donna Ringoringo and then Phrogge Simons. "Until Phrogge stayed out there night and day for a year and three months, people would hear about a bad decision for a day and it would fade. Simons focused the public on the biases and the terrible orientation there towards the lawyers when it should be towards the clients" (Graham, 7 April 1994). In the article Florence was identified as the director of CourtWatch.

What had begun as three women—Florence, Melanie Harrell, and Diana Compton—puzzling over how they could possibly change the family court system in Harris County, had evolved into a well-coordinated, organized, bipartisan political action committee. As a PAC, CourtWatch raised over $80,000, mounted a well-thought-out campaign for reform, and by March of 1994 was celebrating a startling victory in the all-important primaries that determined the candidates for the November election.

Florence Kusnetz was more than the administrator of CourtWatch; she was a key player from the very first moment of her involvement with the group. Florence was the logical choice, Melanie Harrell said, because "she knew people, she knew the law, she was very respected." Although Florence was retired, the success of CourtWatch was the culminating achievement of her career. It was also an affirmation of her personal evolution—from a Brownsville girl to a successful wife and mother, a prominent attorney, a divorce mediator, an innovator, a leader, and a reformer.

CHAPTER 2

Florence

A Woman in Two Worlds

"I was sure my brain had atrophied."

— FLORENCE KUSNETZ

"Faygie, pick up the phone," Howard Kusnetz called to his wife when I asked to speak with Florence.

Florence Kusnetz was Faygie Moglinsky in the 1930s and 1940s when she was growing up in Brooklyn. Howard called her by that name when they met at Thomas Jefferson High School and, affectionately, calls her by that name still. Faygie didn't change her name—in addition to their American names, children of Eastern European Jews are traditionally given Yiddish or biblical Hebrew names, and it was common to call children by those names in Jewish immigrant neighborhoods.

Florence's parents came to the United States some time between 1910 and 1912. Rose Lefton came from a shtetl called Ostrelenka, outside of Warsaw, Poland. Abraham Moglinsky was raised on a farm near a town called Grodno, in Russia. They met in New York, married, and settled down in Brownsville, a Jewish neighborhood in Brooklyn. Most of the people who lived in Brownsville (called "Brunzvil" by the immigrants in their Eastern European–accented English) and the adjacent neighborhood of East New York were Ashkenazim.[1] They were Jews and their second- and third-generation descendants who came to America from Northern and Eastern Europe—Germany, Poland, Russia, Lithuania, Latvia, and the Austro-Hungarian Empire.

When Florence was coming of age in the 1940s, Brownsville was still predominantly Jewish. But as Alfred Kazin wrote in his memoir, because of Brownsville's poverty and seeming lack of grace, for some it was "notoriously a place that measured all success by [one's] skill in getting away from it" (Kazin, 11). (A friend of mine, the poet Richard Fein, described one of Brooklyn's main thoroughfares, Eastern Parkway. He wrote: "It wound into the dens of Brownsville and toward Jews even poorer than my parents, a lower social class my family feared falling back into without so much as saying so, intuitively recognizing those minute class divisions that could be measured by social dividers called avenues . . . below Utica Avenue, the Parkway squirmed off in the distance toward the din of Pitkin Avenue, a brassy notch above the hustle of Orchard Street" [Fein, 92].)[2]

The historian Deborah Dash Moore says that Brownsville was "a world of its own," characterized by an "egalitarianism in tone and manner." Unlike other Jewish neighborhoods in New York at the time, in Brownsville it was possible to find the "entire spectrum" of Jewish political and cultural life (Moore, 62). Also, compared to the Jewish neighborhoods in New York today such as Crown Heights, Boro Park, or the areas along the length of Ocean Parkway from Flatbush to Brighton Beach, Brownsville was predominantly secular. Only a small percentage of the population attended religious services on a regular basis. Florence's parents, like many in Brownsville, were minimally observant and religion did not become important to her until a good many years after she'd left the old neighborhood. For those growing up in Brownsville, Jewish identity didn't depend upon religious observance. In 1925, 95 percent of Brownsville's inhabitants were Jews (Abramovitch and Galvin, 6). Because so many immigrants lived in the community, Jewish identity was firmly rooted in the Jewish culture: customs, language, literature, and shared history and values.[3]

Florence's sense of her Jewishness, her *Yidishkeit*, was unconscious. It came from the signs and symbols of Jewish life visible everywhere, from the trivial to the profound. Although many of these had lost their original religious significance, they were still part of the culture and tradition of the community. One example was the mezuzah, a tiny container in the shape of a miniature Torah or scroll, mounted on the doorjamb of the entryway. In it was a rolled-up paper or parchment printed with verses from Deuteronomy. An Orthodox Jew touches his fingers to his lips and then to the mezuzah whenever he enters or leaves his home. Florence's home had its mezuzah in the doorway where, as in most other Brownsville homes, it was ignored— but it was always there, and its absence would have been noticed.

Like most other women in the neighborhood, Florence's mother kept a kosher home. Everyone knew the dietary requirements, the many rules of kashruth, whether they followed them or not. (Non-kosher foods were not likely to be found in Brownsville shops even if someone wanted to buy them.)[4]

For girls like Florence, Saturday was a day for dressing up, and not just for those observing the Sabbath—it was part of the rhythm of the week. Jewish holidays, even the minor ones, were celebrated by the entire community. Some holidays, such as Purim, were Jewish history lessons. While non-Jews got special outfits for Easter, Florence got her new clothes for Passover or Rosh Hashanah, the Jewish New Year. The Passover seder was celebrated in most households, although it was already changing from a traditional, solemn commemoration of the story of the Exodus to a more raucous family gathering. Chanukah, the Jewish Festival of Lights, was celebrated with the gift of a coin, Chanukah gelt—usually fifty cents but sometimes a silver dollar. "Here's a shekel," fathers would say, dispensing the largesse long before there was a state of Israel, which reappropriated the biblical term for its currency. Even Thanksgiving, the most American of holidays, had its Jewish version—the turkey was invariably preceded by typically Jewish starters and the meal often ended with a sweet noodle pudding rather than pumpkin pie. On high holy days every shop in the neighborhood was shut, and all the schools were closed. In Brownsville, not only the students but the public school teachers were predominantly Jewish.

Because the Brownsville Jewish immigrants came from so many different countries, their common language was Yiddish, the *mame-loshen,* or mother tongue, and when Florence was growing up, Yiddish was still spoken in many homes. There were Yiddish daily and weekly newspapers, Yiddish signs and menus, Yiddish-speaking shopkeepers and owners of countless delicatessens. Cultural programs in Yiddish were broadcast on radio station WEVD (whose call letters were the initials of socialist Eugene V. Debs).

Along with their Yiddish language and Jewish customs, immigrants brought the values of the old country to the *naya velt,* the new world. These values became deeply embedded in the culture of Brownsville. Among them were an abiding belief in education, which would bring not only wisdom but *yikhes,* or status; *takhlis,* a belief that one's activities must be goal-directed and lead to some positive final result; and *tsedakah* and *gemuluth hasadim,* or charity and the obligation to help the less fortunate. Interwoven with these Jewish values was the overarching tradition of social consciousness based upon the principle of *tikkun olam,* the repair or improvement of the world. In Brownsville, these values were expressed, reinforced, and carried out in *landsmanshaftn,* or fraternal and mutual benefit societies, and in other community organizations where the power of group action was understood.

For women, the primary obligation that ranked above all others was to raise their children in a home in which the Jewish culture, the *Yiddishe yerushe,* was preserved—a home in which Jewish values were perpetuated. This home was child-centered and the family was cherished within it. Florence Kusnetz's entire adult life reflects and exemplifies all of these Jewish values. In addition, what Florence absorbed while participating in holiday observances and many other simple acts was a deep, visceral internalization of her Jewishness. However taken for granted and unacknowledged it was at the time, it would emerge many years later in the form of personal religious observance and a commitment to family and activism.

Like many in Brownsville, Florence's parents were uneducated; they spoke Yiddish and broken English. Although her father was able to read the Yiddish newspaper, her mother was illiterate. She started to attend night school but gave it up, Florence says, "in order to have dinner on the table when my father came home from work." In spite of their hard work, Florence's parents were poor for most of their lives, perhaps poorest when she was an infant. Florence was born on March 4, 1929, only a few months before the crash and the Great Depression. She remembers: "My father was a garment worker—a presser. We struggled through the strikes, and the slack seasons, and no work, and labor unrest. In the best of times he made barely enough to keep the family together. And he was so tired."

Although education is highly valued in Jewish society, in Florence's family it wasn't seen as the route to financial success. The Moglinskys chose the other common Jewish route of rising from poverty: through business. None of the Moglinsky children—not even the boys, Jack and Ben—were encouraged to go to college. In fact, Florence was the only high-school graduate in the family. Her sister, Sara, worked as an office clerk for their brother Ben, who had started a novelty hat business. At first he manufactured cowboy hats, but he later signed a contract with Walt Disney productions and became a millionaire after developing the Mickey Mouse hat and all the other Disney theme hats, including the propeller beanie. Ben more than fulfilled his parents' expectations.

Florence was smart and a good student. In 1946 she graduated from Thomas Jefferson, the local high school, near the top of her class, with a college preparatory diploma. "I was the only one in my family who valued

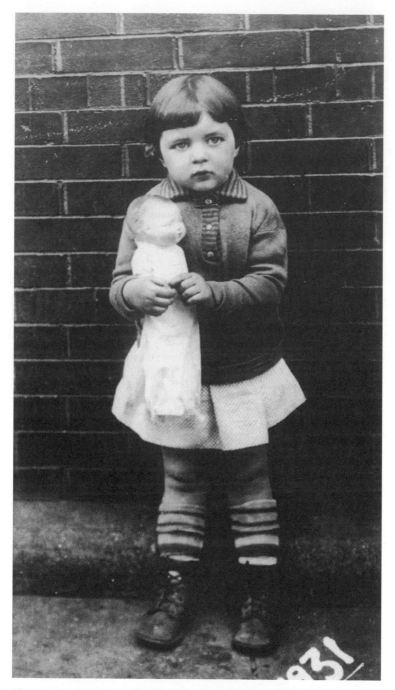

Florence in 1931, age two. Few families in Brownsville owned cameras.
This photo was taken by an itinerant photographer. Photo courtesy of
Florence Kusnetz.

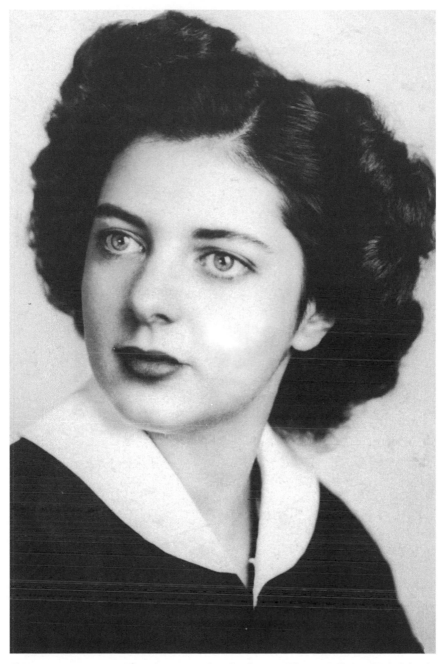

Florence, age seventeen. This photo was taken for the 1946 Thomas Jefferson High School yearbook. Florence was tenth in a graduating class of six hundred. Photo courtesy of Florence Kusnetz.

academics," she says, adding something that always troubled her: "Because of that, it seemed as if I didn't fit into my family very well" (Surface, 3).

Florence always thought she would go to college to study for a career, although most Brownsville women of her generation took courses in business studies. They planned to work as secretaries and bookkeepers, to bide their time until they married and their real life's work began. Florence was one of the exceptions. In spite of the lack of support by her family, in spite of the social and cultural pressures, in spite of the fact that she was not interested in the one approved profession of teaching, Florence looked beyond the limitations to see the possibilities. She applied to and was accepted at the very competitive City College of New York, one of the most highly regarded colleges in the city's university system.[5] But she found a program that interested her elsewhere. Well before the importance of nutrition became broadly acknowledged, when the field was geared to limited therapeutic applications, Florence decided to become a dietician. Yet, while attending a two-week orientation program at Brooklyn's Pratt Institute, she agonized over whether to enroll.

She never did. It wasn't that Florence was intimidated or had lost interest. Rather, when the time came for her to pay the tuition, she couldn't bring herself to ask her parents for the money. "We had free colleges in New York; I could have enrolled elsewhere," Florence says. "But there was something in my background that said, college is a luxury—I need to go to work and start supporting myself. So I enrolled in a business course." And, like most females of her era, she found herself in an office, working as a secretary and bookkeeper, waiting to become a bride. "I was raised to get married and have children," she says. And so she did.

On August 24, 1950, Florence and Howard married and set out for Detroit with all of their youthful enthusiasm, "eager to see the world." (They have not yet lost their eagerness; it's exhausting just to hear about their travel schedule.) In the early 1950s, coming from the relative insulation and familiarity of Brownsville's "sheltering neighborhood," as Jewish historian Deborah Dash Moore calls it, the young couple found that Detroit was quite enough of the world. They settled into their new home, a tiny third-floor tenement apartment in a changing neighborhood where they paid only $28 a month in rent and where, Florence says, "there was a shooting every night." But they were not there for very long; they lived in Detroit for only a year and a half.

Because of Howard's work with the Public Health Service, Detroit was just the first of fourteen moves in twenty years: from Detroit to Cincinnati, Cincinnati to Salt Lake City, back to Cincinnati, to Silver Spring, back again to Cincinnati, and so it went. "It was hard to move, but on the other hand, I made friends all over the country," Florence says about the moves, remarkably without resentment. Her older son Bob was born in 1956 in Salt Lake City, where Florence was taken in and sheltered by the Jewish community. Ironically, it was there, in that bastion of the Mormon religion, that Florence consciously reclaimed her ties to Judaism. And Salt Lake City was where she began to have an understanding of the connection between her ancient faith and her sense of social consciousness. "I began to read everything I could put my hands on about Judaism," she says:

That was when I decided it was an incredibly rich and wonderful foundation that I had already, but didn't know I had. And I really think I became connected to Judaism in those early days by being part of a wonderful synagogue family. People were wonderful to us. When I had my first baby, the sisterhood adopted me and loved me and made me baby showers.

Once my Jewish consciousness was heightened, I began to see that people in the helping professions were inordinately Jewish. Doctors, lawyers, psychologists, social workers. I started to wonder, how come?

Dan was born in Cincinnati two years later, in 1958. Until the boys were old enough for her to start getting bored, Florence was a homemaker, wherever home happened to be. In the 1950s, most young Brownsville couples remained in the neighborhood or found homes nearby—in East Flatbush or the newly developing areas of Canarsie. Few ventured out even as far as Long Island which, at the time, was still mostly small towns and country and farms. The mobility of the Kusnetz family was unusual, but in just about all other respects, Florence's early marriage followed a pattern that was typical for Jewish women of her generation and social class.[6] They were "transitional" women who were described by the Jewish historian Blu Greenberg as having internalized traditional values. They were "generally content" to play the role set for them while their children were still young, but later, when they stepped outside that role and tried to reconcile demands of work, marriage, and children, many complexities and conflicts intruded into their lives (Greenberg, 23). They had evolved from traditional wives and mothers into women who combined career and family. They had become women "split between two worlds" (Dinnerstein, ix–x).

Women like Florence, who were able to step outside their roles as wives and mothers and pursue careers, were a new phenomenon in the traditional Jewish community. They had to overcome multiple significant barriers in order to achieve their educational and career goals. Some of these barriers affected all American women in the period following World War II, while others were related to social class. Some were particular to cultural norms and social class *within* Jewish-American society. Generally, Jewish women who grew up in Brownsville, with their Eastern European, working-class backgrounds, were affected differently than were middle-class Jewish women from Northern and Western European backgrounds—from Austria or Germany, for example—who lived in other communities in New York City, such as the Upper West Side.

Although Brownsville was a poor, working-class neighborhood, young women were expected to be full-time mothers and homemakers; it was considered the only appropriate role for a married woman, especially once there were children to raise. Despite the reality—many of their mothers were shopkeepers or did other types of work in their homes—idealized gender roles persisted, and they were uncompromisingly and rigidly defined.

(There have always been a large number of poor and working-class women in America who, in addition to homemaking responsibilities, worked outside the home. During World War II, when Florence was coming of age, many middle-class married women who were already mothers entered the workforce for the first time. But since they were replacing men who were serving in the armed forces, women were expected to leave their homemaking jobs only for the duration. Though after the war ended many women stubbornly remained in the workforce, most succumbed to the lack of support as well as the lack of career and educational opportunities. Some eagerly, others reluctantly yet dutifully, returned to full-time homemaking and parenting. Once again, since they were no longer a part of the paid workforce, they were thought of as *non-working* mothers [an oxymoron, a contradiction in terms]. Yet World War II permanently altered the face of the workforce by breaking down barriers to the employment of wives and older women. During the war, married women working outside the home had become an accepted fact. Florence was still in high school at this time, too young to have joined this workforce, but her view of women's work was inevitably affected by the image of Rosie the Riveter, who proved [once she had been permitted to try] that she could do a "man's" job.)

When Florence considered whether to pursue a career or devote herself to marriage and family, her decision was constrained by a Cold War rhetoric. The need for a speedy return to normalcy that centered around the traditional family was proclaimed immediately after the end of the war. A concept resurrected from an earlier era, which historians called the "cult of domesticity," began to take shape. As social historian Elaine Tyler May explains, "The cold war ideology and the domestic revival" were "two sides of the same coin." Nothing else, May wrote, "on the surface of postwar America explains the rush of young Americans into marriage, parenthood, and traditional gender roles except the relationship that developed between political and family values"(May, 10). No groups in America were exempt from the pressures of this domestic revival—certainly not Jews, who were still reeling from the devastating effects of the Holocaust (May, 7, 11, 23).[7] In addition, in Brownsville, family values and the cult of domesticity were familiar concepts. They were congruent with the values of traditional Jewish culture, and they forged a strong chemical bond via the energy provided by the propaganda of the Cold War as the family "seemed to offer a psychological fortress" and protection against the dangers of communism (Harvey, 71).

Jewish women of Florence's generation who grew up in Brownsville—the post-war Cold War generation—were not only struggling against the overwhelming currents of mainstream American society but also against limitations imposed by working-class, Eastern European, Jewish culture: a Jewish woman did not need a college education to perform her traditional role; she did not need to prepare for a career. On the contrary, she could anticipate domestic bliss: she was assured that she could find everything she needed in marriage.[8] Florence and the women of her generation took it for granted that their lives would revolve around their husbands and raising a family, although they had some vague sense that they might want to do "something" once the children were grown. True, they might become widowed, but they were young and mortality was something they never even thought about, let alone planned for. Nor did they consider the possibility of divorce and the need to support themselves. In Judaism the *ketubah,* or marriage contract, has always been "imbued with holiness," a "contract blessed by God" (Baker, 143–144). In spite of the importance of marriage and family in Jewish life, divorce is permitted and surely it happened, but it was rare and remote from the experience of most young Brownsville women.

Consequently, like her Brownsville contemporaries, Florence did not have genuine choices, but rather constraints as two cultures—traditional

Jewish culture and mainstream American culture—joined and reinforced each other. And both were fortified by Cold War ideology. In Brownsville, poverty further limited women's educational and career aspirations. Few families could afford to send all their children to college. Generally, if a choice had to be made between a brother or sister, it was not a true choice; men *had* to have careers so they could support their families. Finally, there was a lack of career opportunity; teaching was one of the few professions open to women. In Brownsville, women who thought about careers at all, in spite of the hurdles, planned to become teachers. It was one of the few acceptable professions for a Jewish woman, since a teacher's schedule was viewed as compatible with her role as wife and mother.

Florence was twenty-one when she and Howard married and left for Detroit. Howard had wanted to be a doctor, but in the 1940s and 1950s there were quotas (of about 5 percent) for the admission of Jews to medical schools. Howard was a pragmatist; he earned his undergraduate degree at NYU and then a master's in public health at Columbia. (His very successful career, however, was closely related to his first calling.) He became an expert in occupational health and safety with the United States Public Health Service, one of the uniformed services of the government, and was one of the architects of the legislation that created the Occupational Safety and Health Administration (OSHA) and their now well-known regulations. Howard is still a sought-after consultant.

During the 1950s, Florence and most of her contemporaries were homemakers. At the beginning of the 1960s, however, twenty-three million women, more than one-third of all American women over the age of sixteen, were in the workforce, and half of these women had school-age children. By the end of the decade, a majority of working-age women held paid jobs (Moen, 11). In 1966, Florence was getting ready to join the trend. The Kusnetz family was living in Silver Spring, Maryland; the boys were eight and ten years old. As a good Jewish homemaker, a modern *baleboste,* Florence had always seen her family as her first consideration. This meant deferring to Howard's needs and professional obligations, which carried them from place to place around the country. And it meant "being there" for Howard and for the boys. But Howard was traveling a great deal and often was away for weeks at a time. "That's when I realized that I had to do something more with my life than keeping house," Florence says. She had dabbled in cooking and baking classes, sewing, painting, ceramics, and gardening, "always wanting to learn something new," but they weren't satisfying pursuits and seemed trivial. She was getting restless and depressed. One day, after she'd tried an afternoon of bridge, she thought, "What a terrible waste of time." But, what to do?

The answer came accidentally, after a talk with one of her son's teachers who had gone back to school to get her teaching certificate as an adult student. She told Florence how different it was from when she had been a young student. "Hmmm, maybe I can do this?" Florence thought:

She told me how rewarding it had been to go to college as an older person. She said she got a lot more out of it than she ever did when she was younger. This gave me the idea that it was not impossible for me to go to college at an older age. But of course, this was 1966 and nobody was doing anything like that; it was virtually unheard of.

Before marrying and leaving New York, I had started taking college courses at Brooklyn College, going in the evenings after work—just taking one or two courses a semester—just because I loved learning. Now I wondered if I could become a student again. (Surface, 2)

Nervously, Florence made some inquiries. "I was sure my brain had atrophied," she confessed. When she "finally got up the courage to try it," she enrolled at the University of Maryland in College Park. Slowly, part-time, she began taking classes when the boys were in school—dipping her toes, very tentatively, into icy waters. In 1966, the world of higher education was a cold place indeed for students like Florence, who came to be known as "returning women."

It had been twenty years since Florence had graduated from high school, but she loved college. In spite of the fact that she was one of the few mature women in class during the regular day session, "I knew this was right for me," she says. Once, when Florence was standing in line to register for courses—in the days before computers and credit cards and preregistration, this took hours and hours—one of her classmates kindly, if condescendingly, brought a chair for her to sit on. And not only were the students young, Florence says, but "it wasn't until I was back in college for five years that I had a *teacher* who was older than me." In her first English class, she told her instructor that she hadn't written anything in sixteen years "except a note to the milkman." For their first assignment, students were asked to write compositions about their relationships with their parents. Florence looked around the classroom: "Everyone was twenty years younger than me." Her essay, she thought, would not have been exactly what the professor had in mind. It might actually have been more interesting, though, since Florence's parents were totally bewildered by her desire to return to school. At her age! Thirty-seven! Instead, Florence wrote about her relationship with *her* children.

Although Florence had been tenth in a class of six hundred when she graduated from high school, she couldn't believe she was still capable of earning "great grades." But to no one's surprise but hers, her brain hadn't atrophied at all. And she loved the stimulation. "It was extremely exciting to get out of the house and explore new ideas," she says. Yet, in spite of Florence's new set of all A's, she was afraid to take on more than a couple of courses each semester. She also worried about no longer "being there" for her sons. She struggled to find courses that would get her home by three, but finally relented and gave the boys their own keys to the house. Not surprisingly, they took to the change better than she did. They took themselves off to Hebrew school, behaved responsibly (much to her great relief), and were proud to be trusted.

It wasn't all smooth sailing though. "Sexism" and "ageism" were not yet commonly used words, but the two phenomena existed throughout society, as much in institutions of higher education as elsewhere. Universities should have been exceptions; because of their educated faculties they might have been leading the effort for equity. Quite the contrary. Older students and women, particularly women, were not taken seriously. Florence's experience was typical:

I remember a time when I tried to take an advanced level political science course for which I needed the professor's permission. He took one look at me. He knew nothing about me; he had never seen me before, and he said no. I couldn't go to his class. Because "obviously," as he put it, I had "other priorities."

I looked at him, in shock, and said, "You don't know that. I work very hard in my classes and I think I deserve a chance." And he said, "Okay, why don't you come and we'll see what you can do." It was obvious that he was challenging me to prove him wrong.

Well, I showed up on the first day and all of the wise-ass kids in his class took one look at me and said, "Uh-oh, there goes the curve." I didn't even know what a curve was. I had to come home and ask Howard. But it seemed that they knew I was not in school to party.

On the first day of class this professor assigned Plato's *Republic* to be read overnight. It was a ridiculous assignment. But Florence read the book, understood what she could, and was prepared for the next morning's discussion. Sure enough, as she suspected, the professor called on her first. He continued to do so every day until he realized that she was not only as well prepared but usually better prepared than her younger classmates. (As they feared, her grades were so outstanding that she would later be accused by fellow students in some of her courses of being a "curve-breaker.") Because of our heightened awareness of gender and age discrimination, such overt bias is not likely to occur today. But these were early days.

Florence stuck it out and finally enrolled full time. The family had moved yet again and was now living in Ohio. Because transferring credits from one school to another is always a problem, Florence was afraid another move would jeopardize her standing. But by then, she says, "I was convinced that I was going to see this through"—and she did. In the spring of 1970, Florence graduated from the University of Cincinnati as a member of Phi Beta Kappa, with highest honors, a degree in political science, and a hard-earned confidence in her ability.

Since Florence wanted the boys to be in college by the time she went to work and since she had the financial luxury of not having to go to work, graduate school was a logical next step. But again, she wasn't sure what she wanted to study. Somewhat belatedly, she asked herself, "What do you do with a degree in political science?"

Florence had some vague notion that she might like to study law, "but to tell the truth," she says, "I hadn't a clue as to what law school was like or what lawyers did." She certainly had no idea that in 1970 law was a relatively hostile profession for returning women. Even more recently, with large and growing numbers of women entering the profession, law schools were not welcoming "fortyish" women. But Florence had already been swimming against the mainstream; it's not likely that she would have been dissuaded by that challenge. Actually, it would have spurred her on; she could be very stubborn when provoked. Her vulnerability was her Jewish-mother guilt. "Once again I had this feeling," she says, that it was "not right to take family funds and spend them on myself, especially with the kids growing up and the time growing closer when they would need money for college" (Surface, 3). To further confuse matters, Florence had been offered a fellowship in urban planning, which she thought sounded interesting. Tuition would be free and the fellowship carried a stipend of $400 per semester.

To get some idea of what law school might be like before she made a final decision, Florence sat in on a class in contract law at the University of Cincinnati Law School. "I was turned on," she told me, "amazed that I understood this stuff—I was hooked!" With this began a replay of the conflict Florence had experienced years ago over the financial repercussions of higher education (whether to attend the dietician program at Pratt Institute or to be practical and take a business course). She almost didn't allow herself to follow her desire to study law. But this time there was Howard; he helped her make the decision, although at the time neither of them realized how important his help was. (One of the most important factors in married returning women's success in college is their husband's emotional and financial support.) "Which would you choose," Howard asked her, "if the money were taken out of the equation?" Unhesitatingly she said, "Law!" And that was it. "We'll find the money someplace," Howard said. In the fall of 1970, Florence entered what she calls the "fine old law school" at the University of Cincinnati.

Thirty-odd years ago, there were few women in the legal profession, and fewer still had had an impact on the culture of the law. It was men who made the laws and dominated the law schools, the legal profession, the courts, and the legislatures. That Florence could go to law school and practice at all was an improvement. In her history of American women and the law, Texas A & M Professor Judith Baer wrote that men completely monopolized the profession (Baer, 129). To fully appreciate what Baer meant, and what Florence encountered, it's useful to take a brief look at some of the hurdles women had to overcome.

The first break in the barrier against women in American law came with the suffragist movement, exactly one hundred years before Florence enrolled at Cincinnati Law School. In 1870, the U.S. Supreme Court admitted a woman, Belva Lockwood, to its bar. But at about the same time, in what was the "first sex discrimination case ever heard by the Supreme Court," five justices agreed with Justice Joseph Bradley, who argued that Myra Bradwell, an Illinois attorney, should be "disqualified from practicing law" because as a married woman she was unable to enter binding contracts. This verdict notwithstanding, there were some women attorneys, "few of them, to be sure," practicing in most parts of the country (Baer, 269). But even if they were allowed to practice, women had to surmount another obstacle. There were few law schools in America in the nineteenth century. Of these, still fewer admitted women; in order to practice they had to become lawyers through apprenticeships. In 1910 only 1 percent of students entering law schools were women.[9]

An exception was Stanford University, which opened in 1891 and organized an undergraduate department of law two years later which, in 1908, evolved into Stanford Law School. The first woman to graduate with a law degree was Altha Perry Curry. Stanford was the "only institution among the top law schools in the country" that always admitted women ("Celebrating a Century"). Even so, by 1952 a very small number, only fifty-six women, had graduated from Stanford Law. Among them was Sandra Day O'Connor, who would go on to become the first woman on the United States Supreme Court.[10] From 1948 to 1970, the number of women attorneys ranged between 1.8 percent and 2.8 percent of the total. The percentage of women in law schools was somewhat higher, but this situation would change dramatically after Title IX of the Education Amendments Act of 1972 forbade sex discrimination in educational programs that received federal funds (Baer, 269).

The passage of Title IX produced almost immediate significant gains; once the opportunity arose, women poured into law schools. Clearly they were ready and waiting. Unfortunately, law schools were neither, although they had no choice if they wanted taxpayers' money. The total numbers were still small, but between 1971 and 1974, a single period during which there would have been a complete turnover in a law school's student body, "the proportion of women law students *tripled*" (ibid.). By 1977, the number of women had increased to 9 percent of the lawyer population and more than 25.5 percent of law school enrollments.[11]

Baer believes that Title IX alone "probably did not cause the dramatic increase in the number of women law students, lawyers, and judges that occurred in the next fifteen years." She thinks that civil rights law "rarely works that directly" (Baer, 277). I agree, but in this case, which was helped along by more general gains by the feminist movement, Title IX must account for the steady growth in the number of women entering the law, which some now characterize as the increasing feminization of the legal profession. Whether or not Title IX was the main cause, it was a necessary condition for change to occur. Today, women hold professorships in law schools (Florence never had a female professor in law school), there are women on the Supreme Court and on the highest state courts, and some women are chief justices of their state courts.

Title IX was an outgrowth of the women's movement, which had lain relatively dormant since suffrage was granted to women by the Nineteenth Amendment to the Constitution. The effects and aftereffects of women's roles in World War II, both in the armed services and on the domestic front, contributed a latent energy to the women's movement's revival but, as the abolitionist movement had done a century before, it was the civil rights movement that truly awakened feminism. Once people begin to think about rights for one group, equal or unequal treatment of other groups becomes apparent. Thus, the battle for civil rights was eventually transformed into a human rights struggle. The revival of feminism that emerged in the 1960s—"Women's Lib," it was called at that time—was part of that greater struggle.

Feminist theory provided the intellectual foundation for the women's movement, drawing upon many disciplines including history, sociology, literature, semiotics, political science, moral development, and psychology. There were significant points of disagreement among feminists, as there continue to be, but there was important common ground. Feminist theory challenged the idea that women's inferior status was simply the result of choice or of natural, biological differences between men and women. Together, feminists provided a means for understanding what was demonstrable: that women in America, like minorities of color, had been historically disadvantaged as a result of bias. The attitudes, values, and behavior that defined norms or acceptable standards favored white men, and the behavior of others was measured against those norms. With regard to gender, it was women, as Simone de Beauvoir said, who were cast as different. Not abnormal, but "other."

Feminist theorists raised many questions about what was simply taken for granted as the way things "naturally" were. They asked why, and how, did men come to have a higher status in society? How did women become the "other"? How did the male disposition become affirmed as the standard for normally accepted behavior? Feminists compared the higher value placed upon characteristically "male" traits such as objectivity, detachment, and rationality with the less valued "female" opposites of subjectivity, involvement, and emotion. They began to examine the very idea of difference. Difference is a relative term, as Harvard law professor Martha Minow makes clear in her essay "Justice Engendered," meaningful only as a comparison. She points out that people differ from each other in a wide variety of ways. "I am no more different from you," she says, "than you are from me." Difference is not intrinsic but relational: "A short person is different only in relation to a tall one," Minow says. "Handicapped persons" are compared to the "able-bodied" (Minow, 218).[12]

Feminist theory asked one more probing and complex question. If men are the beneficiaries of an inequitable social system, what needs to be done to fix it? In the early days of the revived women's movement, feminist theorists didn't provide a unified sense of how change could be accomplished. They did, however, provide a rationale for change when many wondered impatiently what these women's libbers were asking for now. Nancy Levit, professor of law at the University of Missouri, asks, more sympathetically, what was "at the heart of feminism." She answers her own question. "At minimum" she says, "equal rights for women and men and equal social opportunities for both sexes" (Levit, 219). And certainly equal economic opportunity.

Women's libbers were making basic demands. They wanted to be freed from gender stereotypes based upon unfounded negative assertions; they wanted to be liberated from coercion to conform to these gender stereotypes and the consequent limitations; they asked to be acknowledged as equally capable. They wanted equity of treatment; that is, in a given situation would a woman have been treated differently if she were a man? (Chamallas, 310).

One outgrowth of feminist theory is feminist analysis as applied to the law. Feminist legal theory, or feminist jurisprudence, is a critique of legal philosophy and history, legal culture, the administration of the law, and the effects of the law upon women—students, professionals, and litigants alike. Although feminist legal theory has gone through several stages during which one hypothesis or another dominated, what unites the disparate interpretations is a perspective tied to the belief that the law, as it is practiced in Western society, systematically disserves women. Most legal theorists who identify themselves as feminists are critical of the status quo. They are not neutral observers and recorders; they have a point of view and are advocates for reform.[13]

Today, the literature in the field is vast. One selected bibliography includes writings on the history and background of feminist theory, feminist jurisprudence, research methods, applications to areas of the law related to family issues, abortion, pornography, sexual harassment, sexual orientation, medicine, philosophy, violent crime, criminal law and procedure, courts and dispute resolution, and employment and workplace issues ("Feminist Theory").

Unfortunately, feminist legal theory came too late to help Florence understand her experiences in law school, an institution that seemed odd to her from the very start, a man's world. Had feminist legal theory been more fully developed, it would surely have helped demystify some of the oddity. But in 1970, just on the cusp of the phenomenon that was to occur with the passage of Title IX legislation, no one had yet explained the dissonant experiences women were having in law schools. Dorothy had landed in Oz.

CHAPTER 3

Gender Bias and the Law
The Blind Maiden

"Law school was like coming into a foreign culture."
— FLORENCE KUSNETZ

I t was 1970. "When I started at the University of Cincinnati Law School," Florence remembers, "one of my profs cornered me in the library, in the stacks, accusing me of starting 'trouble' in his home." The professor reproached her: "Do you know what you did? Do you know what happened in my house last night because of you?" He was so hostile, Florence says, "I thought he was going to hit me." Florence was bewildered; she couldn't imagine what she had done. Then she learned that the professor and his wife had seen her on television the night before being interviewed about her law school experiences.

The associate producer of the show, a TV news program, was the wife of one of Florence's classmates. After a conversation that Florence could only imagine—"Guess what? We have this old lady in our freshman class. She's got two kids at home!"—the producer called Florence to ask if she'd come on the show. "Once a week we interview people of interest," she said. Florence said yes. "So I went down and she taped me. I was going to get five minutes but I got so verbose and it was so interesting, they let me go on for ten. 'So why are you going to law school?' she asked me. 'What does your husband think?'"

The segment, which was shown on the six o'clock news, sparked the argument between the professor and his wife. The professor was indignant: "She saw you on television and now my wife wants to know why *she* can't be going to law school. She said to me: 'See what women are doing now?'" Florence could only respond, rather lamely, "What has that got to do with me?"

In fact, it had a great deal to do with her. This occurred prior to Title IX of the Education Amendments Act of 1972, which forbade sex discrimination in educational programs receiving federal funds. Florence was not simply a novelty; she was a role model for women entering the legal profession at that pivotal time. She didn't have to say, "If I can do it, you women out there can do it." That implicit message was broadcast literally and figuratively. Florence was one of only eleven women in a class of 162. And, at the age of forty-one, she was fifteen to twenty years older than her classmates. For Florence, "Law school was like coming into a foreign culture. No allowances were made for women to introduce any kind of new ideas, to accept women's expressions or opinions if they differed from the dominating male point of view. They didn't know what to do with women in law school. We were a real aberration."

Florence finished her first year of law school in Cincinnati, but then Howard retired from his work with the Public Health Service, and the family had to move again when he took a job with the Shell Oil Company in Houston. It would be the last of fourteen moves for Florence:

When I came to Houston, house hunting in June 1971, the dean of the law school said I could not be admitted as a transfer student since they were admitting the largest freshman class they had ever had and they were all full. He promised that if I waited a year he would admit me then. I told him that after five years of juggling school and home and two cross-country moves, I was operating on sheer momentum. There was a good chance that if I stayed out a year, I would not continue.

When I got back to Cincinnati, I haunted the mailbox. Sure enough, I received a letter from him saying they had decided to admit me after all. I knew then that I would go all the way. I started my last two years of law school that September.

By the time Florence transferred to the University of Houston, several of the eleven women in her class in Cincinnati had dropped out. The situation was not peculiar to Cincinnati; there was a very high dropout rate among women in law schools, particularly in the first year. Women found themselves in an alien and often hostile environment. "Law school was of the men, by the men, for the men," Florence says. "It reminds me of medical research that was all done on and for men. It took generations to realize that women were different." Of course, Florence understands that traditional, conventional wisdom supported just that view: that men and women *are* different from each other—in their biology and, consequently, in their behavior—and that this was a historically and culturally entrenched notion that was resistant to change.[1] Women *were* treated differently from men, although not as Florence meant them to be. Unfortunately for women, the treatment was most often discriminatory (as medical and other researchers have admitted). What Florence was suggesting is that men and women have different needs, which should be addressed in such a way that the end results are equitable. Although she may not have realized it, Florence was taking a position on one of the dominant and persistent controversies in the feminist literature: the sameness-difference debate,[2] which has divided feminists since the nineteenth century (Williams).

As Harvard law professor Martha Minow has said, difference only has meaning if one thing is being compared to another. Feminists agree that "difference" is measured against a presumed norm and, with regard to gender, that norm is male. The controversy stems from the fact that by acknowledging that men and women are different we can plunge headlong into what Minow describes as the "dilemma of difference" (Minow, 228–229). This concept prompts a number of significant questions. Is it better to notice gender differences or to ignore them? By noticing gender differences, are we inadvertently reinforcing and perpetuating negative stereotypes? Or, on the other hand, do we perpetuate stereotypes by ignoring them? The danger in acknowledging difference is that it may backfire by stigmatizing a group not only as different but also as inferior, a problem faced by many who benefit from affirmative action programs.

When Florence was in law school in the early 1970s, feminists were not prepared to engage in such a debate. They believed that to acknowledge difference would inevitably serve to perpetuate gender inequality and discrimination; they avoided that slippery slope. Instead, they argued that men and women should be treated as if they were the same. In 1971, the Supreme Court agreed with this assessment in the "first important equal protection case decided favorably for women," *Reed v. Reed* (Scales, 94–95). The Court decided in favor of the American Civil Liberties Union's Rights Project, which held that women and men were, in legal terms, "similarly situated." ACLU counsel Ruth Bader Ginsburg reasoned, in this case which had to do with women's ability to administer estates, that there was "no demonstrable difference" to justify treating the sexes differently. The principle applied in other areas as well. The problem was that cases kept appearing in which it was obvious that men and women were not "similarly situated"—most notably in situations involving pregnancy. Although many feminists eventually came to accept that it is important to acknowledge difference, at least for legal purposes, in this earlier period there was a great effort to do just the opposite.

While this is not the place for a lengthy discussion of gender difference, some additional comments are necessary in order to fully understand gender bias in law schools and, indeed, in the law itself. Today, the "nature-versus-nurture, biology-versus-culture, genesis-versus-environment dichotomy has broken down" (Ruse). Rather, we know that there is a complex interaction between our genetic dispositions and the experiences that shape our behavior. As boys and girls encounter different situations, they learn to see the world differently, they acquire different attitudes and values, and they learn to behave differently. Those differences are reinforced by experiences in their families and in other social institutions, such as schools. Public schools are expected to fulfill a primary academic function—students are meant to master basic subject matter, skills, and concepts—but they are also institutions in which social and gender norms, those expected and acceptable behaviors which may first be learned in the family, are reinforced.[3]

Like public schools, colleges and universities have a socializing function. In colleges, students are expected to learn how to manage their time, make decisions concerning their course of study, and learn the norms of their discipline. Students do not just acquire information; they are taught to think as historians, sociologists, artists, or scientists do. Nor is it different in professional schools.

In law school, learning how to "think like a lawyer" is as important as learning the law. Law students learn to extract the basic principles in an argument rationally and analytically, and they learn to exclude subjective concerns and sentimentality. Students learn to see the world through the lens of the law; by learning to think like lawyers, they become lawyers. They not only learn to think objectively, rationally, and pragmatically but they also learn to value those traits, which become internalized. For a woman, learning to think like a lawyer has meant learning to assimilate traits that are thought of as typically male. And thus, it has meant learning to think "like a man." This is why—more than thirty years after Florence began her legal studies, as women are about to outnumber men as attorneys and judges—Harvard Law School Professor Lani Guinier chose *Becoming Gentlemen* as the title of her book about female law students.[4]

Florence understands that thinking like a lawyer is different from the "normal" thinking process: "You have to analyze things and separate things that are relevant and not relevant." But there was something else—an attitude, a male arrogance—that permeated the law school. Florence recalls, "The professors were like cocks strutting around and showing how smart they were. They were more vicious to the women, who didn't come to this aggressive approach as naturally as the men."

It wasn't just the women who need to be handled more gently. Men dropped out of law school too; those who could take the combat stayed and became what were called the "piranhas" and "barracudas." The educational method needed to be more humane, more caring, more nurturing.

"I didn't like law school," Florence says. "It was as if the professors were saying, I know it and you don't and look how stupid you are." There could have been an alternative. "Why couldn't they say," Florence asks, "I know this stuff is foreign to you but I'll let you in on the secret; I'll teach you how to do this so that when I ask the questions, you'll know what answers I expect." In fact, many women were so intimidated that they were often reluctant to volunteer in class, even when they were certain of the answer.[5] Florence remembers an incident in class when she was a first-year student:

It was a very complicated case in international law involving semi-fraudulent activities. As a first-year student, you don't know any of the theoretical, legal issues. I was the only one in the class who got it because I knew what they were looking for and I found it. It was not theoretical; it was strictly procedural.

I was shy, I didn't want to draw attention to myself because if I said something wrong I was laughed at, pooh-poohed, derided. The kids were very unkind; it was awful. Finally, the prof said, "Any other theories?"

Bingo! Everyone looked at me and they hated me, because I got it.

Over the years, Florence met many other female attorneys who'd had similar experiences. "The professors always tried to trip you up," she says. Still, she tries to understand:

I know why they did it; they want to toughen you up for the practice of law. But I talked to people going through medical school. I asked if this was the way it was there too. Are they trying to flunk you out? No. Once you're admitted they work their darndest to help you stay in. They're available for you if you need help; they help you get help.

It was the same feeling in Cincinnati and here in Houston. They were never really on our side. It was OK with them if we worked our butts off and got low grades and we decided to leave. It wasn't fair. In Houston no one took us seriously.

This was 1971, it was just after the beginning of the feminine awakening. Women were saying, "Here, we matter too." But when I entered law school, I wouldn't say we were invisible; we were seen as intruders. Nobody believed we belonged there.

Not only was there a lack of support for the women, but there was blatant sexism among male students and professors. One day, Florence was in a civil procedure class held in a huge lecture hall. "There were maybe five women in my class," Florence recalls, "with fifty, sixty, eighty men. The professor came in, looked around, and announced, 'Ah, today is ladies day; this is the day we pick on the ladies,' and every question, as nasty as it could be put, was put to the ladies." The men chuckled, enjoying the women's discomfort.

Florence also took issue with other common practices in law school. "The first impression I got was one of cliques. Everyone had a peer group except for the women. Women were not included in any kind of study group or activity or research project, we were on the outside," Florence says. Yet none of the women came together to help each other. There was only one other woman in Florence's class who had a child. "She and I were so busy with our outside commitments that we had no time to give to developing a peer group." But Florence wonders why "those who had just come out of undergraduate school didn't seem to develop any kinds of connections with each other."

At the time, Florence sensed how important peer study groups were. Study groups are helpful to all students, particularly minorities and returning women.[6] In study groups, as students continue discussion in social settings — over lunch, walking to class — they reinforce what each learns individually. But, like the other women, Florence "felt and remained isolated." The one time the women got together was when Florence organized a protest. "I was so timid at the time," she told me, "I said to Howard, 'Imagine me doing this?'" Timid, perhaps, but also indignant. It seemed very strange to her that in a first-semester course "no woman got over a C but some of the men got A's and B's, and we knew who the smart people were."[7] Florence recalls:

The women got together to decide what we should do about that. We thought that there must be a way to put a number, not a name, on the test booklet, so that this professor wouldn't know whose paper he was grading. He definitely was not playing fair. We went to the dean's office and told him about that idea; he said that he would approve it and instituted a way to do that.

But good students were still getting C's—the girls—so we were livid. We went back to the dean and asked: "Are you sure that the professor wouldn't have had any way to find out whose paper he was grading?" The dean said that they had used a number system, just as we had suggested. So we asked him who had the key to which name goes to which number. He said that it was in the office.

In the office? Where anyone could have access to it? So we figured out that this professor figured out which were the women's papers.

Florence had dealt with overt sexism and ageism in undergraduate school and, in spite of her "timidity," was prepared to deal with them again. It soon became clear, however, that her difficulty as a mature woman in law school was more subtle and indirect. The law, as Florence and others perceive it, "embodies a male culture, a male way of doing things" that dominated both the law school curriculum and methodology.

Traditionally and symbolically, law professor Ngaire Naffine explains, the law is personified as a "blind maiden balancing the scales of justice, dispensing her services with perfect impartiality" (Naffine, ix). The symbol is appealing, but false. The law, as it is still practiced in western society, is neither blind nor female. A convincing body of evidence has been produced by feminist legal theorists to support the position that there is a "deep-seated male orientation in law, which infects all its practices" (Naffine, 2). It is not difficult to understand why. Men constructed the fundamental principles of western law, wrote the laws, interpreted the laws, enforced the laws. Professor of Law Catharine MacKinnon, a feminist and prolific writer, asserts that the law, which seems to be

neutral, abstract, elevated, pervasive—both institutionalizes the power of men over women and institutionalizes power in its male form . . .

Those with power in civil society, not women, design its norms and institutions, which become the status quo. Those with power, not usually women, write constitutions, which become law's highest standards. Those with power in political systems that women did not design and from which women have been

excluded write legislation, which sets ruling values . . . Lines of precedent fully
developed before women were permitted to vote, continued while women were
not allowed to learn to read and write . . . (MacKinnon, 611)

Naturally, the law values characteristics identified as male—objectivity, rational thinking, detachment, competitiveness, and aggressiveness. Those "male" qualities are not necessarily negative (nor are they held solely by men). The problem is that they continue to be valued to the *exclusion* of characteristics considered female, such as subjectivity or relativism, even when approaching a legal conflict more subjectively might lead to a better solution. The taken-for-granted assumption in the law has been that objectivity is always better than subjectivity.

Objectivity (supposing it is even achievable), has become an issue that is the source of heated debate.[8] Objectivity requires a dispassionately rational, detached, and impartial attitude that is attained by relying on what Florence describes as a "rigid, rule-bound way of thinking about legal issues and problems." Theoretically, as Naffine explains it, problems are "decontextualized" and abstracted (Naffine, 53); that is, the legal question is taken out of its context. Therefore, a law student "may pass through the university encountering literally more than thousands of cases with little thought for the human beings to whom they must be applied." Naffine points out that many law school curricula now include nontraditional topics to add a "social and critical dimension" to legal teaching and "to show that law has a real-life setting" (ibid., 29).[9]

While feminist critics do not, of course, suggest that the law should be completely relative, some suggest that guidelines or standards, rather than rules, would enable legal judgment to take individual circumstances into account. The idea "that you can identify an essential human being disconnected from time and place and then endeavor to meet his needs—is fundamentally flawed," Naffine claims. "Impartial justice," she says, "cannot be secured by ignoring the specific qualities of people and by assuming that we are all interchangeable units" (ibid., x). In Naffine's view, which is characteristic of a number of other feminist critics of the American and British legal systems, this is sometimes called "abstract universality" (ibid., 96).

Florence contends that applying the rules abstractly is not sufficient: "You can't really fix a problem without seeing the whole." As a law student, she experienced a conflict which has been described as "thinking like a lawyer" vs. "thinking like a person." She says:

This is where I got in trouble. I had to struggle to narrow down my focus; to stay on the defined written-down laws and precedents even if, in fact, they didn't make any sense in that particular case. Common sense was my big problem in law school. I found there wasn't enough room for common sense, and that's one of the ways in which they change your thinking, to squeeze you into a mold by saying there's no room for common sense because that's too subjective. You have to suspend your common sense and look up the rules and adapt your facts to the rules and adjust your judgment. To me, that's just as subjective because you're not an engineer dealing with equations or science.

As more women are entering law and politics, two areas that have been intimately linked since the beginning of this nation's history, these professions may eventually incorporate more "female" values and attitudes.[10] It is unfortunate, I think, that these values are characterized as female, rather than humanistic. A synthesis of the two approaches (rather than competition between polarized notions of male vs. female values) might result in decisions that are less rule-bound and that focus more on the broader context of the situation. At present, however, the law remains "male"—philosophically, culturally, and practically. In the early 1990s, Judith Baer argued in her treatise on women and American law that there are "many examples of male bias in the content of law," as well as a bias, "intentional or not, [that] pervades law's structures and functions" (Baer, 245). The problems are not yet resolved.

Legal culture is initiated, transmitted, and perpetuated by law school curricula that have been resistant to alternative or multiple perspectives. It will be interesting to see how gender biases, which are embedded in legal culture, are affected by the recent appointment of female deans at some of the most prestigious and elite law schools: Stanford, Duke, Georgetown, and Harvard. Common sense tells us that the culture of these schools will be affected by female leadership; if that is true, we hope the effect will be positive. But as one of my professors was fond of saying, "Common sense tell us that the world is flat." The newest of the female deans is Elena Kagan, at Harvard, who was appointed in April 2003. This is especially satisfying since Harvard, founded in 1817, only began admitting women to their law school in 1953 (Dillon).[11]

In 1870, Harvard's small law faculty was guided by Christopher Columbus Langdell. He significantly shaped the teaching of law by basing the study of law upon the case method. Langdell's method was completely different from almost all teaching at the time, which was based upon lecture and rote memorization through drill; that is, persistent and repeated recitation and repetition. Because Langdell assumed the lawyer's business took place in the courtroom, for the first time students were reading original cases. Rather than memorize secondary sources and interpretations, students reviewed and discussed the arguments of major cases and the relationships among them. The instructor led the discussions by close questioning about "the facts of the case, points at issue, judicial reasoning, underlying doctrines and principles, and comparisons with other cases" (Garvin, 58).

Although the case method was resisted initially, after it was praised by "Louis Brandeis and other successful Langdell students" it was slowly adopted by some elite law schools. The case method proved to be far superior to recitation; it helped students understand basic legal principles and to "think like a lawyer" (Garvin, 59). And, while Langdell's method may have had intellectual consequences for legal education by making the study of law more narrow than liberal, it also made it more professional and serious, producing effective courtroom practitioners. Langdell's general method, although not all of his specific teaching strategies, is still practiced in law schools today and is known as the Socratic method. This method, in fact, dominates almost *all* first-year instruction. But law professor Lani Guinier finds the rapid-fire questioning method highly problematic. She thinks it is particularly unfair to women, who find it alienating (Guinier, Fine, and Balin, 28). In a study of teaching methods and practices at the University of Pennsylvania Law School, Guinier found that such a "competitive approach to training lawyers" not only "inhibits" many women but some men as well (ibid., 2). Many others agree. Professor of Law Michael Meltsner, who directed the First Year Lawyering Program at Harvard in 2002–2003, says that the focus of the Socratic method is to prepare students for litigation in which the law is "viewed as a public contest with winners and losers" (quoted in Garvin, 59).[12]

Because the method is so prevalent, the *Princeton Review* recommends that prospective female law students read Guinier's book, *Becoming Gentlemen,* before they apply to law schools. One law professor refers to the Socratic and case methods of teaching as "initiation rites" that first-year students must endure (Froom).

Guinier's findings confirm Florence's experiences with the Socratic method, although she doesn't totally agree with Guinier's conclusions. Florence believes that the method, used correctly, is designed to make you think on your feet, to think out a response. But Florence says that the method was misused to "trip you up, to mystify the law." She says:

My teachers, who all thought they used the Socratic method, didn't. They didn't put any thought into what questions they were asking, in terms of developing a concept. But they made sure the questions were so devious that whatever answer you gave, they could criticize it. They threw questions at you to show you how stupid you were. Their purpose was to make you feel inadequate and stupid, to make you work harder and to teach you that the law was some mysterious body of knowledge that it took some superhuman superior being to understand. Hopefully, because you're here in law school, you'll be able to get it eventually, but you don't get it yet.

It could have had value later on in the courtroom if it had been done properly, because it could teach you how to switch your thinking process; because in the courtroom you have to be good on your feet, and fast in your thinking. So it has a very valid purpose. But I was never lucky enough to get a teacher who used it well enough that I could get something out of it.

Some of Guinier's female colleagues resent her critique. What it implies, they say, is that "women need gentler treatment than their male classmates" (Mangan, 12). But Guinier defends her point of view: "A school may be treating all students the same; [yet] it may not be treating all students equitably. Some students may not be participating as much, learning as much, or feeling as competent when we insist on teaching them all by the same methods and all in a hierarchical, adversarial, formalistic way. Sameness may not be fairness in this context" (Guinier, Fine, and Balin, 12).

Guinier states that in a study of twenty-four Harvard classrooms, female law students were significantly more likely than male law students to report that they "never" or "only occasionally" asked questions or volunteered answers in class. In addition, professors allowed those with the quickest response time to dominate the class (ibid., 13), a situation that echoes Florence's experiences in Houston more than twenty years earlier. In Guinier's survey, women students reported that "men ask more questions, volunteer more often, enjoy greater peer tolerance of their remarks, receive more attention from faculty during classes, get called on more frequently, and receive more post-class 'follow-up' than women." Guinier reports that a study "at eight different law schools across the country found that male students speak disproportionately more in all classes taught by men" (ibid., 12).[13]

According to Carl Monk, executive director of the Association of American Law Schools, tough Socratic questioning is giving way to less combative forms of instruction (Mangan, 14). This is to be applauded, along with changes that address other problems. Law school methods and curricula are finally catching up to the reality of women's presence and needs in law schools. And, prompted by a relentless feminist critique, there have been significant inroads into male bias on the part of the professors.

The field has also seen an increase of women on law school faculties. Florence never had a female instructor—neither in Cincinnati nor in Houston. A study conducted by the Association of American Law Schools found that during the 1999–2000 school year 31.5 percent of the faculty were women. The percentage of female deans was, expectedly, lower: 10.9. Although women are still the minority, these figures represent a clear improvement.

Many assume that more female instructors will result in courses that are less competitive and more focused on teamwork. Professor Ann Shalleck teaches such a class in family law at American University. In this course she applies methods to legal education that have come to be associated with what is now known as "feminist pedagogy."[14] Shalleck's approach, often referred to as clinical legal education, is based upon progressive teaching principles, particularly the integration of theory and method. Shalleck uses such strategies as role playing followed by small group discussion not only to "explore the relationship between lawyer and client," but also to "enable students to look at legal doctrine, legal institutions, legal alternatives, and theoretical assumptions embodied in the law in the context of a real life" (Shalleck, 229). Clinical teachers also utilize such methods as models and simulations. Ideally these methods should not only be practiced by female instructors, but also disseminated among and accepted by predominantly male faculties. The "institutional cultures at individual schools" will, however, ultimately determine how amenable or resistant they are to the introduction of clinical teaching methods ("Advice for Women on Choosing a Law School").

There is further evidence of change, not just in method, but also in course offerings at some law schools, such as those advertised by Washington College of Law at American University in which "serious attention is given to ways that the structure and operation of the law can affect men and women differently" ("Women's and Gender Studies"). And in addition to changes in formal curricula, efforts are being made to warm up what has been called a "chilly climate" for nontraditional students on college and university campuses.[15] An example is Women in Law, an association at the University of

Kansas Law School that sponsors a mentor program for incoming students, presents speakers at brown bag lunches, provides information to law students at an annual Career Forum, and generally advocates for women students ("About Women in Law").

The fact that law schools are only beginning to catch up with the reality of women's needs is an example of what historian Joan Hoff calls the "broken barometer syndrome," that is the lag time between the start of political action and an ultimate improvement in status. Women have been entering the legal profession in large numbers for more than thirty years, since the passage of Title IX legislation in the early 1970s. But it was not until 1996—more than twenty years after Florence and her contemporaries experienced the shock of "coming into a foreign culture"—that the American Bar Association's report on the State of Women in the Law Schools finally recommended attention to issues of sexual harassment, academic and family support services, and career services. The ABA also encouraged individual faculty members to "better tailor their courses toward women students." The ABA recommended including "a broad range of issues that will be more appealing to women, using 'effective language' (i.e. using gender neutral language and 'hypotheticals'), using a variety of teaching methods and grading techniques to avoid giving some an 'arbitrary advantage,' and using gender-neutral testing methods" (ABA Watch). That handwritten in-class exams are now frowned upon recalls Florence's experience in which the women in her class consistently received lower grades than the men, as handwriting often gives away gender.

Unfortunately for Florence, neither the gains achieved by the women's movement nor Title IX affected the way law schools functioned in the 1970s. She was there too early—on the very cusp of the phenomenon—to have experienced the positive effects ultimately brought about by the huge influx of female law students. Nor, as she began her career, did she feel the positive effects of the growing number of women entering the profession.

CHAPTER 4

Ethical Dilemmas

Practicing Family Law

"I don't know if I chose family law or it chose me."

— FLORENCE KUSNETZ

"Y̲ou're a sap, you're a fool, what is it your business what she does with the money after the case is over? This isn't the way you practice law."

The occasion for this eruption was the conclusion of one of Florence's first cases. Florence describes the day as the happiest of her new professional life. She was fresh out of law school and working at her first job, an internship in a small law firm in Houston. "I was a young lawyer, very aggressive and eager to prove my mettle," Florence says. The client was a woman named Gussie. She was the very first client that Florence got on her own, and she needed child support. "She was a nurse at a local hospital with several children to raise, struggling to make ends meet. Gussie's husband was several thousand dollars behind in his payments; no one had enforced the law," Florence recalls.

Florence had an arrangement—what she facetiously calls a "mutual exploitation" arrangement—with Seymour Lieberman, a lawyer who shared an office with two other attorneys. She was grateful to have the job. When she began to look for work, Florence realized that "the world was not looking for a forty-four-year-old, entry-level female lawyer. I really pounded the pavements, visiting large and small law firms. I was willing to start anywhere" (Surface, 4). Lieberman and his associates provided Florence with an office, a desk, and a typewriter. In return she worked for $250 a month as an apprentice doing research, preparing documents, and attending real-estate closings, "but that's not much help if you don't know how to fill in the forms." As part of her apprenticeship Florence could work on cases independently if, as with Gussie, she'd acquired them on her own.

Florence successfully collected five or six thousand dollars from Gussie's husband, a bus driver. For the first time, Gussie had a lump sum of money. Florence was concerned that it would just slip away:

I asked her: Gussie, what are you going to do with this money? She said, "I don't know, I'll pay off some bills, I'll get the kids the things they need." So I said to her, Gussie, from what you told me, I know that you've been paying on your house for ten or eleven years and you still owe money on it. You have it on a "contract for sale," which is not a normal way to buy a house because it's without a mortgage. If you default on one payment you have no equity so you lose the whole house, it reverts back to the owner. Why don't you find out how much you owe on your house and pay it off?

Florence called the owner, a man who negotiated such contracts for sale in the black community. "They pay and they pay and they pay, and if they miss a payment, he gets the property back," Florence explains. "Then he contracts it to somebody else and keeps getting the money. It's a common way of dealing with poor people who don't have down payments. They never build up equity." When Florence learned that Gussie needed only another few thousand dollars to pay off the balance, she convinced her that "it [was] in her best interest to pay off the balance." Gussie's sister, who worked in a bank, was able to get her a loan for the difference.

The owner was "aghast," Florence says. "He gave me a hard time because he really didn't want to sell the house, but he had to if she met the terms of the contract." Florence was overjoyed when she succeeded in getting Gussie the deed to her house, both for Gussie and for herself as well. She was soon deflated, however, by the reaction of the attorneys in her office. They were "irate at what I was doing even though it didn't affect them or the work I was doing with them." Florence defended herself: "She's paying me, I said. I'm working for my client's best interest. Why shouldn't I do this? She doesn't know what her options are and I can see what her needs are. Was I wrong to suggest that she might do this? She's smart enough to know that what I'm saying makes sense and she was able to do it."

But her colleagues wouldn't let it rest. "They went on and on; they made my life there uncomfortable; they made me feel like I was the dumb one."

It wasn't until later that Florence came to believe "how typically male this whole scenario was." In law school, Florence learned that she was a woman in a man's world. In her professional life she was learning the same lesson. Myra Dinnerstein's characterization of "women split between two worlds"

referred to women like Florence who began their adult lives as typical homemakers, presiding over their domestic world (Dinnerstein, ix–x). When they
began jobs or careers, they entered the public world. When Florence's career
began in the early 1970s, the public world was the world of the law, which was
completely male-dominated. "The men lawyers I worked with in courts and
elsewhere focused on the end result: you get to where you're going, you're
finished, you go on. They didn't see the big picture. Women see things differently from men; we see things in a broader context with a broader focus.
You didn't fix one problem without seeing the whole." Consequently, it is
reasonable to infer, as Florence did, that men and women would develop
different attitudes toward the law and the way it is practiced.

At this point, it's too soon to determine the impact, if any, that the large
and growing number of female attorneys will have upon the way the law
is practiced, although the demographic change since the passage of 1972's
Title IX legislation has been startling. By the late 1990s 45 percent of those
newly admitted to the bar were women. Because of the numbers, many
attorneys believe gender bias is no longer an issue. They think that talk
about a gender gap is "overblown." One was quoted as saying that "women
should grow up and stop whining" (Rhode 2000, 39).

But numbers alone tend to mask problems of gender bias, which is central
to the story of CourtWatch. The 1994 Gender Bias Task Force of Texas
report was only one of "some sixty surveys" nationwide that "consistently
[found] substantial race and gender disparities," such as glass ceilings in law
firms and law schools, lower salaries for women than men, and other evidence of a persistent gender gap.[1] While "progress has been substantial," the
agenda remains "unfinished" (Rhode 2000, 38). Cultural change is a very
slow process. Since women in the law are a relatively recent phenomenon,
they have not been in a position to make substantive changes in legal practices or legal culture.

When Florence established her legal practice in the early 1970s, she was
following the tradition of a few women with incredible determination who
managed to practice earlier in the century, when women were rarely admitted to the bar. There is an understandable fascination with the histories
of these first women lawyers; they are empowering stories of how women
coped as they "prevailed over great obstacles" (Bowman, 629).[2] But their
stories are more than that; they expose the paradoxes or the "double bind"
of the female attorney who was (and still is) caught in a "dilemma" (Bow-

man, 625). They provide a glimpse into how the women dealt with the "contradictions between the socially defined" images of women and of lawyers: "Shall she model herself upon the stereotypically male image of an attorney and risk being accused of inappropriate aggressiveness? Or shall she heed the advice . . . to act more femininely, talk more femininely, walk more femininely—and risk the judgment that she is passive and unsuited to the life of the courtroom?" (ibid.).

Life stories of women who entered the law more recently than those pioneers have also been written, and they include firsthand accounts of the hurdles that, like Florence, they overcame in gaining respect and recognition as professionals: "Those few women who gained admission to the bar could not compete for work on an equal basis with men. Often, they could find work only as law librarians or legal secretaries. When they did actually practice, they might be hidden away in the recesses of law firms, where they could not offend customers" (Baer, 276).

Women who were hired by law firms were often asked to take on work that men would never be asked to perform (Bowman, 628). One example is none other than Sandra Day O'Connor, who has reached the pinnacle of professional success as the first female United States Supreme Court justice. After she graduated from Stanford, with honors, she was offered a job as a stenographer in a law firm! That was in 1952. The situation was better for Florence in 1972; the profession was still hostile to women but gender discrimination was not quite so overt.

Florence remained in her apprenticeship with Lieberman just long enough to establish her own general civil practice. She says:

I went into a lot of courts: county court, probate court. I remember going into court and I was the only woman. Lawyers, judges, bailiffs, all they wanted to do was hold your hand. They were absolutely condescending.

There were some older women who had gone through law school in the sixties who were very nice to me (a few; I would say half of them). Because practicing law is so different from going to law school, they offered to help. And I did call them; I'm not proud. If I need it, I call for help.

They were extremely cognizant about what my needs were, as if to say, "I know those bullies out there, and they're going to bully you. And here's what you do: don't pay attention to this one, and this one is worse, and that one's gonna make you feel like two cents."

In twenty years of practice, Florence says, she never had any male lawyer "reach out a hand to help or to be nice; it was very adversarial."

In the 1970s, Florence believes, women going into law were not planning, nor were they encouraged, to be trial lawyers. At that time, what appealed to women was a chance to help people rather than to "fight wars," she says. "Women were more willing to talk, to settle, to work things out." Florence thinks that men didn't see it that way. Men were saying, "What? Why should I talk settlement? I'm being paid by the hour." Over the years she has seen a change, Florence says, but when she first started practicing law "a lot of women didn't need to support themselves; they didn't need the big incomes right away. And frankly, they weren't as competitive. It's a very nice thing to see your name in the paper, especially in high-profile cases. We had a lot of those, every big city does. But the women didn't need to see their names in the papers. Women weren't so power-hungry, or money-hungry."

Florence experienced the full range of treatment that other women have encountered in the courts from judges, opposing attorneys, and even witnesses, experiences which have been described as ranging "from the apparently well-meaning to the consciously insulting to the blatantly bigoted." One judge referred to an attorney as a "little girl," another was "complimented" for being a "fashion plate" (Baer, 271). The *Gender Bias Task Force of Texas Final Report* cites other instances of "hostile, demeaning, and discriminatory gender-biased treatment in the courtroom" that was experienced by many female attorneys. One attorney recalled: "Despite the fact that I had a two-piece suit on, carried a 'lawyer's briefcase,' and stand 5′11″ tall, the . . . judge asked me in a loud voice, 'What can I do for you little lady?'" (*Gender Bias Task Force Report*, 37).

Florence recalls: "In my first year of practice—seventy-three or seventy-four—I had a bailiff pat me on the head like a little girl; I was as old or older than he was!" She also remembers an opposing counsel who made faces at her in court "just to spook me," she says. She couldn't imagine that he would ever do that to a male attorney. "The funny thing is," Florence says, "he referred a client to me about six months later." She couldn't understand why. "I thought he hated my guts." When she called the attorney to ask him about the referral, the situation became clear. It was a difficult family law case. "Of course I sent her to you," he explained. "You're the one who can help her. She's hysterical; she's a hysterical woman." Florence argued, "She's not hysterical, she's a woman in distress; she needs a lot of help. She needs somebody who will listen to her." Florence did listen, to her and to many others. "I got tons of clients from word-of-mouth because everybody knew that I really gave each case special attention."

After about five years of general practice, Florence decided she had to lighten the load. She had already stopped taking criminal cases:

I had no stomach for that. With all the plea bargains and everybody in the system knowing everybody else personally, it was a real good old boys system, and I never felt comfortable there. So I gave up criminal law and concentrated on civil.

But I looked for an area of expertise. If I was going to put all this time into practicing law, I wanted to do what I did better and differently than most people, otherwise why bother? My time has always been extremely precious to me; I hate to waste time.

I was finding out that most lawyers hated doing family law. Many lawyers would say, "As soon as I can afford it, I'll give it up."

But Florence's heart, she had learned, was in family law. "I don't know if I chose family law or it chose me." Either way, it was a good match; she was very good at it and she liked doing what she was good at: "I'm good at contracts too, I can write the best contract of anyone I know, but didn't give me the same satisfaction as helping move someone through a treacherous and difficult and devious system. I seemed to have more of a tolerance for problems of the family and I'm sure it was because I was twenty years older than most of them when I became a lawyer. Also, I was not in the practice of law to support my family and there was no pressure on me to produce income. I had the luxury of doing something I truly wanted to do."

Jewish culture predisposed Florence (albeit unconsciously, she thinks) to work in family law for several reasons. It was compatible with her social consciousness and with the concept of *tikkun olam* (the obligation to "repair" the world). It was an area of the law that intersected with a deeply held Jewish value—the importance of the family.

In biblical times the obligations and rights of the husband and wife, the protection of children, and the disposal of property had already been defined for Jews. But it was Rabbinical law that "modified and humanized" the marriage laws (Shepherd, 32–34), changing women's status from chattels, the property of fathers or husbands, to that of protected inferiors. The new laws safeguarded the woman's property and ensured the basic obligations of the man to provide his wife with food, clothing, and sexual relations.[3]

In the early Middle Ages, polygyny was still practiced in European Jewish society. But in the eleventh century an important ruling made it essentially impossible for a man to take more than one wife. In addition, by this time, a man could no longer divorce his wife without her consent. The marriage contract, the ketubah, was "women's protection against desertion." Later on, courts, *bet din,* were established in the Jewish villages and towns of Europe to settle acrimonious civil and domestic disputes, a tradition that was carried to America by Jewish immigrants. (Although Florence hadn't been aware of it, there was a *bet din* system in Brooklyn that was formalized only a few years before she was born.)[4] As an attorney, Florence would be dealing with the tenacious remnants of these predecessors of contemporary family law.

The tradition of the wife as a protected inferior, symbolized by the term "paterfamilias," made its way into Roman law and eventually into British common law. Common law, historically, allowed husbands to "chastise" their wives using "reasonable force"(Chamallas, 19). In Britain, the original "rule of thumb" allowed a husband to beat his wife "with a rod or stick, so long as it was not wider than his thumb" ("Family Violence," 5). Despite this rule, until the seventeenth century in some parts of Europe and into the nineteenth century in England husbands could actually *murder* their wives without punishment. Even animals "were protected legally before women and children" ("Family Violence," 1).

Subsequently, family law arrived in the colonies with the British settlers and, as in biblical times, regulated marriage and divorce. Family law identified the "reciprocal rights and duties of family members" and apportioned "power and responsibility among husbands and wives, parents and children" (Baer, 123). A father's right to physically "chastise" his child is well known. Less well known is that in colonial Massachusetts a father had the right to *kill* a disobedient child (Fitzgerald, 433). And, as in Britain, husbands had the power to chastise or, as it was called here in the United States, to "correct," his wife. When the right of force was finally abolished, it was supplanted by a doctrine of "family privacy," which enabled the legal community to look away when what we now call domestic violence occurred.[5]

Family law in America has changed dramatically since the nineteenth century when, as in Britain, the doctrine known as couverture gave the husband complete economic control over his wife. Wives had "no right to hold, acquire, or convey property, retain their own wages, enter into contracts, or initiate legal claims" (Rhode 1999, 127). These issues were grievous to early suffragists. Elizabeth Cady Stanton said, "This whole question of women's rights turns on the pivot of the marriage relation and, mark my word, sooner or later it will be the topic for discussion" (quoted in Sachs and Wilson, 148). Changing these "old patriarchal laws" was a notable success of the women's suffrage movement (Baer, 125).[6]

One major reason for the changes in family law since the nineteenth century is not only that roles have changed within the marriage but that the definition, nature, and concept of family itself have changed, making family law one of the most complex and difficult areas in American jurisprudence. Harris County Family Court Judge Linda Motheral says she was drawn to family law because she was interested in people, not business or property: "Family law allows you to enter the personal dynamic, it impacts people's lives in important ways. And it touches so many lives: 50 percent of American families and a huge number of children are affected by contentious divorces, conflict, and sometimes by poverty." She is correct, of course. At the beginning of the twentieth century only one in five hundred marriages ended in divorce. By mid-century the number was one in three; estimates are now that it is one in two.

Despite family law's importance in modern life, it is low in prestige in the legal hierarchy. Yet it actually has gained status; matrimonial and child custody cases used to be looked down upon "at best, as paralegal," (Rhode 1999, 134). Family law's low status is due to a number of factors. It doesn't pay as well as other areas; family lawyers deal with ordinary people who can get very emotional; and, Judge Motheral says, "domestic disputes are messy, you have to get into people's private behavior, their bedrooms." Many male lawyers are generally averse to family law for these very reasons, and there is more prestige in high-profile, high-money jury trials.

Whatever the reasons, family lawyers are harshly and unjustly demeaned by their colleagues in other areas of the law as "bottom-feeders," Motheral says. Another Harris County Family Court judge, Bonnie Hellums, agrees: "Family court judges are low in the hierarchy. The 'civs' and the 'crims' feel like they're real judges. It's true nationally, it's true statewide, and it's true locally. And it's amazing to me because I'd love to get some judges from across the street, to get them to listen to a family case, because they'd be blown away. Because then they've got to handle the emotions, and they've got to deal with kid stuff, and they've got to deal with property. And the law changes more rapidly in the family area than in any other area of the law. It's a very sophisticated practice."

Judge Mary Sean O'Reilly, one of the contributors to the report of the
Gender Bias Task Force of Texas, adds:

*There's a kind of schizophrenia about family law. It's not real law—it's divorce,
it's kids, it's pots and pans, it's not real, it's just family. It's not a big civil litigation, it's not building bridges, or breaking contracts or shooting people up at the
dime store. It doesn't deal with power, or big bucks, or high visibility, or making
the Fortune 500. How can pots and pans possibly be as significant as doing a big
business deal, or a real estate deal, or defending O. J. Simpson? How could it
possibly be so important? It deals with family issues, which are women's issues.*

I have come to believe that there is yet another reason that family law has
low status in the legal hierarchy. It is not only because family law deals with
women's issues, but because it is an area in the law that is female dominated,
and thus devalued. Family law practice shares the stigma with some other
professions—such as elementary school teaching and nursing—of being
"women's work." In fact, until the 1970s, family law was the one area in
which women were encouraged to practice. The commonly held view was
that women were *suited* to dealing with domestic crises, "hysterical women,"
emotional situations, intimacy, and, of course, children, and this perception
has not been totally extinguished even now. The converse was also believed
to be true, that women were not suited to other areas of the law. It was said:
"Women can't be shining lights at the bar because they are too kind; in
criminal law women can't handle discussions of sex; women are not good
corporation lawyers because they are not cold and ruthless; women lack
a high grade of intellect; women in firms will alienate clients; and finally,
women are poor employment risks . . . [they] lack ability, dedication, and
emotional stability; they feel an obligation to home and family" (Sachs and
Wilson, 190).

By their own admission, however, and in the record, women have shown
themselves to be quite capable of a so-called "macho" ethic in courtroom
battles, complete with sports and war metaphors. But many women become
unhappy with the "role of gladiator."[7] Judge Hellums remembers the turning point for her. She had just successfully completed a case. "The wife
turned around and said to me, 'Why did we butcher that man; I was married
to that man for forty years? Why did we leave him bleeding on the floor?'
I thought, there's got to be another way to do this." Florence, too, regrets
that early in her career she "went for the jugular." Both women followed the

letter of the law and achieved justice for their clients, in our conventional understanding of the concept. But whether the process was humane, ethical, and moral was what troubled them. When she was a student, Florence took an ethics course with a professor who was the senior partner in a law firm. "The whole thrust of his ethics course was," she says, "watch yourself but make as much money as you can without breaking the law. I can't imagine that if I had a female professor I would have come out of an ethics class with that message."

The perception that there is a male set of ethics and another, different female set of ethics has been the subject of discussion in the feminist literature for the past twenty years. A bit more recently it has been debated within feminist legal theory. The moral dilemma that Bonnie Hellums experienced—attaining justice for her client by having done something morally wrong—exemplifies the conflict between what Harvard psychologist Carol Gilligan described in her 1982 book *In a Different Voice* as an ethic of justice versus an ethic of care. Gilligan's powerful theoretical model remains controversial and is still being discussed and applied to a number of diverse areas of study including philosophy, psychology, education, sociology, and jurisprudence. It is worth exploring for the issues it raises for family law; Florence found it particularly relevant for the insights it prompts and the possibilities it suggests.

Gilligan's theory of an ethic of care resulted from her work with Lawrence Kohlberg, with whom she was associated at Harvard. Drawing upon the work of Jean Piaget, Kohlberg had constructed a "stage theory" of moral development by studying the way subjects of different ages made decisions about right and wrong.[8] He posed hypothetical scenarios and then asked subjects of varying ages questions about what would be the right thing to do in such a situation. The scenarios posed moral dilemmas for which there were no objective right or wrong answers. (The most famous of these is called the "Heinz dilemma." Briefly: Heinz is a man whose wife is deathly ill. The medicine to cure her exists, but he can't afford to buy it. He tries to negotiate with the pharmacist, but to no avail. The question is, would it be right or wrong for Heinz to break into a pharmacy for the drug?)

Kohlberg then illustrated how children's abilities to make moral or ethical judgments change as they mature intellectually. He found that there was a "hierarchy" of moral development: children base their judgments upon ever more sophisticated and "higher" values. Young children make judgments about right and wrong for personal and pragmatic reasons. For example, in the Heinz dilemma, they decide that the act is wrong because they might be caught and punished for breaking into the pharmacy. As children's intellects develop and they can comprehend more sophisticated and abstract ideas, Kohlberg maintained, they begin to make moral judgments on the basis of abstract rules or laws. Finally, in the ultimate stage of moral development, he said, they make judgments according to universal principles of right and wrong, using an ideal of abstract justice—absolute, objective—that can be applied equally to all and is independent of personal consequences. Kohlberg took it for granted that abstract justice was the ideal, the highest value to which one could refer in making moral or ethical decisions.

But Kohlberg, it turned out, had based his theory almost exclusively on responses by male subjects, thereby tacitly fixing a male-referenced standard as the norm.[9] Subsequently, as additional studies included females and gender comparisons were drawn, Gilligan found it odd that girls didn't seem to demonstrate the same high level of moral development (an especially interesting turn of events, since women have historically been depicted as morally superior to men). Gilligan reasoned that Kohlberg's theory described *male* moral development and proposed an alternative model through which to assess female moral development, based upon a different set or hierarchy of values.

A "hypothesis cannot be tested adequately," Gilligan said, by examining only male behavior; something is "missed by the practice of leaving out girls" (Gilligan 1986, 325). For example, boys tend to adhere closely to rules when they play games. Gilligan found that girls, on the other hand, tend to bend the rules if feelings might be hurt or friendships might be threatened by applying them. Likewise, boys tend to adhere more closely to the notion of abstract criteria of right and wrong in making moral and ethical judgments. Girls' judgments are often more relative and contextual, taking into account how a decision might affect another person. Boys tend to develop an ethic in which justice is the highest value while girls develop an ethic of care, Gilligan says, in which relationships are the highest value. Consequently, boys and girls tend to respond to questions about right and wrong differently. When boys and girls speak about what is moral, Gilligan concluded, they often speak in "different voices." These different male and female orientations to the concept of justice are carried forward into adulthood.

Gilligan's "different voice" theory is not without its problems.[10] Critics claim that, in addition to other methodological problems, she based her conclusions and generalizations upon the limited sample in her study. She is also criticized for assigning moral superiority to women's concern with relationships and what Professor Joan Williams calls a "celebration of feminine domesticity" (quoted in Smith, 290).

But the longer-lasting debate has to do with yet another controversial aspect of Gilligan's theory: in the ongoing sameness-difference debate, she supports the notion of difference. "Emphasizing males' association with abstract rationality and females' concern with interpersonal relationships reinforces longstanding stereotypes," warns Stanford Professor of Law Deborah Rhode. In order to "make sense of gender dynamics," she says "we need frameworks that neither overstate nor undervalue gender difference" (Rhode 1999, 176–177). Not an easy balance to achieve.

Over time, Gilligan and others have responded to critics by refining and amending the theory. Some criticisms are not with the different voice theory so much as with its interpretation and application. Because the theory is so accessible, because it seems to confirm women's experiences, because it is "memorable, handy, and easy to oversimplify, there is the temptation to use Gilligan's work in a shallow way, to distill it into a neat formula" (Scales, 97). For example, the concept of different voices has been presented as a simple dichotomy, as either-or. But, to be fair, Gilligan never claimed that either sex used one or the other "voice" exclusively. On the contrary, Gilligan thought, as Martha Chamallas explains, that "most people, males and females, used both voices or orientations in defining and resolving problems" (Chamallas, 64). Gilligan claims that two moral voices can exist: one speaking about justice, that is "equality, reciprocity, fairness," and another that "speaks about connection, not hurting, care, and response" (quoted in Mashburn, 188). An ethic of care, then, does not mean that women disregard criteria related to abstract justice in making moral and ethical judgments. Rather, these criteria are not taken for granted as the only, or even the best, available. Gilligan argued "in favor of transforming the moral domain by bringing the two voices together in an inclusive way that required changing both orientations" (Chamallas, 65).

If there are different voices, is such a synthesis possible? Are the voices compatible? Some speculate whether there might be a middle ground that incorporates other theories together with Gilligan's notion of an ethic of care.[11] Clearly, there are opposing and still unresolved arguments. But the notion of two ethical systems provides an interesting and useful lens through which to examine the law, particularly family law.

Family law, which falls under the umbrella category of civil law, covers a wide range of areas as well as a large and constantly increasing volume of cases that may involve: "divorce, annulment, and property distribution; child custody and visitation; alimony and child support; paternity, adoption, and termination of parental rights; juvenile causes (juvenile delinquency, child abuse, and child neglect); domestic violence; criminal nonsupport; name change; guardianship of minors and disabled persons; and withholding or withdrawal of life-sustaining medical procedures, involuntary admissions, and emergency evaluations" (Babb, 31).[12]

In conversations with Florence, other family law attorneys, and judges, I heard repeatedly how applying the rules and procedure of family law to domestic disputes in a strictly abstract, non-contextual, impartial, and objective way—which is consistent with an ethic of justice—creates a particularly bad mismatch. Domestic disputes are highly emotional situations that tend to be unique and idiosyncratic. Still, the system traditionally operates by attempting to apply the law mechanically and objectively. The problem, Florence says, is that the resulting decision "may be technically correct and morally wrong." It may ultimately intensify an already stressed relationship that usually must continue long after a case has been concluded. If family law were *also* informed by an ethic of care, that is, by placing a higher value on relationships, the family court system would function very differently.

A related issue is that family law is part of civil law, itself an adversarial system. "In certain circumstances," Florence concedes, "the law has to be adversarial because you have two people at opposite ends of the truth." In family law, however, rather than resolving conflicts, the adversarial nature of civil law often exacerbates tensions. Florence believes that

there's no reason a husband and wife have to be a plaintiff and a defendant. They both have grievances, almost always. Almost always they both are right. Almost always the two don't see eye to eye about some things but they do over other things. A domestic dispute is not the kind of dispute that lends itself to an adversarial action. That is appropriate in disputes that lend themselves toward definitive resolution. You have a problem, you solve the problem and you go on your way. You don't usually have an ongoing relationship. You want to get it over with and get on with your life. If you're suing your brother-in-law and you know you're going to be seeing your brother-in-law for the rest of your life you might want to avoid a conflict that will spill over into your family. The closer relationship you have, the more enmity. The only way to avoid this conflict is by taking the case out of the adversarial system.

Relying on the rules that govern civil procedure, or what is known as "black-letter law," has built-in problems for the resolution of domestic disputes. Rules of evidence, for example, sometimes "don't make sense in family court," Florence says, "particularly in child custody cases." This is especially true when there are allegations of sexual abuse, as in the Parker-Casterline case documented in *America Undercover: Women on Trial.* This was the case in which the father's prior conviction for rape was not admissible in evidence. Many rules lend themselves to abuse, and "the lawyers exploit that," Florence charges. "They use the rules to delay and to increase costs."

On my first visit to Houston in 1999, I had dinner at Florence's home with a group of women who had been involved with CourtWatch. Among them was Claudia Williamson, who was talking about what she called "the mercenary mindset of the lawyers." She had been through a wounding divorce procedure and claimed that her husband's lawyer said things that were "totally untrue." His attitude was, as Claudia described it: "Hey, I'm just doing my job, ma'am. He hired me and that's what I'm hired to do." But "what he was hired to do," Claudia said, "was to destroy me, although he followed the letter of the law—whether in fact it was ethical, appropriate, or moral." The proceedings began in 1993. It took until 1995 for Claudia to finish paying her attorney and "to climb out of the black hole," she said. Judge Bonnie Hellums, a successful CourtWatch candidate in 1994 who is still on the Harris County Family Court bench, was at that dinner meeting. "Two years is par for the course," she told Claudia, "you're right there in the norm."

Something that especially infuriated Claudia was the way rules of evidence were manipulated by her husband's attorney. But, Claudia concluded, "in the end it didn't matter because the judge was asleep anyway," which provoked an outbreak of hilarity and gales of knowing laughter around the table. Claudia may have been joking but some of the women knew that that actually happened in the court.

Diana Compton, one of the CourtWatch founders, was also at the dinner meeting. She had gone on to law school and, like Florence, become a family law attorney. She was disillusioned: "I'm taking families through this horrible process and nobody comes out satisfied. The clients hate me in the end because the outcome is always bloody. They hate the system, they hate the judges, and they hate the fact that they're poorer and not better off. They had their day in court but nobody listened."

Florence understands Diana's feelings. In the summer of 1980, when she had been practicing law for several years, she received an application to

become a family law specialist. By that time, she had been an attorney for
seven or eight years and had an ever-growing family law practice. She also
had an ever-growing frustration with the system. Florence remembers: "I
was looking at the application and all the questions were totally procedural.
What they were asking would have been just as appropriate for trial law
or probate law. How did this demonstrate that someone was prepared to
be a specialist in family law? Most attorneys go through the motions, they
become certified in order to raise their fees. This rubbed me the wrong way.
This was the first niggling sensation I had that I wasn't doing what I really
wanted to be doing in family law." [13]

Florence began to do some serious soul-searching: "I began to see that
nothing was getting better," she says. "The cases were getting bloodier." She
asked herself, "Is this what you want to do, is this what you went to school
for, is this what you had in your mind as a sense of justice, is this what you
were put on earth for? Shouldn't you be bringing some equity and justice
into the world?" Something felt very wrong.

Florence did some research. She checked out books on arbitration, conciliation, "whatever I could read," she says. She began to think about creating
a better system, an alternative system. But her research was sporadic; she was
busy with her work. And then, Florence says, "One day I open the paper,
it must have been April 1981, and I see a front-page article about this man
named O. J. Coogler. He had invented a system called 'Structured Mediation' and was giving courses all over the country to train family mediators
to resolve disputes without litigation. I said, 'Eureka—somebody has done
this. I don't have to do it!' He had started in North Carolina, then moved to
Atlanta and on to Washington D.C., setting up mediation centers wherever
he went."

Florence called Coogler and registered for the next forty-hour training
course—eight hours a day for five days. As it turned out, it was very bad
timing. Just the week before the course was scheduled to begin, Florence
had to bring her mother, who had been very seriously impaired by a stroke,
to Houston from Brooklyn. She hired a woman to care for her mother while
she was away, but "the week that I was gone was very traumatic," Florence
recalls. "I really wanted to be here to look after my mother. I was very torn."
But Florence was also very determined. She was "hoping it would work
out, praying that it was as good as it sounded—and it was." She remembers
with much satisfaction, "Coogler was a dynamic personality. He had two
trainers with him, a lawyer, Steve Erikson from Minnesota, and another

trainer, Virginia Stafford. There were twenty-one people in the class from all over the country. A handful were lawyers, the rest were from the helping professions. It was the first time I heard the term 'helping professions.' I asked them to define it. I didn't understand why lawyers were excluded from the category. It was the most eye-opening experience, a truly life-changing experience, an epiphany. It was exactly what I was trying to create."

Florence was so excited. "I found a way to take my clients out of the system." She couldn't wait to come back to Houston, thinking, "This is so good, it makes so much sense. Wait until I tell everybody what I learned. I thought everybody would be so excited. I was thinking the judges, and the lawyers, and my clients, everybody who was involved in divorce, was going to love this. Because it makes so much sense. How could you not love something like this that is going to help people?"

Florence is still surprised at her own naïveté. "I was old enough to have known that things are not that easy," she says. She starting talking to everyone about mediation, explaining the concept, defining it, defending it— and defending herself. "They think I'm crazy," she thought. "I get into a conversation with one judge, telling him how wonderful this is, and he says, 'Come back when you have something in place.' When I come back, he says, 'Oh yeah, mediation, I do mediation all the time. That's what a judge does.' He didn't get it; none of the judges got it. The lawyers got it, but didn't want to hear about it."

Mediation, as Florence defines it, "is a voluntary process in which parties to a dispute, with the help of a neutral third party, explore ways to negotiate their differences and reach a satisfactory resolution." Florence also defines what it is not. It is not arbitration, in which a third party makes the decision. In mediation, the individuals involved make the decision. It is not legal negotiation, in which lawyers, in an adversarial process, represent each party in the dispute. In mediation the parties negotiate for themselves. It is not counseling, nor is it therapy. It is task- and goal oriented, aimed at resolving disputes over issues that the individuals identify. In divorce mediation these may have to do with property, custody, child support, visitation, and contractual alimony. Mediation cannot replace the traditional adversarial system, Florence says, "where that is necessary and appropriate."

Although mediation has advantages for lawyers as well as for the courts, it took some persuasion for them to see it that way. And many never did. At an annual national meeting of matrimonial lawyers in 1983, an attorney made an appeal to her colleagues to make the divorce process less "horrendous" by considering the use of mediation. One Houston attorney, J. Lindsey Short Jr., responded by saying, "That's fine if you want to take the social worker's point of view" (quoted in Patner). Other objections were more reasoned: that mediation was not appropriate in every case, as in cases involving domestic violence in which the process might enable one party to overpower the other if the mediator was not skillful.[14] Some were concerned that agreements drawn up by non-attorneys might not conform to code or might have other problems. They had quite legitimate reservations; mediation was not a panacea. But most Houston divorce lawyers were not interested in working out the bugs.

Fortunately, there were a few family law attorneys in Houston who discovered mediation at the same time that Florence did. In the second week of July 1981, when Florence returned from taking the mediation course, there was a note on her desk. It read, "Just found out you went to the mediation training. We're going next week. When we come back, we'll do this together." The attorneys were Don Graul, Alece Egan, and Judy Dougherty. When they got back, the four joined forces. "We formed a core of lawyers who were determined to bring mediation to Houston," says Florence. They mounted an education campaign.

In those days, "mediation was not a household word," Florence says. That is an understatement. In September 1981, when she began her own mediation practice, separate from her law practice, Florence ordered stationery. What she got back from the printer read "Divorce and Family Mediation Services." When the group arranged to be listed in the Houston yellow pages, they were listed under "Meditation," Florence says—now amused— "along with the yoga people." The next year they got the listing changed to "Mediation," but "they put the yoga people with us." The third year they finally got it right.

Later that year, the four attorneys introduced divorce mediation to the Houston Bar Association. They included an experienced mediator in their program, a mental health professional. But she wasn't a lawyer. They didn't realize what a mistake that was; they were met with complete disdain. Florence recalls, somewhat bitterly, "We were laughed off the stage. The attorneys were incensed that a non-attorney would have anything to do with divorce. They ridiculed us and practically walked out on us. We soon learned that lawyers saw mediation as an economic threat. Few seemed willing to consider whether it would benefit their clients."

The four colleagues began to look for others who would support mediation. They focused their attention on social workers and psychologists who were already doing some form of marriage counseling. By 1983, they had organized a local mediation group that met monthly to discuss problems. "We did a lot of peer review to find out what worked and what didn't," Florence says. As Florence remembers it, there was a complete absence of competition. The group was committed to finding a way for divorce mediation to become an accepted and common prelitigation process. Some of the early members of the group, in addition to the original four, were Bruce Mitchell, who went on from mediation to law school; Marie Mullineaux, a Houston social worker; Susanne Adams, a non-attorney mediator; and Maureen Peltier, an attorney-mediator who still practices in Houston and who is part of yet another effort to make the process of domestic disputes more humane, the outcome of which is called collaborative law (discussed in Chapter 5). They were, Florence says, "dedicated, tireless advocates of mediation."

There was little success with the family court judges, however. The group was offering private mediation services separate from their legal services, but those who couldn't afford the fees had no alternatives to the courts. Florence remembers approaching the judges and, one after another, being rebuffed. Even as other Texas counties were embracing the process, Judge Robert Webb said, according to Florence, "What do we need mediators for? That's what my associate judge does." Judge Henry Schuble told her, "Florence, I'm happy to see you but if you're here to talk to me about mediation, forget it. I'll never put mediation in my court." Schuble's reasoning was that mediation would erode his power. Judge Huckabee refused to offer mediation as an alternative to the more costly and painful court proceedings. It wasn't so much that Huckabee was against the concept of mediation, but that Houston lawyers were adamantly opposed to it. According to an article in the *Houston Post,* family court judges admitted that Houston Bar Association ratings were "crucial" to their reelection. The lawyers were indispensable for both political and economic support. The judges "make no bones about soliciting campaign contributions from big law firms to wage county-wide races." Huckabee denied that he was opposed to mediation because of pressure from the lawyers, but "in the next breath he adds that it would be political suicide to order mediation in his courts" (Grandolfo).

In the midst of this opposition came progress in the person of Harris County District Judge John W. Peavy Jr. Peavy, Houston's only black judge, took the step that was still unpopular with his colleagues: he endorsed the use of mediation, prior to the formal court hearing, for couples who were scheduled to come before him. Most of these cases involved already divorced couples involved in custody disputes. Judge Peavy had come to believe that mediation, already in use by this time in half of the fifty states, was a viable option: more informal, more comfortable, less traumatic, and less expensive than the courts. What enabled Peavy to offer this alternative—a special, no-charge, on-premise mediation service—was that several divorce mediators, including Florence, had agreed to volunteer their professional services. On a Tuesday morning in October 1985, Peavy announced: "This morning, trained mediators are available to meet with you in an attempt to define the issues that can be settled prior to a hearing and hopefully develop clearer communication between the two of you . . . The court encourages you to take this step prior to actually coming before the court for a decision. All of the data we have available shows the settlements reached in mediation are more satisfactory to the parties in the long run" (Gilbert).

On that first day two cases were settled by mediation. It was an important day for what had by then become a project sponsored by two relatively new organizations: the Houston Bar Association Alternate Dispute Resolution Committee, and the Mediation Network of Greater Houston. In both cases the litigants had no idea prior to that day that there was an alternative to "the only route they knew—the courts" (Gilbert). Divorce mediator Judy Dougherty said, "It's really looking like it's going to be a success, I'm real hopeful. The fact that a judge is doing this makes all the difference in the world." Dougherty was delighted. "We need to have [divorce mediation] legitimized. People will pay attention if they feel like the court is saying it's an OK process" (quoted in Gilbert). Dougherty's optimism was, unfortunately, premature.

Although Judge Peavy was very impressed and recommended the volunteer program to other judges, and Florence was hopeful that mediation was "slowly coming into its own," there was stonewalling behind the scenes. Florence later learned that the family court's administrative judge, Bill Elliott, "hated what we were doing so much that he forbade the judges to initiate any kind of mediation in their courts." As administrative judge, Elliott had the power to control the agenda of the courts. Florence remembers a conversation she had with Elliott:

I asked him, "What do you have against mediation? Everybody's doing it. In Dallas they have a wonderful program. In Austin they have a program. What's the problem here in Houston?"

He said, "Well, I'll tell you. There is no certification, and I don't believe that mediators are qualified. The reason I'm saying that is because even a butcher can call himself a mediator and hang out a shingle." (Surface, 4)

Professionalism *was* a serious issue, and the practitioners knew it. The Houston groups, who were already organized, contacted mediators in Dallas, Austin, and San Antonio. The first meeting of the Texas family mediators was held in the basement room of a public hospital in Austin. A group of about twenty, they decided to take the name "Texas Association of Family Mediators." Florence became the group's first treasurer and, in 1990, its president.[15] By that time, however, in addition to family and divorce, mediation had moved into many other areas. The organization realized that to broaden its membership it had to drop "Family" from its name. This was fairly simple, but qualification, training, and certification were more difficult problems to resolve since mediators came from such varied professional backgrounds as law, social work, and psychology. There were also "thorny ethical issues," Florence says.

In 1987, a major development occurred. It was a great victory for mediation advocates and provided the credibility they were seeking. The state of Texas passed the Alternative Dispute Resolution Act (ADR), requiring both general and family mediation training for anyone, attorneys and non-attorneys alike, who wanted to practice mediation. And it was also made clear that, although it was not mandatory, mediation *had to be considered before trial* for all family law cases that involved children. (This was later amended concerning cases involving domestic violence.) Darrell Jordan, president of the State Bar of Texas, announced the new statute with pride.

There were also a number of other improvements to the system. In addition to mediation and jury trials, the act provided for non-jury trials by a retired district judge agreeable to both parties, mini-trials, and arbitration. Jordan urged attorneys to become familiar with these methods, which were no longer considered experimental and were already being used to resolve not only what are derisively referred to as "barking dog disputes," but also some major commercial cases.

Florence, who had been active all over the state in promoting mediation and who fought for this legislation, was extremely gratified. "Even though Texas was not in the forefront of promoting family mediation," she says, "it ended up with one of the best ADR statutes in the country." It seemed as if the battle finally had been won. Judges all over Texas—in Galveston,

Dallas, Fort Worth, Midland, Lubbock, and Austin—began making referrals to mediators in private practice and in court-connected programs. Admittedly, the process still was not without its flaws and problems. Yet "all found it to be a great asset in giving people a forum for expressing their anger, their fear, and finally for getting down to the business of making arrangements for their children during and after divorce," Florence says. But not in Houston!

"Only in Harris County," Florence remembers, still astonished, "did the judges, led by Judge Elliott and Judge Daggett, refuse all attempts to consider referrals to mediation as proposed by the statute."

While the battle may have been won, the war wasn't over. But Florence would prove to be a formidable adversary.

PART TWO

CHAPTER 5

Florence, Melanie, and Diana
"Housewives Dabbling in Politics"

*"Victims of the system started coming forward and it was just apparent
that something had to be done—and it had to be done from the outside."*
— MELANIE HARRELL

At one point in the 1994 election campaign in Houston, Melanie
Harrell told me, someone she knew tried to demean the growing
power of the court reform movement. He characterized the cadre
of CourtWatch volunteers as nothing more than disgruntled "housewives
dabbling in politics." Melanie remembers the incident: "This was a guy I
went to high school with, who was married to someone I used to work with
as a CPA. I was very fond of her. She and I were talking at my high-school
reunion and I was telling her what I'd been doing, when her husband made
that remark. It made me furious at the time, he was so condescending! But
now, it's pretty funny, considering how naïve we were."

At that time, Melanie had been involved with the family court reform movement for several years. In fact, she had provided the State
Supreme Court Task Force to Investigate Judicial Appointments with
important and useful information concerning the so-called good old boys
network that allegedly operated in the court system. The task force so
angered some family court judges, "the most likely targets of criticism," that
fliers announcing the public hearings, which had been prepared by Randy
Burton of the Houston-based advocacy group Justice for Children, were
removed from the Family Law Center. The fliers, Judge Dean Huckabee
said, were a "bunch of crap" that "convicted the judges before the hearing"
("Inadmissible," 47).

By the early 1990s, attention was focused on several Harris County Family Court judges as a result of "three years of nonstop protests, an FBI investigation, and widespread accusations of corruption, cronyism, and indif-

ference toward the people they served . . ." (Makeig, 20 May 1997). Many, including Florence Kusnetz, Melanie Harrell, and Diana Compton—the three dynamic women who made up the nucleus of what was to become CourtWatch—could see that the family law system was imperiled. Diana believed that in Harris County it was irreparably broken.

In 1987, the Texas legislature had passed a statute supporting the use of mediation. But even if the parties to a dispute were completely honest and committed to the process, mediation was not a panacea. And mediators soon learned that some problems didn't lend themselves to negotiated settlements; some domestic disputes needed to be settled through the courts, such as the many cases involving spousal or child abuse. Critics believed that collaborative decision making was not possible between a victim and abuser for a number of reasons. They cited the significant imbalance of power between the victim and abuser—an abuser might use mediation as an opportunity to continue his control and manipulation of the victim. Furthermore, critics claimed, the victim could reveal very little in a mediation session because of fear of retaliation. Indeed, there were serious concerns that the mediation session itself might provide an opportunity for retaliation, since there was growing evidence that violence escalates when an abused woman tries to leave a relationship, and a violent spouse would know exactly where his partner was expected to be at a given time (Thoennes, 2).[1]

Mediation was having other growing pains and problems. Some mediators were poorly trained in black-letter law; that is, the rules, codes, and procedures that make up the written law. These are statutes passed by state legislatures that constitute rules for the operation of the legal system. Florence uses a helpful analogy to explain what this means: "Think of black-letter law as similar to the Constitution; it includes everything except interpretation and opinion."

"Many mediation agreements *were* defective," Florence says. "A lot of documents were prepared that would not hold water" because mediators didn't know the codes or understand the legal technicalities of black-letter law. Fortunately, just one year after her graduation in 1981 from the South Texas College of Law, Maureen Peltier joined the informal group of mediators that Florence had organized in Houston. This young attorney took on a helpful project; she developed a checklist for the mediators from the thirty or forty pages of regulations. And, over time, other problems were worked through as well, although recalcitrant judges were still unwilling to implement new methods of dispute resolution.

The judges' position seemed perverse since, apart from their other values, mediated agreements had a major advantage for the courts: they helped relieve very crowded dockets. The judges should have loved them for that reason alone. Mediation was being embraced elsewhere in the state—Dallas, for example, had an exemplary program (Grandolfo). Except for Judges Peavy and Motheral, however, the family court judges pretty much ignored the process—that is, if they were not openly hostile to it. Florence was irate. "Our judges have no guts," she told State Attorney General Dan Morales, and added, "Courts everywhere are moving toward ways to reduce costs of litigation, but Houston's family court judges are blocking reforms that help the public because they're afraid of the lawyers' response, and they're afraid they may draw an opponent in the next election" (quoted in Morales).

With most Houston lawyers and judges resistant, the small group of Houston attorneys who supported mediation turned to professionals in other fields to disseminate information and extend its use. They contacted psychologists, social workers, marriage counselors, and others "who also wanted to see families spared the agony of the courthouse," Florence says. Eventually they were successful in their efforts and, in time, even many lawyers turned to mediation, albeit in an amended form.[2] By September 1994, shortly before the election, the new position of Harris County Family Court Mediation Coordinator was created.[3]

Even after the introduction of alternative methods of dispute resolution, many clients wanted advocates who were completely on their side and not disposed to compromise. They were quite within their rights. Women, often with good reason, were fearful of being taken advantage of by their husbands. Wives are usually at a financial disadvantage; older women, particularly, are often not in control of the family finances and may not know the complete value of the estate.[4] "The wife may own one half of the assets," Florence says, "but may not have access to it without the husband's approval or signature. Often the money is in his name. He can use it or he can move it beyond her reach." Men may be victimized as well, of course, and not only those with limited means. There is opportunity for abuse along the entire range of the financial spectrum.

After mediation was introduced in Houston, some couples who might have been amenable were turned against the notion by attorneys who both distrusted the process and were more at home within the adversarial system. Sadly, more than a few attorneys were completely unrestrained, giving rise to the numerous sport and combat metaphors that critics used to describe their behavior. So-called Rambo lawyers didn't hesitate to use fierce battle tactics. They relied on "the legal arsenal to bludgeon the other side," said one attorney, the chairman of a committee that was trying to redraft a code of ethics for the American Academy of Matrimonial Lawyers. These attorneys, he continued, "inflict lasting damage on family relationships that must survive a bitter divorce" (quoted in "Finding More Room"). Roy Cohn, the attorney famous, or infamous, for serving as counsel to Senator Joseph McCarthy, is quoted as saying that in a divorce "you're at war. Only one side wins" (Rhode 2000, 86). Some spoke brutally about "pulling out all the stops, going for the jugular" (Sayler). One well-known (and expensive) Houston divorce lawyer said his charge of $500 per hour was for "combat pay." Attorneys such as these rejected the notion accepted by many others in the profession: hardball litigation did not prove love for clients or even guarantee winning a case. But it did—and still does—hurt the profession by damaging its image (Sayler). "Divorce ethics," Florence says derisively, "what an oxymoron!"

Aggressive family law attorneys not only hurt their profession; they hurt their clients. Some clients were goaded into accepting the scorched-earth tactics of their lawyers, who exploited highly charged domestic situations and often made them far worse than they were to begin with. "Family law litigations," Diana Compton says, "are tortured situations, and the way the system was used, the estate was depleted; everyone was angry in the end." Above all, the children were hurt. "It was verbally espoused that [the lawyers] were operating in the best interest of the children, but it was a lie," Florence says. "They were operating in the best interest of the parties, in a system that operated in the best interest of the one who had the most money and the most power." As one family lawyer put it, "Has it occurred to you that in a divorce action, children can be a valuable commodity?" (quoted in Rhode 2000, 86). Although children did have advocates appointed by the courts (attorneys or guardians ad litem), the system for appointing ad litems in Harris County was charged with being rife with corruption. Melanie Harrell provided extensive data in support of this claim to the state Supreme Court task force that had been investigating judicial appointments (and later to the FBI and IRS as well).

By 1991, it was noted in the local press that negative attitudes and practices were spreading within the Houston legal community (Manson, 7 July 1991). Some attorneys lamented an increase of "bitterness" in family law cases as well as the rise of a "personal, adversarial approach to the practice of law," with more personal animosity and rudeness among attorneys (ibid.). It was, however, a situation not unique to Houston. Increased incivility had not gone unnoticed by numerous state and local bar associations. In fact, beginning in the early 1990s, incivility in adversarial practices had become a "central focus of concern" of the American Bar Association, which is charged with being the watchdog of the profession *(ABA Watch)*.

An important example of incivility concerns pretrial discovery, a process "whose goal," Florence explains, "is to determine truth." Neither side has all the facts, and "each side gets information from the other side in order to get both stories, to get a clearer picture." Consequently, each side is required to disclose facts relevant to the case that may, and often do, lead to settlement. "But to some family lawyers," Florence says, "fairness and civility are beside the point, they don't want you to know everything they have." They use strategies that subvert the intention of discovery.

Law Professor Deborah L. Rhode is an acute critic of adversarial system abuses. "Some rules and procedures governing civil law can be used by attorneys for evading, exhausting, or exploiting an adversary," she writes, making pretrial discovery "anything but." Attorneys withhold information by asserting the attorney-client privilege "without an adequate basis"; they misplace or reshuffle documents "to prevent an opponent from locating relevant materials." Attorneys advise clients not to confirm uncontested facts. They create so-called document debris by prolonging questioning on matters that are peripheral or of "dubious relevance." They engage in various types of "unreasonable scheduling practices, such as arranging depositions in order to impose maximum inconvenience and expense; refusing reasonable requests for extensions; delivering documents under time constraints that will prevent adequate responses or that will force opposing counsel to work over holidays, weekends, and vacations." Some attorneys engage in indefensible conduct toward opposing counsel "such as obscene language, and sexually or racially demeaning comments." They may use such questioning techniques as "probing for peripheral but humiliating disclosures," they may object to reasonable inquiries, or they may inappropriately coach witnesses and instruct them not to answer. And they resort to "sharp practices," such as exploiting an adversary's inadvertent error. When such tactics are used and when the opposing counsel "feels entitled to respond in kind, the cycle becomes self-perpetuating" (Rhode 2000, 82–86).

Problems related to the abuse of the adversary system are most troublesome in family law. Rhode says, "The breakup of a marriage rarely brings out the finest aspects of the human spirit, and vengeful spouses have found no lack of professional accomplices" (ibid.). Like attorneys in other areas of civil law, family lawyers can manipulate the litigation process by taking advantage of black-letter law. In Houston, Florence says, there was "blatant" misuse of the rules of evidence to exclude relevant and important information. Using legal technicalities to cause delays and increase costs in an already costly process, Rhode says, can turn litigation "into an expensive war of attrition" (ibid.).

The normal appeals process also caused additional difficulties. Litigants in the family courts are often unhappy with the outcome of a trial and can become convinced that they have been treated inequitably. "But," Florence explains, "the way the law is, you cannot appeal a ruling of the court until you have a final judgment. That means you have to go through the whole case and *then* appeal what the judge has done." This procedure, which is crucial or it would be possible to appeal every ruling of the judge as he went along, is also very costly. Some corporations and industries (for example, the tobacco and drug industries and, unfortunately, even the Justice Department) use the appeals process precisely because they have the resources for repeated appeals while their challengers often do not. In family law, the cost of appealing a judge's decision can be prohibitive. By the time a couple gets to the end of a trial, they usually can't afford to appeal and start all over again. Pro bono work is only offered to the very poor, and in Houston the cost of a custody trial could range from $50,000 to $200,000. Florence argues that the appeals process is especially problematic in family law for that reason: "Rich people can afford to get their day in court. Poor people lose everything they have, including their homes. They beg and they borrow, and they go to their parents for money, and they mortgage their homes. They suffer the bad decisions because they can't afford to go for a good decision."

Consequently, if they were unhappy but out of money, they were also out of luck. In addition, Florence says, an appeal didn't guarantee a reversal, since "in most issues of dispute, the discretion of the family court judge would stand," even when the ruling was "contrary to common sense." In other areas of law, such as criminal law, there is a very narrow area for judicial discretion because the law is so well developed. Family law is different. Florence claims, "There is no way, in family law, you can codify. Changes in society have been so vast and so rapid in the last fifty years. Nothing changes more rapidly than family law. Certainly there has to be structure, you have to have criteria, and they have to be objective. But all examples can't cover everything that can come up in daily life. This is legal, and this is legal, and this is legal, but then you get to a door and you say beyond this point it's illegal. That's when the judge decides."

One of the most serious problems in the Harris County Family Courts in the years leading up to CourtWatch was precisely in the area of judicial discretion—or rather, its abuse. There were numerous cases, many having to do with serious cases of alleged child abuse, documented in the local newspapers in which the discretion of a family court judge was severely criticized.

By 1990, when Florence had been practicing law for almost twenty years, she had reached the point where she refused cases that were headed to trial. If the potential clients rejected mediation, she told them, "I can be your lawyer and I can try and settle your case but I don't believe in family court trials; the system is not the way I would have it. I will represent you to get the best settlement you can get. However, if the other side blocks the settlement you will have to change attorneys."

Today, even if Florence's clients were on their way to the courthouse, they could choose another alternative to the conventional litigation process: collaborative law. Florence met Stuart Webb, founder of the process, at a conference.[5] His idea was simple, though radical in the adversarial world of family law. Each party to a domestic dispute would be supported and represented by a lawyer, but the four people would sit down together and would collaborate without compromising the legal rights of either party. Together, they would try to work out an agreement on relevant issues such as custody, child support, or division of property, *before* they went to court.

Collaborative law attorneys agree that the adversarial system is inappropriate for resolving disputes among people who are likely to have ongoing relationships. If there are children involved, litigants will certainly have to deal with each other long after their day in court. The "win-at-any-cost" approach did not work to the benefit of the families involved. It prolonged litigation and drove up legal fees, since it's impossible for an attorney to take a family law case on a set fee because the situation is too unpredictable. "It is easier [for the disputing parties] to show anger than restraint and to go for short-term gratification than for long-term benefits," Florence explains. "You're dealing with a husband and a wife, a father and a mother, who are emotionally involved with each other. They want to sock it to the other

until they both go broke. The emotional issues interfere with rationality."[6]
Florence continues,

*If you charge a set fee and you settle sooner, you've overcharged them. Or it drags
on and you're working for nothing, forever. So you have to charge by the hour.*

*It can happen in other litigation, but there you're dealing with businessmen
who know their self-interest and who know that when it gets too expensive, they
settle.*

After learning about collaborative law, Florence and Maureen Peltier initiated the practice in Houston. They believed that collaboration could restore
some civility, sanity, and rationality to the process, in addition to reducing
its cost. They asserted that "attorneys can zealously represent their clients
in divorce and child custody cases without taking on the characteristics of
a pit bulldog" (Manson, 7 July 1991). Furthermore, "since 90 percent of all
cases settle before trial," Florence pointed out, "it is not a sign of weakness to
talk about negotiating a settlement" (ibid.). By February 1991, Florence and
Peltier had assembled a group of lawyers who declared themselves committed to making family law more responsive to the needs of their clients. They
chose the name Attorneys for Negotiated Resolution (ANR).

Although some attorneys were already practicing collaboratively, Florence and Peltier thought a coalition of attorneys could be more effective
in promoting the concept. In a letter to the legal community calling for
a meeting, Florence set out the reasons she believed collaboration would
attract clients: people looking for attorneys would select those who promised to work for the best possible settlement instead of the bloodiest trial;
an affirmative public statement from attorneys who identify with this style
of practice would bring clients who seek justice, not vengeance; and a new
image would bring public support and restore some of the respectability
that the profession had lost.

The first meeting was an exploratory session, an exchange of ideas that
resulted in a statement of policies and procedures that was subsequently
applauded in the media for trying to bring decency back into family law disputes without compromising anyone's legal rights.[7] The primary stated goal
of the ANR was to manage family conflict in such a way that the possibility of post-divorce litigation would be reduced and, above all, the children
would be protected. The attorneys meant to do this by correcting some of
the most egregious adversary system abuses. For example, ANR attorneys

opposing each other in disputes agreed that they would not take any uni-lateral action unless reasonable efforts were made to notify each other of events that might affect the clients. Another major point addressed discovery abuses. The lawyers agreed to full disclosure and sharing of all relevant documents by both parties within a specified time frame.

Critically important to the success of any lasting negotiated settlement was educating the parties involved so that they would be better prepared for the painful process ahead. They needed to understand the emotional impact a divorce would have, both on them and especially on their children. They had to grasp the importance of family code provisions on custody, child support, spousal support, and issues of confidentiality. They had to become aware of the many confusing court procedures—filing, temporary injunctions, sworn inventories—and the costs involved. They had to consider the need for outside resources such as mediators, psychologists, accountants, tax attorneys, business brokers, appraisers, financial planners, and so on. They also had to understand the risks and benefits of contested litigation; that is, going before a judge or jury in a costly trial. The details were bewildering.

In 1991 Houston collaborative law was a groundbreaking idea. More than a decade later, it's still atypical. A May 2004 *New York Times* article states that collaborative law has just "recently made its way to New York." Collaborative law practitioners "generally meet in the equivalent of support groups" because the method is not based upon thought processes that are familiar to most lawyers (Gross). ANR also encountered this problem. Well-meaning attorneys, interested and willing to make a commitment to practicing collaborative law, were not trained in family dynamics; family law certification focused almost exclusively on trial experience. To remedy this, ANR organized seminars in which they shared instances of successful techniques and information on such topics as effective communication and negotiating skills. By March of 1992, ANR, which had begun with fourteen attorneys, claimed sixty-two members. Since then its growth has been modest but steady, both in the Houston area as well as throughout the country. By 2004, according to originator Stuart Webb, "forty-five hundred lawyers nationwide have been trained in the protocol" (ibid.).

Judge Sean O'Reilly thinks that collaborative law is a good approach. "It's a public declaration to stay on the high road, to retain civility. A commitment by the families and their advocates to remain non-adversarial," she says. But what would be better, she and others believe, would be to take family law out of the adversarial, civil system, formally and entirely. A recommendation O'Reilly wrote for the *Gender Bias Task Force Report* was somewhat understated: "Adversarial proceedings in the family law courts often are not in the best interests of the parties" and "the adversarial process may operate to aggravate gender inequities" (*Gender Bias Task Force Report*, 116). Accordingly, O'Reilly recommended an alternative that would take the form of a Family Resolution Center. She elaborated in the report:

My reflections and recommendations are focused on my seven years of experience as a family law trial attorney which have now been exceeded by my nine and a half years on a family court bench in Texas.

I am adamant in my conviction that we need major legislative changes in the approach we take to family law in this state. We need a new language and an interdisciplinary system that will ultimately remove family law matters from the courtroom.

*If we develop an inclusive system of mediated resolutions to family conflicts that incorporate educators, health care persons, and accountants, then we will make great strides in both preserving the life of a family after divorce and fairly dividing the assets acquired during marriage. When I speak of a new language I mean an entirely different way of thinking and articulating the reality of family life as we move into the twenty-first century. (*Gender Bias Task Force Report, 105)

Unfortunately, such thinking and innovative state legislation was, and is still, highly unlikely to occur. Collaborative law may be the next best thing.

In 1990, at about the same time that Florence and Peltier were organizing Attorneys for Negotiated Resolution, Florence was awarded one of ten Women on the Move awards in the Houston metropolitan area (out of a field of several hundred nominees). The award commemorated her pioneering work in establishing a mediation system, her advocacy and legal work, and her outstanding contributions to her profession. It was sponsored by a number of groups, among them Texas Executive Women and the editors of the now-defunct *Houston Post*. When a journalist asked why she was so good at working with families, Florence replied without hesitation, "I was a grown-up and a whole person before I was a lawyer."

Not long after launching Attorneys for Negotiated Resolution, Florence decided to retire. She was past sixty, she had been practicing law for twenty years, her sons were grown and pursuing their own careers, and

Howard had retired. It seemed the right time to get out of the oppressive Houston summer heat, do more traveling, spend time with her grand-children, gather friends and family together for holidays, and get to those projects she'd been putting off, such as writing her memoirs. Florence closed the door on her law practice in 1992 and shut down her mediation practice in 1993. But her fantasy of a leisurely retirement was not about to materialize—not just yet. Not long after she retired, Florence received the phone call from FBI Agent Kathy Loedler that put her in touch with Melanie Harrell, the young woman who had caused quite a stir downtown at the Family Law Center.

About a year earlier, in September 1992, Melanie had testified before the Texas Supreme Court Task Force that was investigating judicial appoint-ments. As opposed to looking at appointments of judges *to* the bench, the task force was examining repeated appointments of individuals *by* judges to serve as guardians ad litem.

Ad litem fees varied wildly and were not predetermined. A basic fee was paid by Harris County Child Protective Services, but an additional amount could be negotiated between the disputing parties and the judge-appointed ad litem. The fee might be less than what an attorney would earn in the same amount of time on his or her normal practice—in the case of an indi-gent litigant, for example. On the other hand, in a scathing critique of the system a coproducer of two PBS documentaries on child abuse claimed that it was "not unusual for these fees to reach over $25,000" and yet still not have a ruling on a case (Helton, 1).

"When the ad litem system works," Susie Alverson of Justice for Children says, "it can be an effective way of making sure children are properly taken care of" (quoted in Barth, 70). The problem in Harris County was that the system both wasn't working and was also vulnerable to abuse. There had been complaints for several years concerning the way family court judges assigned ad litems. Attorneys were affected differently depending upon whether they were in or out of "the loop"; those in the loop were generally appointed to the more lucrative cases.

For attorneys not in the loop, taking ad litem cases was not generally something they wanted to do. Why would they want to be appointed to cases that were added to their normal workloads for less than their normal fees? Often they were the "new, young people who got assigned," Florence says. "It was not a fair fight." But if they were appointed by a judge, they had to take the case; they had no choice. Some judges appointed the first attorney in sight when they stepped out of their offices; some lawyers learned how to evade being chosen by avoiding certain floors of the family court building. They called the third floor the "Bermuda triangle" ("In the Loop").

Attorneys who were in the loop, members of the legal community claimed, were part of "an elite clique" who were beneficiaries of alleged "cronyism." They were the "lawyers who courted special favor with judges" and who "received preferential treatment" (Piller, 25 August 1991). These were the lawyers who got those "often-hefty fees" for court appointments. For attorneys who were repeatedly appointed, it was called "easy money" (Greene, 11); 62 percent of Judge Allen Daggett's ad litem appointments, for example, went to two attorneys. One, Michael Stocker, was appointed more than four hundred times between 1987 and 1991. He received more than a third of Daggett's 1,071 appointments during that time (Piller, 26 August 1991). Other judges—Robert Webb, Henry Schuble, and Bill Elliott—each appointed their own favorite attorney "at least one hundred times" (Piller, 25 August 1991). Melanie's report highlighted such flagrant abuses in the appointment of ad litems in Harris County.

It would not have been indefensible for judges to repeatedly select the same attorneys if they were particularly suited to the role, well trained, or readily available. And the judges claimed, quite reasonably, that they wanted to work with attorneys who were known to them and who understood the process. One prominent family law attorney, Earle Lilly, defended the practice, although he referred to it as "playing favorites." He is quoted as saying, "The public doesn't understand, if they appoint an [inexperienced] ad litem, they don't know what the hell to do" (quoted in Piller, 25 August 1991). Judge Dean Huckabee claimed that he would only work with attorneys who had the "expertise and integrity and ability to handle that particular situation" (ibid.). But according to numerous reports, although some ad litems were excellent attorneys, often that wasn't the case. Many were unprepared to deal with children's issues. Some were "uncaring and incapable of making responsible recommendations to the court," and some never even met their charges prior to arriving in court for the trial (ibid.). They simply made an appearance in court, made a recommendation, and collected a substantial fee. It was said that some cases were "decided quickly and negotiated in the hallways of the courthouse." Those interested in visiting and observing the court system were encouraged to do so but cautioned not to "expect to see attorneys and judges busy interviewing children" (Helton, 1).

There were additional problems. Some appointees were state legislators who might be counted on for political favors. Judge Bill Elliott gave

21 percent of his ad litem appointments to state legislators (Gillece, 12).[8] Melanie Harrell learned that Elliott appointed U.S. Representative Gene Green twenty-four times when he was a state lawmaker and chair of the State Senate's Jurisprudence Committee. State Representative Senfronia Thompson was "tapped by Judge Bill Elliott twenty-six times between 1989 and 1991" during the time that she was chair of the Judicial Affairs Committee, which controlled bills that affected the judiciary! (Lenhart). "So," Melanie Harrell told me, "Elliott was appointing the chairs of both legislative committees—one in the House, one in the Senate—that dealt with the judiciary."

Attorney contributions to judges' election campaigns was another major issue. It "riled critics that many attorneys who get ad litem appointments have contributed to the campaigns of the judges who appoint them" (ibid.). One unnamed critic said, "If you aren't in the little entourage of lawyers that help [judges] get reelected, you're out of luck." He went on to say that he "felt compelled" to attend a thousand-dollar-a-ticket event in order to remain "on equal footing" with other attorneys (quoted in Piller, 25 August 1991). Although the judges and some attorneys claimed that their contributions did not influence the judges' decisions or appointments, there was a clear appearance of impropriety, which was an issue in itself. And, illogically, even those family court judges who ran unopposed were able to receive campaign contributions. Dean Huckabee had never been opposed in ten years on the bench. Robert Webb had been on the bench since 1978 and had never been opposed (Gillece, 12).

That Melanie Harrell was able to assemble data concerning ad litem appointments was a remarkable feat. She said that it was very difficult to get data in a useful form, since a list of contributions made by attorneys to judges' campaigns was the only information publicly available. "Because ad litem fees were paid by the litigants and there was no data collection, the problems couldn't be proven," she explains, "and there was no way of knowing what went on under the table, at the alleged poker games, etc." When Melanie gave a copy of the report to the task force, it caused a "sensation." One attorney who was on the contribution list was at that meeting. "She elicited the fury of the chairman," Melanie says, "when she commented in front of the task force that contributions were simply part of the 'cost of doing business.'"[9]

What provoked Melanie into attempting such a seemingly impossible task was the Parker-Casterline case—and Diana Compton's support.

Melanie and Diana met when they attended Houston Community College. The two women, both Houston natives, had much in common and became good friends. Melanie was a CPA and Diana held a Bachelor of Business Administration degree in finance. They were "two moms with two babies, six months apart," Diana said, by the time she saw the "horrible story" presented on Channel 13 (ABC) by television reporter Christi Myers. Diana phoned Melanie, who was in the middle of cooking dinner. Later that day Melanie watched a rebroadcast of the report on the Parker-Casterline custody dispute. The women were particularly "outraged," Melanie says, when Mary Frances Parker "was sent to a mental hospital for being hysterical while the kid was sent off with her father, a convicted rapist."

The case was only one—though perhaps the most disturbing—of a number of troublesome custody and child abuse cases that had recently been in the news. ABC subsequently organized a televised "town hall meeting" to call attention to these and other problems in the Harris County courts, but it was the plight of Mary Frances Parker that, Diana claims, finally got Houston to take notice of "what was going on down at the Family Law Center." Although they didn't know what to do, Diana and Melanie had decided to act. "We can't have judges who appoint cronies who won't protect children," Diana said. Melanie had an additional reason: "I had a young child and I guess I identified with Mary Frances as a fellow mom. The more the case unfolded, the more outraged I felt. Then all the other victims of the system started coming forward and it was just apparent that something had to be done, and it had to be done from the outside. The Mary Frances Parker case was in 1991. We had just had an election in 1990. There was going to be four more years of these judges." The women pooled their financial knowledge and analytical skills and put them to work.

Diana had become involved with child advocacy soon after her own baby, Betty, was born. Before the Parker-Casterline case, there was no scarcity of child abuse cases that had caught media attention. Some were particularly ghastly: children who were deliberately starved or beaten to death. And here was Betty, loved and secure. Diana thinks back: "Although it sounds sentimental, when I looked at her I told myself that every single child on this planet is just as precious as she is, just as innocent as she is, has just as much potential as she does, and is just as deserving as she is."

But, unlike most people, Diana didn't leave it at that. She went that one step further and decided to become an activist. As a stay-at-home mom, she had the time. And, she says,

I felt an obligation as a citizen to stand up for children who weren't being pro-
tected by our family court system. It was my moral duty. Some situations reach a
point where they are so offensive and unjust that you just feel compelled to stand
up and say, "This is going to stop, and if it's only up to me, so be it."

Because I wasn't involved in any way at the time with family court, I knew I
could speak out without repercussions. Families caught in the family court tangle
of special interest weren't able to do so.

Diana began investigating child advocacy groups. She first became involved with an organization called Children at Risk, serving for a time on
their board. A watchdog organization, it collected data on child health, education, and poverty. Then Diana learned about an organization in Massachusetts called KID-PAC that monitored legislators' positions on children's
issues, supporting some and lobbying others. Diana decided to start a similar PAC (political action committee) in Houston. She describes herself as
having been very naïve and very idealistic. "I thought I could just go out
and do it by myself," she says. "KID-PAC was an idea before its time. Several
influential people took it seriously, including the savviest politician in the
county, Commissioner Steve Radack, but most voters seemed to shy away
from the word PAC. It got to be very frustrating trying to explain that the
only way to make some politician do the right thing by children was to
expose them through political advertising."

Still, in 1989–1990, Diana did manage to get her KID-PAC organized,
enlist a few volunteers, and raise a modest amount of money, with which
she started a newsletter. After Children at Risk issued a report calling attention to the poor quality of life of many children in the Houston and Harris
County area, KID-PAC donated money to help sponsor a mayoral election
debate. The debate, which took place in October 1991, focused on children's
issues. Diana thinks that "it was the first public indication ever in Houston that children's issues were a viable political pressure point." But a few
months after the debate, Diana had to discontinue KID-PAC—she had
decided to become an attorney. In August 1992, she was due to enroll at the
South Texas School of Law.

The balance in the KID-PAC account ultimately paid for Melanie and
Diana's later acquisition and duplication of judicial records. When they
acquired computerized copies of ad litem appointments, they found that
there was "no information about dollars, just numbers of appointments
by judges of particular attorneys." Campaign contribution reports, on the
other hand, were not computerized, but did include specific amounts. "I

took these reports," Melanie says, "such as they were, and reentered all the data on my computer to get the total number of appointments and the total dollars in campaign contributions for each attorney in every court." After several weeks of analyzing the data, Melanie wrote a report correlating campaign contributions and judicial appointments, "but I didn't know what to do with it," she says. The women searched for organizations that might be interested in the data and began to attend meetings. By that time, there were a growing number of groups in Houston that were sharing their experiences in the family courts, holding meetings on a regular basis. Among them were TFER (Texas Fathers for Equal Rights); Grandparents Raising Grandchildren; Mothers Without Custody; Justice for Children, and CODES (Citizens Organized for Divorce Ethics and Solutions) (Piller, 26 August 1991). In addition, there was a Victim Assistance Center.

Diana describes CODES as an organization for men and women "who had been through the system, who had lost their money, and who were dissatisfied about what happened with their divorce." As a result of the Parker-Casterline custody dispute, the group began discussing "judges not understanding about child abuse." The leader of CODES was Jolene Reynolds, the woman who, Diana recalls, first contacted Lee Grant, after which "a producer came to Houston to conduct interviews." The producer was Grant's husband, Joseph Feury.[10]

America Undercover crew members had initially been sent to Houston to research a documentary on divorce, but "when they started hearing [abuse] stories in divorce support groups, they switched subjects" (Hodges, 1). Cases involving child sexual abuse were extraordinarily troublesome. Child advocates claimed that judges simply had a difficult time believing how common child sexual abuse was. At least one Houston attorney blamed lawyers themselves for the situation, since they too often used accusations of sexual abuse as a tool to gain custody for their clients even when the claim may not have been justified. One journalist, in an article with the rueful title "Unheard Voices: Children, Abuse, and the Courts" wrote,

There seems to be a widespread courthouse belief that allegations of sexual abuse are only the newest weapons in custody litigation.

Judges in the divorce courts are sick of hearing about sexual abuse, say child advocates. Judges are jaded by false allegations, say lawyers. They are overwhelmed by the complicated nature of these cases, which only add to already overcrowded dockets, say the judges themselves. (Sowers)

After Grant's crew and producer paid a visit to Houston, Lee Grant herself came to talk with participants in alleged child sexual abuse cases in which the use of judicial discretion had been questioned. In these cases, because black-letter law didn't provide sufficient direction, judges were permitted broad discretionary powers.[11] (Melanie Harrell was among those interviewed by Grant, although she wasn't identified in the film.) Ultimately, *America Undercover: Women on Trial* focused on three Harris County cases and one case that occurred in Bee County, elsewhere in Texas. The cases were initiated by four women: Sandi Hebert, Ivy Raschke, Sherry Nance, and Mary Frances Parker.

The Hebert case involved Mike Hebert, a lieutenant in the Houston Police Department. His ex-wife Sandi, a public-school teacher, went to court for a hearing to change visitation for their younger son, five-year-old Wayne. The reason, according to Sandi, was that the boy, who had been in therapy after his parents' divorce, told his therapist that he had been sexually abused by his father (Sowers). Child Protective Services verified that abuse had occurred, although the father adamantly proclaimed his innocence.

The judge in the case was Dean Huckabee. After a private meeting with the child, Huckabee was incensed. He ruled that the mother had "mental health problems" and that it was "a classic case of brainwashing" (quoted in Hodges, 1). Although the hearing was supposed to have been about changing visitation—no one had raised questions about Sandi's ability as a mother, and Mike Hebert had not sued for custody—Huckabee awarded tempo-rary custody of the child to the father. When Sandi heard this, she began to shake and wail. Huckabee then told Sandi's attorney, Dinah Bailey, that if Sandi didn't "compose herself she'd be forcibly removed from the build-ing."[12] He did not permit her to say goodbye to her son.

Despite repeated appeals, Sandi didn't see her son again for three years. When she did, she was not permitted to tell him why she hadn't seen him in all that time, or even why she didn't say goodbye.

In another Huckabee case, two children were placed in the custody of their father Bob Roberts after his ex-wife Ivy Raschke claimed that he had beaten and sexually abused her in front of the children. The son, Derek, wrote to Huckabee numerous times, pleading with the judge to return him to his mother. Once again, Huckabee claimed that the boy had been brain-washed and that the mother had severe mental health problems. And once again, he wouldn't let the mother say goodbye to her children.

Eventually Derek ran away from his father. Although he was not forced to return, and his sister Sasha was also allowed to go back to her mother, the father's custody was never revoked. In a bizarre twist, Charles Martin, the court's psychological expert in the case, later had his license revoked when *he* was charged with abusing *his* child (Hodges).

In the Bee County case, Sherry Nance, a mother of four, killed both her husband Tom, whom she had accused of abusing their son, and his father, her father-in-law. Even after Child Protective Services made a video in which the boy explicitly described the abuse, the judge had awarded custody to the father's parents. What drove Sherry to a murderous rage was that the father had then moved in with his parents and the boy. When she went out to their ranch to confront them, a gunfight broke out in which Sherry was seriously wounded and the two men were killed. Sherry was convicted of murder and given a life sentence. But, she says, "My son is not being sexually molested, and that's worth it" (quoted in Hodges, 1).

With regard to the Parker-Casterline case discussed in Chapter 1, the scene that took place when Judge Daggett was unable to seat a jury was described in *Women on Trial* by Christi Myers, who first broke the story on Houston television news. Melanie Harrell and Diana Compton were at that hearing. Diana recalls: "It was incredible. Christi understated the vehemence and anger that erupted in the courtroom when T. Wayne Harris [attorney for Casterline] asked the panel if they would have a problem giving custody of a child to someone convicted of sexual assault. Several people shouted and almost all hands shot up in the air. When the jurors spilled out into the hall, they were all fuming and so indignant."

Casterline withdrew his petition (Piller, 3 July 1991). Mary Frances was left with $20,000 in court-related costs but, echoing Sherry Nance's comment, she said, "I can take anything as long as I've got my child and she's safe" (quoted in Barth, 71).

Women on Trial was telecast only twice in Houston before HBO took it off the air, a consequence of separate lawsuits against Time-Warner Entertainment (which owns HBO), director Lee Grant, producer Joseph Feury, researcher and co-producer Virginia Cotts, and Randy Burton of Justice for Children. Libel suits were brought by Huckabee, Hebert, and a psychologist named Kit Harrison, who were all shown in the film, which they claimed was biased and defamatory. Grant had characterized the family courts in Harris County as "medieval in their punishment [and] irrational in their decisions." The plaintiffs characterized the show as "sinister and powerful" (Hodges, 1), although they couldn't have known, at that time, how powerful it would actually prove to be.

Attorney Randy Burton, who had been chief prosecutor for the Harris County District Attorney's Office in their Family Offenses Section, later founded the watchdog and advocacy organization Justice for Children. Photo courtesy of Randy Burton.

Randy Burton defended his position: "I stand by everything that I said about the problems with the family court system. I think that this lawsuit is merely one more attempt to silence the critics of the family court system. I think that the suit will provide an excellent opportunity to tell the truth about what's going on in the family courts" (quoted in Piller, 3 July 1991).

Burton added, in an article he wrote for the *Houston Chronicle,* that the *Women on Trial* cases were not isolated examples, as was claimed by former Harris County Family Law Judge Alvin L. Zimmerman. "The real truth is that it is unfortunate that the HBO special was only confined to an hour," Burton wrote. "Had there been additional time, perhaps the true enormity of the horrors occurring daily in the family court system in Harris County could have been told" (Burton 1992).

By the time *Women on Trial* was aired in October 1992, there were already many vocal critics of the family courts. Donna Ringoringo and Rose Abraham, both believing they had been victimized by the Harris County Family

Court system, had already been picketing outside the Family Law Center for several months (discussed in Chapter 1). Although the film did not initiate the protest, it did intensify interest in the long list of allegations and charges that had been mounting against family court judges for several years. It also rallied the support of various Houston women's groups, who joined the picketers, and it motivated Ringoringo to significantly escalate her protest.

By the end of December, Ringoringo's vigil at the Family Law Center had been noticed by national news and television organizations. She had shackled herself to the building when efforts were made to remove the protestors, and then she went on a hunger strike which lasted twenty-two days. Although the project never materialized, film producer Robert Baker was drawn to her story and considered telling it as a made-for-television movie. Baker referred to Ringoringo as a "modern day Gandhi, taking on a system she perceives to be unjust" (quoted in Greene, 29 December 1992).

Hyperbole aside, the protest continued for more than a year under the subsequent leadership of Phrogge Simons, who took over for Ringoringo when she was hospitalized. The site in front of the Family Law Center in downtown Houston was occupied day and night. County officials "tried a variety of tactics to bring an end to the round-the-clock protest vigil," but the protestors fought back (Marshall). At first, the protestors used the bathroom inside the Family Law Center, "but county officials declared an end to that practice" (ibid.); Simons then found an office building that agreed to the use of their facilities. When a judge declared that cots were not permitted, Simons lined three cots up and draped a banner over them that read, "Remove corrupt judges, not cots"—a clever move, some had to admit. "I'm in compliance now," Simons said, but "if I want to sleep on my sign at night . . .?" (quoted in Greene 1994). Then chaise lounges were brought in; they had not been expressly forbidden. File cabinets, on the other hand, were another issue. There is a wonderful photo of a demonstrator, Jim Nash, defiantly checking his files, although State District Judge Scott Brister had ordered the file cabinet removed.

The demonstrators received a great deal of moral support from attorneys going in and out of the courthouse, as well as from litigants and passersby, but there were some altercations. Attorneys Darlene Smith and Sharon Gardner were offended by some of the signs, especially two in particular that implied that their firm was involved in bribing judges. After unsuccessfully petitioning to have the signs removed, Smith and Gardner decided to remove them themselves. A "short scuffle began," which then "escalated into a verbal sparring match" (Greene, 30 December 1992).

"There were so many things happening at the same time," Diana Compton says, "it's almost impossible to keep track of any kind of chronology." Meanwhile, the list of alleged court abuses continued to grow. Even if charges couldn't be proven there was a clear perception that there were many problems. Harris County Family Courts and some of its judges were accused of gender and racial discrimination, favoritism, and cronyism resulting from party politics; they allegedly made improper use of campaign funds. There were allegations of fraud and collusion. One family court judge, Henry Schuble, was actually charged with fraud. The Internal Revenue Service was involved with one investigation, while the FBI was investigating allegations that included corruption and bribery.

Around the same time, in the spring of 1993, Florence kept her word to Agent Loedler and phoned Melanie Harrell. There were about twenty people at the first meeting of what would become CourtWatch, including Nancy Sims, a highly skilled political consultant. She had been asked to attend the meeting by Sue Schechter, a state legislator. At the meeting, Diana pushed for organizing a political action committee like KID-PAC; she remembers that Nancy Sims agreed. "Yes, that's the way to go," Sims said.

And that was the way they went.

CHAPTER 6

The Election of 1994
"The Babes That Slew the Goliath"

"Luckily the ringleaders were so arrogant—the ones who insisted that the pleas and demonstrations were only sour grapes—that they didn't take us seriously. Until it was too late."

— DIANA COMPTON

There was bound to be controversy connected with CourtWatch. The women of CourtWatch believed that they could fix what they saw as an ineffectual system—worse, a harmful system—by employing the same political processes that had kept the judges on the bench. But they had to convince the voters, and to do that, they had to keep pressing allegations concerning the old boys network, indifference, cynicism, collusion, and corruption in the family courts. According to Florence, John Hill, a former Texas Supreme Court Chief Justice, dubbed the Texas judicial system the "the laughingstock of the nation." If that were so, Florence claimed, the Harris County family court system "may be the biggest joke of all" (Kusnetz, 27 January 1994).

Controversy was inevitable for several reasons. CourtWatch, which had an aggressive anti-establishment campaign that put it squarely in the spotlight, was described as an "increasingly vocal oversight group" whose influence grew throughout the election campaign (Makeig, 18 September 1994). With the help of some sympathetic county employees, CourtWatch volunteers managed to comb county records, trace political contributions, inspect dockets, and check out rulings. The *Houston Chronicle* said that "when they lambaste a judge, it is invariably backed up by statistical research, and people listen" (ibid.). That was bound to ruffle some feathers. CourtWatch screened and selected some judicial candidates for endorsement but rejected many others, which was bound to hurt and anger those who were rejected. And despite bipartisan endorsements, some thought that the organization favored Democrats.

The Houston system for electing judges is highly politicized. As long as judges run on party lines, there will be partisan rivalry, which is naturally heightened during any election campaign. And 1994 was not just any election campaign. It was the first time that many Houston judges were opposed in their bid for reelection in almost two decades, and it was women who were mounting this charge against powerful men. After the primary elections in March, Glenda Joe, a leader in Houston's Asian-American community, said that CourtWatch members were seen as "the babes that slew the Goliath" (Rodriguez).

CourtWatch was bound to provoke the "housewives dabbling in politics" attitude, as it was characterized by an acquaintance of Melanie Harrell's. Other demeaning, derisive, and dismissive comments were also made about the women. An article in the *Houston Chronicle,* which objected to criticism of the courts as unfair, personalized the protest by claiming that the "common denominator" among the activists was mothers who had lost their custody battles (Zimmerman). The author implied that the protests and demonstrations were a result of nothing more than sour grapes. One reporter, describing Phrogge Simons, who was maintaining the protest at the Family Law Center, evoked the image of a frantic woman, "quick to launch into accusations involving racketeering, fraud, extortion, bribery, and idiocy" (Makeig, 18 September 1994). Tom Stovall, the district courts administrator, dismissed the demonstrators as disillusioned. They go to the family courts, he said, "hoping for a fairy godmother with a magic wand to resolve their bitter dispute," but in the family courts, unlike criminal court or even juvenile court, he added, "no one wins." Even so, Stovall begrudgingly admitted that he hadn't seen as much interest in the judicial election "in at least 35 years" (ibid.).

Some of the CourtWatch volunteers were, indeed, housewives. And some were disgruntled. The Harris County Family Courts were thought to be especially hostile to women—this was one of the principal reasons that family court reform became a women's issue in Houston. Florence correctly believes that "everyone who goes through the system is victimized," but "women perceived themselves as more victimized."[1] In Houston, this perception was justified. It was confirmed by a statewide gender bias task force report.

The Gender Bias Task Force of Texas was created in 1991 to examine whether gender bias existed in the judicial system, and if so, to determine its extent and nature and make recommendations to address the problems.

The task force found that gender bias was pervasive in Texas. There was gender-biased language in legal statutes, gender (as well as social class) bias affected access to the judicial system, and gender bias was found to exist in courtroom interactions that affected the litigation process, including biased treatment of litigants and of female attorneys. There were differences in fees that male and female attorneys received for court appointments. And gender bias was found in areas of "substantive law," which included decisions concerning divorce and division of property, custody and visitation, child support, domestic violence, and criminal and juvenile sentencing. Although there were some biases against men, gender bias in the legal system affected women more negatively. Thus it is not surprising that CourtWatch was made up almost entirely of women. "Everyone," Diana says, "seemed to have a family court horror story." (But it's interesting to note that none of CourtWatch's leadership had been divorced.)

CourtWatch had made specific and targeted attempts to recruit men; Florence thought that there would be "a lot of fathers who would be interested in reform." She was a bit puzzled:

I didn't realize it was a woman's issue until we started CourtWatch. We tried to enlist as many people as we could, across a broad spectrum—male, female, different ethnicities, different ages, different economic and social levels. We wanted a really representative cross section of backing for CourtWatch, because all people are subject to abuses in the court.

But it didn't turn out that way. Family issues are perceived as women's issues. Family concerns are conceived of as women's concerns.

CourtWatch did get a range of supporters among the two hundred volunteers who worked for the organization: poor, rich, divorced, not divorced, black, white, Asian, Mexican. But they were women. Florence thought about this a great deal. She thought it unfair to men to suggest that women have a "corner on ethical or moral behavior," yet women related more to the reforms dealing with children and families that CourtWatch focused on. "We did have men coming to some of the early meetings, but they didn't come back," Florence recalls. "They gave us their ideas and they left. One left when it became clear he was not going to run the organization." And some women also left. As in the beginning of any organization, there's a period of attrition. Florence says, "Some people come to one meeting and you never see them again. Some come to two meetings and you never see them again. So it took us about five or six meetings before we distilled enough people who were seriously interested and began to make policy decisions."

At this point Florence was the nominal head of the group, but all decisions were, and continued to be, made by consensus:

We discussed and discussed and decided that we would all agree. And this is how we would go about it: we would try and raise money and then we would try and develop positions. And then we would go public.

Then everyone said, "OK, we need a leader," and I became the director. I didn't like the word "chairman" and I liked "chair" even less. I'm still looking for a non-gendered word.

We had to have a treasurer. Melanie, because of her experience and being a CPA, was the logical choice.

One man did remain interested and involved as a member of the executive board throughout the life of CourtWatch. He was not married and had no children. "He was a good soul," Florence says. Lance E. Wilks was a business insurance agent and a director of Justice for Children. In the Court-Watch publication announcing the board, Wilks was described as someone who hoped "to educate the public about how the family courts sometimes inflict pain upon abused children and the parents who try to protect them." And although they were not members, other men were extremely helpful and supportive to the organization. Brad Gaber, a graphic designer and illustrator, created the eye-catching CourtWatch logo; Howard Kusnetz set up and operated the CourtWatch database; Randy Burton, founder of Justice for Children, and Eugene Cook, professor at the University of Houston Law School, were available for advice.

It was not only CourtWatch that consisted primarily of women; the candidates the group selected and endorsed were also mostly female. Actually, the endorsement of so many women gave CourtWatch's actions the appearance of a feminist agenda, but the female challenge to the male-dominated courts was not by design on the part of CourtWatch, nor was it unique to Houston.[2] It was one result of a natural professional evolution. Women had begun entering law schools in significant numbers after the passage of Title IX legislation in 1974, and by 1994, many of these female lawyers were seeking judgeships. An article in *Texas Lawyer* reported that in 1994, in addition to a number of female judges who were running for reelection across the state, fifty-four women were challenging sitting judges or running for open seats (Connelly).

Family court reform became a woman's issue in Houston because divorce seemed to be a woman's issue, illogical as that may be. More women than men initiated divorce, yet in 1994 women were still generally disadvantaged in divorce court proceedings.[3] The primary reason was that wives were often at a financial disadvantage; husbands were usually in control of the family income, property, and finances. Many women did not understand how to deal with their family's assets, or even know what those assets were.[4] Most women could not afford high-powered attorneys—many were homemakers who had been out of the job market for years. Even those women who did work outside the home almost always earned less than their husbands. One male attorney thought, however, that too much was being made of the difference in earning capacity. He said, in his response to a survey by the Gender Bias Task Force of Texas, that suggesting that "differences in earning capacity should be entitled to compensation—sounds like communism" (*Gender Bias Task Force Report*, 48).

Property settlements were the only way to ensure any degree of financial security after a divorce in Texas—it was the only state in which wives couldn't sue for alimony. The state legislature tried for years to pass alimony laws but never succeeded; the issue was "a perennial loser in the Texas legislature" (Elliott 1994). Florence explains some of the negative consequences of this singular circumstance:[5]

Because Texas is a community property state, it is assumed that if the couple has assets, the wife or husband will get half or a sizable portion.

If the unemployed spouse (usually a homemaker) has no earning skills, the courts have the authority to give her more than half of the assets. For example, an older woman spends her life rearing children and helping her husband get ahead, and he then runs off with his young secretary. This is supposed to compensate for alimony.

Of course, if there are no assets, she is screwed. I had some of these cases—no fun!

Writing for the Gender Bias Task Force, Judge Sean O'Reilly agreed with Florence's assessment. She wrote that the "divorce process can be tantamount to a sentencing of poverty" and "total devastation in a long-term marriage" of twenty or twenty-five years, for example. She elaborated:

That would mean, by way of just a general scenario, a woman would now be in her early fifties with no education past high school, no skills or job history, going through a period of emotional trauma at a time when she has parallel health issues that may be surfacing for the first time . . .

And then I would like to juxtapose to that scenario a woman who has been in a marriage of even eight or fifteen years with two children and no education past high school, no job skills or job history.

For the younger woman it can be a sentencing to poverty at least through the minority of her children. It may mean the children have no educational opportunities past high school themselves. And for the older woman, it can mean that she is in a malaise of depression and minimal subsistence for a decade or longer as she waits to qualify for Medicaid or Medicare.

*In either of these scenarios there is often no financial resource for car purchase or repair, basic grooming, clothing, and dental or medical care, and the many day-to-day out-of-pocket expenses that all of us experience. (*Gender Bias Task Force Report, *46)*

In Houston, as elsewhere, while husband and wife were equal before the law, they were "rarely equal in fact" (Baer, 157).

Custody was the one area of family law in which women were seen as having an advantage. It's true that in *uncontested* cases the mother is usually granted custody. (Some researchers speculate that this is the primary reason that more women than men initiate divorce actions.)[6] But in the relatively small number of cases when custody disputes actually do occur, the outcome for the mother is not at all assured. In *contested* custody cases, fathers normally obtained custody (Levit, 120; *Gender Bias Task Force Report*). Because the primary guiding principle behind custody decisions is the "best interest" of the child, and because the mother usually has the inferior financial status, the mother was (and still is) likely to lose. According to Baer, "fathers have won custody because of their greater income, even when the mother's lower income results from the fact that she has been a full-time homemaker. Fathers have won because the mother has a full-time job, and because she is unemployed. Fathers who have remarried have won custody because they now can provide a two-parent family" (Baer, 148).

In Houston, custody could be used as leverage by a husband and father who was not truly interested in becoming the primary caregiver in order to intimidate the wife into accepting a lesser settlement.[7] It was used to draw out litigation until a woman's funds were exhausted. And women, too, used custody as a potent weapon. For some it was the weapon of choice. For others, due to what Florence calls an "imbalance of power," there was no true choice; it was their only weapon. They used it despite the fact that it might have been in the worst, rather than the best, interest of the child. Sadly, vulnerable children, the innocents, had to be protected from their own parents. And from their parents' attorneys.

Custody issues raise a genuinely difficult problem for attorneys, who are in an adversarial system in which the primary obligation is to the parents, not the children. In Houston, the apparent cynicism of too many family lawyers made the problem even worse. One well-known, successful, and highly paid attorney admitted that he didn't always win custody suits for the *better* parent but, he boasted, he *did* always win. Other attorneys who may have had misgivings, Diana Compton learned, were entangled in a system controlled by powerful judges to whom they were vulnerable: "We could not believe that the family court attorneys were buying into the system. Some of them *were* complicit. But I soon found out that many of them were uncomfortable, yet felt helpless. We had to make a change without involving them."

Children may have their own attorneys or guardians ad litem, but even when they are effective, "there isn't an overall attempt to focus on what's happening to the children *during* the period of divorce," Florence says. She has long advocated that to correct this situation, there needs to be an evaluation of the children's position:

They say the children's interests are paramount, but their interests are not represented adequately. In the very beginning steps need to be taken to explain to the parents what's happening to their children, what's going to happen to their children, and to ease that.

All orders should be built around a plan for the children, instead of "first do all this to protect the husband and the wife and then see where the children fit in." Their needs have to be factored into any settlement that determines child support, access to the children, and even the conduct of the parties.

In an article Florence and Melanie coauthored for the *Houston Chronicle,* they referred to the research on the effects of divorce on children that had recently been completed by noted child psychologist Judith Wallerstein and published in her book *Second Chances:* "Her work showed that it was not the divorce that left long-term, harmful imprints on the children.

Rather, it was the conflict surrounding the divorce" (Kusnetz and Harrell, 14 March 1994).[8]

Repairing the system on behalf of the children became a key and dominant issue for CourtWatch. Because children can be exploited in the domestic wars, the primary responsibility of the family courts should be to see that they are not used as weapons and to determine what is truly in the best interest of the child. CourtWatch held that with only a few exceptions Harris County Family Court judges did not rigorously protect children. (Linda Motheral, one of these exceptions, had been appointed to a vacant post by then-Governor Ann Richards and was an outstanding example of what a family court judge might be and do.) The family courts were erratic—inconsistent, unpredictable, unreliable, and often biased. They suffered from overloaded dockets and judges who were ill-prepared both temperamentally and professionally to deal with emotional family disputes, and they were beset with endemic problems that resulted from family law being trapped inside the adversarial system. In addition, family courts struggled with problems that arose from conflicting jurisdiction. Florence explains:

The family courts have jurisdiction over adoption, divorce, visitation, child support, and any problem that arises from these matters. However, if there is a "peace bond" issued by a sheriff or constable with the purpose of keeping an angry husband away from a fearful wife, then a violation of that bond would end up in criminal court.

If one of the parties to a divorce is arrested for fraud or any infraction of the criminal code, then it is handled in the criminal courts. And evidence from one court is not usually admissible in the other.

Consequently, a family could have one case in criminal court and another in family court at the same time. If this weren't complicated enough, another case might be in juvenile court due to a problem, for example, concerning an adolescent child. And finally, a case could be in civil court for other reasons, such as a suit for money damages. Since there was no unified court system—one which would place matters related to a single family under a single judge—a family might face litigation in several courts with several different judges at the same time, with none of the judges knowing what was happening in the other courts.[9]

Because the family law system was so flawed, Florence and others came to rely on mediated or collaborated settlements. "I came to the point where, in good conscience, I could not take my clients to court for a trial," Florence says. "I could never take a family through the legal system without having them chewed up and spit out . . . It's brutal" (quoted in "Women on the Move"). Diana Compton, who became an attorney with the express intention of practicing family law, could not tolerate the system and even now, ten years later, does not practice family law.

One of the primary goals of CourtWatch was to change the system for the benefit of families and, above all, the victimized children. The groundwork for this had already been laid by Diana's previous child advocacy work with KID-PAC, Melanie Harrell's report to the Gender Bias Task Force, and Florence's work in alternative dispute resolution, including mediation and collaborative law. From their first meeting, Florence and Melanie "got all fired up, decided to get involved and find a solution to the problems in the family courts," says Florence. Together with Diana, they formed a good team. Looking back, all three women told me that although they were very different, there were few instances of conflict or rivalry. "For the most part," Melanie says, "we were just interested in taking care of the problems." She was "comfortable to be treasurer" but was "a little reticent about putting myself out there." Diana felt similarly. They agreed that Florence was the best choice for director. She was known in the legal community and she had expertise in the courts. And Florence was less restrained. "If I don't do it," she thought, "nobody's gonna do it, and it's not right." The women's styles and personalities complemented each other; they worked out a well-functioning division of labor. Diana believes, and the others agree, that Florence was just what the organization needed. She offers this example: "In my opinion, Florence made a key opening strike when she gave a press conference and specifically targeted judges by name. Nothing like that had ever been done before. It was bold and brilliant and generated a lot of press right off the bat. She didn't tell us she was going to do it. She just did it—and I'm glad she did. It was the perfect thing to do."

Not long after that press conference, it became clear that CourtWatch had struck a nerve. There were "a lot of undercurrents," Florence says. She began to receive intimidating letters from lawyers. "I'll be watching you," one letter said. "How dare you do this? How dare you try and upset the system?" said another. Then, following a meeting of the family law specialists of the Houston-Galveston Bar Association, a friend told Florence that a prominent and influential lawyer had announced that he knew "for a fact" that Florence had been forced to retire because of complaints. Florence was "livid" and called him immediately. She recounts the following conversation:

I asked him, "Why didn't you check this out with me before you go and spread lies like that? Where did you get this information?" He said that he heard it from one of the judges. I said, "Didn't it occur to you that those judges already see me as a foe, and it would be in their best interest to destroy my reputation and, therefore, destroy my credibility?" "Well," he apologized then, "I'm sorry, Florence." And I said, "You'll have to take action to retract that statement, and if you don't, I'll sue for defamation of character. This is going to stop right now."

Clearly, attorneys as well as judges were feeling threatened by Court-Watch's potential influence. CourtWatch had decided on nothing less ambitious than improving the family court system by removing five of the nine sitting judges from the bench and at the same time eliminating the patronage system these judges had established over the almost twenty years of their tenure. They hoped to accomplish this radical reform by taking political action.

The group decided to become a PAC, a political action committee. That decision may have made all the difference. It provided CourtWatch with a precise focal point: the judicial election of 1994. Florence says,

It was not a foregone conclusion that this organization would engage in political action; we discussed if that was one of the ways we wanted to go. We asked, "What is a PAC? What do we do?" We would have to get an IRS number because we would be raising funds. We would have to be approved as a PAC.

My original idea was for a citizen's watchdog committee, but we would not have been able to take political action, to endorse candidates. There are a lot of restrictions on non-profits. But because contributions to a PAC are not tax-deductible, it's the only non-profit organization that can exercise political influence. Because of that, we decided it was the way to go.

But first, they had to choose a name. "Diana favored Court Busters because *Ghostbusters* was popular at the time, but we agreed on CourtWatch," Florence says. (The full name of the organization was CourtWatch: A Committee for Family Court Reform.) While the term "courtwatch" was not original—it was actually a common name for such organizations—it was a good choice since it made an unambiguous statement.

Next the group needed a carefully drawn plan of action. They had to make the issues extremely clear in order to educate the public. And they had to offer genuine, credible, and viable alternatives in the form of judicial candidates who, if elected, would implement needed changes. The women knew that they were facing a formidable task: they were going to confront influential men who had major political party support. If they were going to take political action, they needed to know "the political movers and shakers," Florence says, "and how you operate in the political sphere." That would require the help of a political consultant. It was tricky; Court-Watch was nonpartisan, but the consultants in Houston were not. Although CourtWatch interviewed several consultants, the only one they "really, really liked and who was really interested in helping happened to be a Democratic political consultant," Florence says. Her name was Nancy Sims; she worked for Quantum Consultants. Her role was to advise CourtWatch on how to carry out a political campaign rather than promote their candidates—an important distinction.

Sims had to justify to her company the time she would be spending with CourtWatch. She couldn't donate her services, Florence says, "but Nancy was so excited to be doing this, she offered to charge the rock-bottom rate." As Florence remembers it, they met in her office once a week. "She was invaluable; she had the contacts we didn't have. We really could not have done it without her professional expertise." Melanie thinks Sims actually gave the organization a lot more time than she charged them for, and Diana agrees.

Sims's commitment to the organization cost her more than time and dollars. She received a great deal of hostile criticism for her role as CourtWatch consultant, from Democrats as well as Republicans. The Democrats said she was helping an organization that was not only supporting Republican candidates, but was critical of judges who were Democrats. The Republicans said she was a consultant to some Democratic candidates supported by CourtWatch, and therefore appeared to be promoting her clients, not simply advising the organization. Diana believes that Sims was the unsung "hero of CourtWatch."

Diana is modest, however—she herself is even more of an unsung hero. "After CourtWatch was up and running and growing and getting some buzz," Diana decided to "take a backseat and not play a public role." That is the reason she only appears early in the literature, although she did attend "every strategy meeting" and stuffed more envelopes than she cares to recall. There were two reasons for Diana's decision. The first was practical, as she had just started law school. The second was personal. Diana's husband, she says, "was uncomfortable with her taking a controversial and very public position." Out of respect for his reservations, she kept a very low profile.

"Now we had a name and we had a logo," Florence thinks back, and a two-phase strategic plan that Sims had devised. In this first, organizational phase, Melanie was dealing with the IRS to get a tax number and filling out a multitude of forms so that they could qualify as a PAC, file, and become registered. "The next step was very interesting," Florence recalls:

We thought, "Who is going to know what CourtWatch is?" None of us was known in the community. I was known in the legal community but not in the general community. So Nancy said, "The way to do that is to get an advisory board. You borrow their names and you put them on the stationery."

We figured out that each of us—Melanie, Diana, and I—should call people prominent in the community. We would ask if they were willing to lend us their names to show that they supported what we were doing. Even if we didn't know, people at that level already know what an advisory board is.

And it was incredible. We got a cross section of the entire Houston popula- tion. And we did it all in about two weeks.

Eighty-one people agreed to lend their names to CourtWatch. There were PhDs and EdDs and MDs and JDs—lawyers who Florence says "were willing to stick their necks out because they knew us." There were two state representatives. There were black ministers and white ministers, Latino business leaders, bankers, philanthropists, the head of the Houston Area Women's Center, the head of the Rape Hotline (who happened to be Arthur Ashe's sister), professionals from the "therapy community" whose names would be recognized by activists, a radio personality, law professors, an advertising executive.[10]

Florence is still moved when she recounts those two weeks of constant telephoning:

The most dramatic thing that happened to me was I would start with my list in the morning and make calls to people I knew, maybe not well. I would tell them what we were doing, that we were starting a PAC and that I needed their help because no one was going to know me or the organization.

The first question they asked was, "Do I have to come to meetings? I have no time to come to meetings." I said, "Absolutely not, I don't even plan to call on you to do anything. I just want to borrow your name so that the community knows that someone out there knows us and knows that we're not kooks." Then they would agree to serve on an inactive advisory board so we could use their names on our stationery.

Almost everyone said yes; maybe one or two said no. It got to the point where I was sitting at the phone with tears streaming down my eyes because three people in a row said to me, "Florence if you're involved, I know it's OK and you can use my name for anything." Three people in a row said that to me and I started to cry because I had no idea that they even saw me in that light.

Once the working executive board (Diana called them "worker bees") and the inactive advisory board were in place and the various paperwork was filed, CourtWatch moved on to the next organizational step: raising money. Fortunately, Florence, Diana, and Melanie, professional women with some resources to spare, were able to come up with some seed money of their own for basics such as stationery. Florence admits:[11]

We chipped in for the money at the beginning, until we started fund-raising, until the money started coming in to pay our printing bills, etc. We never got the money back. Melanie put a lot of money in, I put a lot of money in, Diana put money in. I figure that I myself probably put $5,000 into CourtWatch. Most of the other members didn't have it.

Nancy let us run up a tab until we had the money to pay her. I think it was $1,000 a month.

Clearly, CourtWatch couldn't function as a political action committee without money for political action. Again, Sims came up with a plan. It began with setting goals and proceeded logically, with small and progressive steps, through the fund-raising process. The plan called for initially raising funds from within the organization and then progressing to direct-mail and special-event fund-raising. Each activity had a specified timeline and target date. Sims explained the plan in an internal CourtWatch document: "Political fund-raising is a unique process which requires people [who are] enthusiastic and committed . . . to give of their hard earned cash, purely because they believe it is the right thing to do." But when people solicit money from others, they also have to "make a personal commitment to the cause." Therefore Sims recommended establishing a committee of PAC members to solicit funds and pursue the collection of pledges from within the membership. Ellen Brodsky Gaber, a licensed CPA and a member of the executive board, took on the daunting task of coordinating the two hundred volunteer fund-raisers. Sims provided specific and detailed instructions:

Here's how it works. Three to ten people agree that their primary shared goal is to raise money for the organization. In their initial meeting these fund-raisers analyze the membership—determining the ability of each member to give to and raise money for the PAC. The list is then divided equally with each person accepting responsibility for making contact with a number of individuals.

A phone call should be made to ask for support and then a specific *dollar amount [should be] mentioned as the requested donation from that individual. When the person has agreed to become a donor, offer to send a follow-up letter with an envelope for remitting the check. Then thank the donor for the contribution and repeat the amount. (I.e., "Thanks so much for your $250 commitment.")*

Remember, if you are turned down for one amount, be persistent, *and ask for the next lower category. (CourtWatch internal document)*

The fund-raising plan also proposed having teams of PAC members who would reach out to family, coworkers, friends, and acquaintances. The teams were described in the plan:

The "Watch" Crew—This team will have the goal of raising $5,000 each over the course of the year. Each individual will receive a watch with the logo on it once she has reached her goal.

The "Crayola" Club—This team will have the goal of raising $1,000 each for the effort. Once their goals are achieved, they will receive Crayola drawings from abused children, framed and with thank you letters.

The "Ivy Leaguers"—This will be the grassroots fund-raising team. Their goals will be to raise $100, $250, or $500 in small contributions. Once they have achieved their goals, they will be given small potted ivy plants. (CourtWatch internal document)

To motivate the volunteers with rewards such as these seems a bit condescending. And other aspects of the plan, Florence felt, were a bit too simplistic. But, she says, Sims was very flexible about implementation. Court-Watch used the strategies that seemed suited to the group and their goals and rejected the others. As Florence recalls:

We started putting together fund-raising letters and sending them out. We had to decide who to send them to. We weren't going to send them to everybody, because

we didn't have that kind of money. And we had to print enclosure cards and
a self-addressed envelope that we wanted them to send back. We formulated a
letter, all on one page, and worked really hard on it. Most of the work was done
right here on Howard's computer, because I didn't have my own computer at
that time.

And Melanie was blown away, because we would talk about it in the morn-
ing and in the afternoon I would fax her the first draft. She asked, "Where do
you find the time? You really are into this." But she got convinced that this was
gonna happen.

There were numerous fund-raising letters that were sent at different
points in the campaign. The first, sent in November 1993, set out Court-
Watch's major issues of concern. It began:

Will your family's future be in the hands of a family court judge? You would
want the best judges for your family, but voting for judges can be overwhelming
if you don't know who they are and what they stand for. 1994 will be different.
CourtWatch will endorse candidates who share our goals of:
—helping victims of child abuse and domestic violence
—increased use of mediation to reduce conflict and cost
—reform of the court-appointment system
—campaign finance reform.

Ultimately, according to Florence, CourtWatch raised close to $80,000
from four hundred supporters. With two exceptions, she recalled, all the
donations were small: "We had one donation of $10,000 from a wealthy
woman philanthropist who came to one of our 'Meet the Candidates' open
houses. We had one female attorney who gave us several $5,000 donations
because she believed in what we were doing. Our smallest donation was $8,
from one of my Hadassah ladies."

Most of the money was spent on advertising the CourtWatch message to
the public. This included printing costs, mailing costs, and renting a post
office box and some ads in local newspapers. CourtWatch even rented bill-
board space, which "cost several thousand dollars each for the month they
were up," says Florence.

After the controversies in which some of the family court judges had
been embroiled during the previous five or so years, it's difficult to imagine
that anyone in Houston could have been uninformed about whom *not* to

vote for. But naming the judges for the record was CourtWatch's first major political move. On November 9, 1993, just four months before the primaries and one year before the general election, articles about CourtWatch's first press conference appeared in both major Houston newspapers, the *Chronicle* and the *Post*. There was no mistaking the intention of the new bipartisan group. The *Post* article's banner read, "PAC aims to oust 5 family court judges." CourtWatch, it said, planned to "turn up the heat on the simmering Harris County Family Courts controversy, targeting five incumbent judges for ouster and calling for reform via the ballot box." Readers were reminded that the family courts had "come under fire in the last year from critics complaining about alleged bias toward women, poor representation by court-appointed attorneys, and the appointment of lawyers who are politically connected to the judges through political contributions." Florence, who was identified as the director of CourtWatch, charged that "many of our judges reward their supporters through a political spoils system known as court appointments" (Schwartz, 9 November 1993).

At the press conference, CourtWatch announced that they would endorse candidates for the primary in March, and subsequently for the November election, as soon as they conducted an extensive screening process. Their "first salvo was fired," when they identified the five judges they would oppose: Henry G. Schuble, Dean Huckabee, Allen J. Daggett, Bill Elliott, and Robert S. Webb (Asin 1993). (Judge Bob Robertson, who would have been the sixth, had died on September 30. His associate judge filled his vacancy.) The *Chronicle* article explained CourtWatch's objection to these judges' reelection, referring to statements made by Melanie Harrell. "These judges," Melanie said, "are not sensitive to child abuse and family issues, do not use mediation enough to resolve cases, and have not educated themselves on family issues" (quoted in Asin 1993).

Huckabee and Elliott, the only judges available for comment, defended themselves rather feebly. Huckabee questioned whether the CourtWatch members had ever seen an entire family court trial. Although he should have been aware that Florence, Mary Gollin (another executive board member), some of the volunteers, and a number of advisory board members were attorneys, he said, "Ask lawyers and they'll tell you I'm a fine, fine judge." Smarting from the CourtWatch opposition, Huckabee later claimed that it was Florence's attempt at revenge since he had denied her request to be installed "in a county office, at county expense, to serve as mediator for litigants in their courts" (Rodriguez). (He seemed to have overlooked the

fact that Florence and several of her colleagues had offered to serve as mediators pro bono; they had been simply requesting a space in which to volunteer their services. Judge Peavey later agreed to permit the four mediators,
including Florence, to volunteer one morning a week in his court, which
they did for three years.)

Bill Elliott simply dismissed CourtWatch's concerns. "That's ridiculous,"
Elliott said. "I think the judges over here are sensitive" (quoted in Schwartz,
9 November 1993). Elliott had been on the bench since the Houston family
court was created in 1976.[12] He was "a legend in Texas," Diana says. Prior to
taking the bench he had been a legislator. Then, as county commissioner,
Elliott hired Barbara Jordan as his administrative assistant for welfare issues;
Jordan was the first black person to hold a major county administrative job.
(Jordan went on to become the first black woman elected from the south to
the U.S. House of Representatives.) It was Elliott's advocacy that led to the
construction of the now-besieged courthouse, the Family Law Center. As
the family court's administrative judge, a position he'd held for the previous
twelve years, he was responsible for the various efforts to evict the protestors
at the courthouse.

Elliott had long been outspokenly skeptical of child sexual abuse charges.
He was remembered for having said that he had a very difficult time believing a father could abuse any child, particularly his own (Gillece). He allowed
that one or two actual cases of abuse did occur, but he maintained that it was
the subsequent interviews with psychologists and medical examinations, not
the abuse, that damaged the child. Elliott believed that charges that family
court judges ignored child abuse cases and allegations of insensitivity were
"overused" (quoted in Nichols). He claimed, not without justification, that
"no one leaves family court happy, it was the nature of beast" (ibid.). But
Elliott defended CourtWatch's right to protest. It was "the American way,"
he said. And, in any case, he made it clear that he was not "threatened by the
group's plan to oppose him" (quoted in Asin 1993). Perhaps his confidence
was a bit inflated, since in all his years on the bench he had never had to face
opposition.

Neither had Allen Daggett been opposed since he first took the bench in
1976, but he had been skewered in the headlines for the previous two years
for his alleged bias and mishandling of the Parker-Casterline case. And Casterline's attorney, T. Wayne Harris, was one of two attorneys who received
more than half of Daggett's ad litem appointments. Harris was cited in
Melanie's task force report on judicial appointments, along with Daggett's
other favorite, Michael Stocker, who was Harris's former partner.

Judge Henry Schuble had been unopposed in the previous election, but since then had run into serious trouble. According to a federal civil lawsuit, an individual had solicited a $10,000 bribe, claiming that he could influence Schuble's decision in a divorce case; Schuble was accused of fraud for allegedly scheming with the estranged husband and others to destroy the wife's business (Zuniga). Schuble would not comment when the accusations were announced.

Robert S. Webb, the last of CourtWatch's targeted judges, had presided over a notorious case of alleged child sexual abuse by the father. In that case, Webb accepted a report claiming that there was no *psychological* evidence of abuse. However, the psychologist's report was based upon an interview with the child in the presence of the accused father. In spite of damaging physical evidence—a rash on the inside of the child's thigh, evidence of rape, and a diagnosis of a sexually transmitted disease, the judge returned the child to the father (Gillece, 15). Webb had never been opposed in an election.

"Longtime incumbents [such as Webb] were rarely challenged, often scaring off prospective opponents with early and eager fund-raising," one reporter wrote. "'Democracy' has been something of an abstract concept in Harris County's family courts" (Ballard and Connelly, 1). The situation was even more offensive because the judges who were unopposed were able to amass campaign funds.

But the reform movement was about to change all this. For the first time, many incumbents had opposition. They would have to mount a genuine campaign and justify their right to reelection. They would also have to use what remained of their "attorney-financed slush funds" which, Florence charged, they freely spent on "undocumented entertainment, travel, and even car payments." She was fearless. "It's all in the public record," she said.

By early December 1993, barely one month after CourtWatch announced its challenge, the group celebrated an unexpected and astonishing victory. Four of the targeted judges—Webb, Schuble, Daggett, and Elliott, all Democrats, all in their sixties—decided to retire! At sixty two Schuble was the youngest.

At first, only Webb, Daggett, and Schuble announced that they would not seek reelection; Elliott insisted that he would run. What changed his mind is not known, but a good deal of speculation occurred. One proposed scenario was that the Democratic Party chief Ken Bentsen had been approached by a person or persons who threatened to expose alleged shady deals that Elliott had swept under the rug. Bentsen could have become convinced that the party would be embarrassed by an examination of the judge's background and convinced Elliott to step down. Others thought that a well-known and powerful lawyer who had been involved with the judge, and who would have been embarrassed by an inquiry, brought pressure to bear. But Elliott insisted that the raging controversy over the family courts had not influenced his decision at all. "Just time to saddle up and move on. Enjoy some life," Elliott said when announcing his retirement. "I've been down there a long time." However, his other comments about "judges against judges, lawyers against lawyers" made his disclaimer seem disingenuous. "There's a great deal of confusion, a great deal of tension, and a great deal of unhappiness around family court," Elliott said. "It's just an unhappy place" (Schwartz, 8 December 1993).[13] When Elliott announced his retirement, Diana Compton crossed his name off the list of candidates with a firm dark stroke that ended in a bold exclamation point.

They were "falling like flies," noted a report in *Texas Lawyer* about the four retirements. Readers learned, however, that the retiring judges were not abandoning their power just yet; they were not leaving the field totally open. Rather, they were throwing their support behind "semi-incumbents," who had been serving as their associate judges in the family courts. These hopefuls immediately began to solicit campaign donations, and one didn't need to read between the lines of the *Texas Lawyer* article to realize that its readers were being cautioned that support would be sought primarily from "the same family attorneys who have been giving generously to the sitting judges for years" (Ballard and Connelly, 31).

Interestingly, the same article contained a sidebar referring to the war chests of the retiring judges entitled, "Family Judges Retire With Surplus Campaign Cash." Because most of those judges had never been opposed in previous elections, they were "taking away more than memories." There was a good amount of money left in their coffers, despite "energetic spending of their campaign funds on such items as car repairs, entertainment, and portable phones" that was made possible by lax criteria and vague reporting regulations. The regulations were equally vague concerning how the judges could dispose of the funds after they retired, but the rule was that over a period of six years they would be able to continue to dispose of the money in a variety of non-political activities (Ballard and Connelly).

Recently deceased judge Bob Robertson's campaign account contained the largest amount of funds: $47,073. Judge Robert Webb's $36,106 was a close second, Elliott had $6,890, and Daggett had $5,325. Judge Schuble's fund was the one exception. Schuble, who spent $1,790 in the first six months of 1992 on entertainment at various Houston restaurants and paid $1,258 for his mobile phone in 1993, was leaving the bench with a deficit in his account.

In the end, of the five incumbents who were challenged by CourtWatch, only Huckabee refused to step down. He had "numerous endorsements, from police unions to the Association of Women Attorneys" and was preferred, if marginally, by the Houston Bar Association ("Family Court Judges"). "We've been investigated by the FBI, the district attorney, the Justice Department, everybody," he argued. "Where are the indictments?" (Makeig 1994). Others wondered the same thing.

Immediately following the retirement announcements, when it became clear that insiders, or those referred to as semi-incumbents, would be seeking the vacated seats on the bench, CourtWatch tried to get a sense of who else might be interested in running. CourtWatch offered to help prospective candidates—financially, with the media, with public relations, with the campaign itself—"but people were afraid," Florence says. Then, "slowly, people started coming forward to say, 'Yeah, I'll consider running—what are my chances?'"

CourtWatch needed a structure for selection that would be fair. Remembering the inadequacy of the family law certification process, which judged applicants almost exclusively on trial experience, the CourtWatch system was designed to be more comprehensive. The screening committee, composed of the executive board and Diana Compton, did want to know about a potential candidate's trial experience, but they were also interested in much more. They came up with a two-part screening device: an extensive written questionnaire followed by an in-depth interview (see Appendix D). The questionnaire asked for details about the candidate's background and experience, including the number of trials and appeals they had been involved with, along with details about those trials; past and present political affiliations and political campaigns; and whether the candidate had been subject to disciplinary action of any kind. In addition, CourtWatch wanted to know about the candidates' volunteer work and organizational affiliations and asked for lists of supporters and campaign contributors. Most important to CourtWatch's endorsement was a potential candidate's professional goals and their perspectives on a number of issues. And finally, if they were endorsed (whether they were elected or not), they were asked if they would pledge their commitment to improving the family courts and supporting CourtWatch's positions on key issues. CourtWatch sent the questionnaires to all eligible candidates who had announced their candidacy during a specific filing period in December 1993. And, Florence says, still with satisfaction, "they started coming back. All of a sudden we had eighteen candidates. Understandably. It was the first chance for people to break into the system." Shortly before the primaries, State Representative Sue Schechter applauded CourtWatch. "This is the best example of what the private sector can do to solve a problem," she said (quoted in Madden).

The screening committee scheduled interviews in Lance Wilks's conference room. (Wilks was the lone male on CourtWatch's executive board.) Each took a minimum of one hour, and sometimes two hours. Occasionally there were back-to-back interviews. "It was a massive effort, " Florence remembers. "We tied up Lance's conference room for days. A lot of it was on the weekend, and we eliminated a lot of candidates who were unqualified as we whittled down." Afterward, CourtWatch brought their advisory board up to date on their decisions and also asked for additional donations. Florence reminded the board about CourtWatch's accomplishments to date: numerous speaking engagements (Florence says that she "made twenty-six speeches before the primary election, and Melanie must have made as many as I did"), extensive television and news media coverage, and a mailing of ten thousand "endorsement cards." Since the group was non-partisan, they made their endorsements based solely on qualifications. And they were planning a mailing to all Democratic and Republican voters who historically voted in party primaries—an additional 100,000 cards that would cost $30,000 for printing and postage. The plea for additional funds ended with a reminder: "There are approximately 400,000 children who will remain under family court jurisdiction until they reach the age of eighteen. Family court judges with integrity and sensitivity can help these children survive the emotional trauma of divorce. We believe the candidates we endorse are prepared to do just that."

There were eight open seats on the bench, since Family Court Judge Linda Motheral was unopposed. CourtWatch had endorsed three Democrats and four Republicans for their parties' nominations in the March 8 primary elections. The endorsed Democratic candidates were Beth McGregor, an accomplished trial attorney who was hoping to fill Schuble's vacated bench; A. Robert Hinojosa, an incumbent who had been recently been appointed to fill the vacancy created when Bob Robertson died; and Dinah Bailey, a former Harris County prosecutor who was vying for Elliott's seat. CourtWatch also endorsed Annette Galik, an attorney who was running in the Republican primary in the same district as McGregor; Georgia Dempster, the Republican candidate in Hinojosa's district; and Doug Warne, the Republican candidate in Bailey's district.

The final CourtWatch endorsement went to Republican Bonnie Crane Hellums, a former Rice University dean who was also a licensed professional counselor, a marriage and family therapist, and an attorney whose ten years of legal experience was primarily in family law. If Bonnie—her campaign slogan was "Give 'em Hellums"—won in the primary, she would oppose Dean Huckabee in the November election; Huckabee was unopposed in the Democratic primary. During the campaign, when Hellums challenged Huckabee for taking contributions from attorneys who practice in his court, Huckabee came up with the counteraccusation that Hellums had taken a possibly illegal contribution from a printing firm—of $372. "She ought to be surprised I haven't gone to the DA's office about that," Huckabee said (quoted in "Family Court Judges"). Hellums explained the circumstances, and nothing came of the charge.

Amidst the charges and countercharges was one that appeared immediately before the primaries in *Texas Lawyer*. This time, it was CourtWatch that was being criticized for not having spent the money it raised. Florence and Melanie quickly responded with a letter to the editor. In addition to justifiably chastising the reporter for not having questioned them prior to writing the article, they submitted a detailed and itemized listing of expenditures in support of candidates—Melanie had kept scrupulously accurate records. (CourtWatch was not actually required to report at that time, but it was important to allay any concerns. At that point CourtWatch had spent over $25,000.) They also made it clear that none of the executive board members had been litigants in the family courts, nor did any have a "financial stake in the election's outcome." Unfortunately, the damage had already been done. Although their letter arrived on March 1, the editor's note said that "it arrived too late for publication before the March 8 primary" (Kusnetz and Harrell, 14 March 1994).

Nevertheless, the primaries proved to be CourtWatch's biggest and most important victory since the retirement of the initially targeted judges. The women, Diana remembers, were "ecstatic" about the outcome: "I will never forget the night of the primary. We won election after election. It was total vindication. Florence, Melanie, and I celebrated quietly at my house. We were filled with a deep satisfaction. The people of Harris County agreed with us—and together we threw the judges out."

Six of the seven CourtWatch-endorsed candidates won. "We did it!"

Diana Compton, Melanie Harrell, and Florence Kusnetz at Diana's home on the night of
the primary election in March of 1994. When they realized that most of the CourtWatch
candidates had won, they broke out the champagne and celebrated. Photo courtesy of
Florence Kusnetz.

CourtWatch wrote to its friends and supporters. "The family courts are
now open to great opportunities for change." It was a "clear mandate for
reform," Florence said. By defeating the semi-incumbent associate judges,
the primary had been even more important than the election in November
would be. For the most part, the forthcoming election would be a contest
among respected and qualified candidates, and no matter what the outcome, "Houston voters pretty much tossed the alleged rascals out on their
ears" (Hull and Boardman, 13).

And it was the year of the woman. Most of the candidates who had
secured their party nominations were women. In two of the coming races,
both candidates would be women—with Linda Motheral already on the
bench, it was guaranteed that there would be at least three women in the
family courts. In six of the seven other contests, at least one candidate was a
woman. CourtWatch anticipated that women would do well in November,
because voters would be influenced in their favor by reports of cronyism
among the all-male family court bench.

After the primaries, Diana compiled an "organizational assessment" in which she noted that the primaries proved that CourtWatch had achieved an "unprecedented success" against "enormous odds." Among CourtWatch's strengths, Diana commented, was that it had a core leadership and volunteers who were committed to change. There were no "victims" of the court within the organization's leadership who might have had a personal, vested interest in a certain outcome. Since they were "on the moral high ground," they'd had "overwhelmingly favorable" coverage in the media. Who could argue with their "stated goals of ethical and responsible family courts?" Much of the public, especially those who'd had personal experience in the courts, was tired of "corrupt politicians and lawyers."

But even with all these strengths, Diana was aware that it was a dangerous time for the organization. For CourtWatch also had its weaknesses. There was an appearance of gender bias in the selection of the endorsed candidates. The leadership was getting tired, and unfortunately there was little hope of finding others, at that point, to take up the slack. CourtWatch had already tapped out its friends and supporters, and the group was having trouble raising money to continue its campaign just as it was going into its final lap. "We seem to have won already in the eyes of some—can't get complacent," Diana wrote. Nor did they. Somehow, they found the reserves of energy to repeat the consuming and exhausting screening process for the general election, selecting the candidates they would endorse from among the primary winners. Now, because six of their seven candidates had been successful in the primaries, "a swarm of candidates sought endorsements from CourtWatch" (Rodriguez). When a probate judge approached Diana and asked to meet with the screening committee to get their endorsement, she remembers feeling very satisfied that CourtWatch was being taken seriously. She had to explain, however, that they were interviewing only family court judges.

The screening committee repeated their process: they sent out interview forms to all of the candidates they had not met with before the primary, and they set up personal interview times. The committee ignored party affiliations, scrutinizing each of the sixteen candidates requesting CourtWatch endorsement and endorsing the better reform candidates. One "sitting judge," Florence says, "was reform-minded, but we had a problem with his judicial temperament." He was known to have had a problem controlling his temper in the courtroom. "We thought we could do better if we were going to reform the court." And, he refused to come for an interview. "It was just arrogance," Florence says. CourtWatch endorsed his opponent.

To inform the public of their endorsements, CourtWatch sent out a glossy brochure with an eye-catching photo of some babies and the question, "Will Your Family's Future Be in the Hands of a Family Court Judge in Harris County?" Inside were pictures and brief biographies of the final judicial candidates. The brochure concluded with a caution: "Nine judges control divorce, custody, and child support cases and their decisions affect millions of people. Such powerful judges should be chosen carefully."

Now that each party had settled on its candidates in the nine judicial districts, for the general election CourtWatch endorsed a slate that was slightly different from the primary. In one district, CourtWatch continued its endorsement of both Georgia Dempster and Judge Robert Hinojosa, Republican and Democratic rivals. In another district in which they had supported both candidates in the primary, CourtWatch decided to support Beth McGregor (Democrat) against Annette Galik. CourtWatch neither opposed nor endorsed Judge Peavey or his rival Don Ritter, and they wholeheartedly supported the single unopposed incumbent, Linda Motheral. The other candidates CourtWatch endorsed were Bonnie Hellums (Republican) against incumbent Dean Huckabee; Sherri Cothrun (Democrat) against incumbent John Montgomery; Associate Judge Deborah Wright (Democrat) against Lisa Millard; Dinah Bailey (Democrat) against Bill Henderson; and Associate Judge James Squier (Republican) against Sandra A. Peebles.

For CourtWatch, the final months leading to the November election were a frenzy of activity on behalf of their candidates: interviews, canvassing, soliciting donations. "CourtWatch got lots of public exposure, lots of public appearances; we got a lot of play and a lot of press coverage," Florence says. They held press conferences and organized a variety of events. They made speeches. "It was a very exciting time."

It was also, Diana recalls, "a very scary time." The women continued to encounter threats and harassment. Diana relates one story: "I had a lot of hang-up calls. Once I went out to my car and an SUV with two men in it were watching my house. Of course, being me, I jumped in my car, and when they peeled out, I peeled out after them. They drove about seventy miles an hour through my residential neighborhood with me right behind them. Finally they got away. I was too angry to be scared at that time. That came later. But I figured we must be having an effect if people were staking out my house."

As in the primaries, CourtWatch endorsements were divided among Democrats and Republicans. Unlike the primaries, however, they were now more heavily weighted in favor of Democrats. Because of this, and because

Nancy Sims was a Democratic political consultant, three days before the November 8 election CourtWatch's credibility was called into question.

On November 5, the headline in the *Houston Chronicle* announced, "CourtWatch Is Embroiled in Dispute." The reporter, Lori Rodriguez, wrote that the group was charged with being "politically tainted" as a result of its relationship with Sims. Critics claimed that there was a conflict of interest, since Sims, in addition to advising CourtWatch, was directing the campaigns of two of their endorsed candidates, Beth McGregor and Dinah Bailey. A number of critics were quoted in the article. "At the very least," one former CourtWatch member maintained, "it has the appearance of a conflict of interest." Another former supporter, Jolene Reynolds, believed that the organization was "a Democratic dominated group." And Annette Galik, who had been endorsed by the group for the Republican primary but whose rival, Beth McGregor, was selected for the general election, referred to the CourtWatch endorsements as "tainted" (Rodriguez). A month earlier, "apparently unhappy that she did not win its endorsement," Galik accused the organization of being "just a Democratic donkey in the sheep's clothing of nonpartisanship" (quoted in Ramsey, Makeig, and Walt). Glenda Joe, a CourtWatch advisory board member, was disappointed in the organization for dropping their support of Galik. Joe, who had dubbed CourtWatch "the babes who slew the Goliath," now charged them with doing "exactly the same thing" they had criticized: "promoting their friends" (Rodriguez).

CourtWatch denied any Democratic influence. Sims echoed the denial. Florence and Melanie reminded the public that before they had done any screenings at all or decided on any endorsements, they had targeted five *Democratic* judges for removal from the bench. Melanie said, "Nancy had nothing to do with who we endorsed; she was not on the screening committee, she was not asked to contribute to discussions [about] candidates, absolutely not" (quoted in Rodriguez). Melanie continued, emotionally and persuasively:

This is not a big political conspiracy fronting for any political party. We're a bunch of moms trying to save our children whose lives could be changed at any time because of a decision by a family court judge. And we're willing to use our money, our time, and our energy to do it.

That is the only agenda we have.

As it turned out, the debate proved to be moot; the Democrats never had a chance. All of the Democrats, save the unopposed Linda Motheral, lost in the great Republican sweep of 1994 that routed Democratic contenders throughout the state and carried George W. Bush into the governor's mansion in Austin. As Bonnie Hellums describes it, "Texas used to be a strictly Democratic state, but now it flip-flopped."

"I can still feel the crushing disappointment," Melanie says, "when the election was decided by partisan politics and not merit or qualifications." Yet in the end, of the nine judges who were on the bench when the reform movement began, seven were gone. (In addition to Motheral, Montgomery retained his seat.) CourtWatch and the reformers had made a "tremendous difference," says Florence:

It meant that from that time on, people were free to vote against the incumbents without fear of retribution. We didn't have the entrenched judges who had been on the bench for fifteen or twenty years who ruled by intimidation. After the election, I was introduced in public as "the woman who turned the family courthouse upside down."

"CourtWatch was powerful!" Melanie recalls, and asks:

Where would the courts be today if Diana hadn't picked up her phone when she saw Mary Frances on TV? Or if Florence hadn't shown up? Where would we be as individuals? I can't answer those questions but I do know that somewhere, a child's life is better because of the work CourtWatch did. That's enough for me—if I had to do it over again I wouldn't change anything. Dedicated individuals with a just cause can make a difference. Maybe housewives should dabble in politics more often.

For Diana, CourtWatch remains significant:

Our success with CourtWatch was one of the proudest moments of my life. I was proud of every single thing we did: the way we conducted ourselves, our motivation, our diligence. Everything about CourtWatch shone with white-hot heat of indignation, that justice appeared to be for sale in Harris County, and that children were paying the price.

CHAPTER 7

Houston
After CourtWatch

"The courthouse is a different place. Now the doors are open and there's a breath of fresh air in there."

— FLORENCE KUSNETZ

lorence and I were talking recently about Houston's prominence in national headlines since a succession of business, governmental, and other scandals, beginning with the Enron debacle, erupted in 2002. Florence says that "living in Houston is like living on the front page; it's a world unto itself."

One place, however, that's no longer in the headlines is the Family Law Center. No one with whom I've spoken, not even the most severe critics, claims that the Harris County Family Courts still have the problems with which they were riddled in the years before CourtWatch. The courthouse is a far different place than it was ten years ago. But there is still room for improvement, and, as Melanie Harrell points out, "some nagging questions remain." She wonders, "Exactly how far did the corruption extend and who-all was involved? Why was the federal investigation stopped? We will never find out, of course. We can only speculate."

At the time CourtWatch was organized there were two ongoing federal investigations that seemed to go nowhere. One was an Internal Revenue Service task force investigation into "widespread corruption in the Harris County courts" (Ledgard 1993). The prosecutor was Mike Shelby, who now is the U.S. Attorney at the Justice Department office in Houston. Shelby won a single conviction: probate court Judge Kenneth "Pat" Gregory was convicted for diverting $28,500 in campaign funds for his personal use and then failing to include that sum in his personal tax return (Luque, 10 July 1993). Randy Burton was hopeful; the handwriting was on the wall, he thought. The public had a "golden opportunity to reshape" the court system. Burton believed that it was "the beginning of the end of the good old boy system" that had been "taken for granted" at the courthouse. "These are exciting times," he said (Linkin and Hensel). Unfortunately, Burton's optimism was premature. Despite assurances that the task force had only begun to explore the tip of the iceberg, despite Judge Gregory's agreement to cooperate with the ongoing investigation of other officials, and despite Mike Shelby's confidence that more indictments would be forthcoming, no additional convictions developed from the IRS investigation.[1]

The other major FBI investigation concerned alleged bribery and misconduct among "campaign contributors and close associates" of both probate and family court judges (Graham, 5 March 1994). Melanie Harrell, who had been interviewed on television about her report on ad litem appointments, was contacted in 1992 by both the IRS and the FBI; she gave them copies of the report. When she "walked them through the data," as she says, an FBI agent told her that the report had saved them three months of work. In March 1994, FBI spokesman James G. Conway affirmed that the bureau would not drop its investigations of the Family Law Center, which had already been underway for more than two years. But, less than a year after Conway's assurances, the investigation was, in fact, dropped.

By the end of 1994, all of the Democratic family court judges (with the exception of Linda Motheral, who had run unopposed,) had either resigned, retired, or lost their seats in the November election. No indictments had resulted from the federal investigations despite electronic eavesdropping and the review of numerous documents, court files, travel records, and witnesses. And by the end of the next year, much of the accumulated evidence, the "reams of information," was useless due to a five-year statute of limitations. There was speculation that the investigations had been "purposely mishandled for political reasons" (Graham, 20 January 1995). Clinton, a Democratic president, was now in the White House; there was a new attorney general—and the investigation had targeted all Democrats. Melanie says it was assumed that "the FBI investigation was squashed." When she tried to contact the FBI, no one returned her calls. "They were out of the picture," she told me. By this time, Melanie had met with Florence and CourtWatch was underway. "I'm so glad we hadn't relied on the feds," Melanie said.

At that time, Gaynelle Griffin Jones had been appointed U.S. attorney by President Clinton. She headed the Justice Department's Houston office, through which the FBI investigation of the family court judges was managed. A brief digression into the story of Gaynelle Griffin Jones, who was besieged with controversies, is worth telling as it exposes some serious issues related to politics and the judicial system.

Jones was a longtime Democrat. Consequently, many inferred that she was reluctant to pursue the investigation of Democratic judges. In addition, it was disclosed that Jones had made a contribution to a "mostly Democratic political action committee that falsely claimed to be nonpartisan"—not CourtWatch, but a group called Citizens for Qualified Judges. Mike Shelby, then the assistant U.S. attorney, had successfully prosecuted Judge Gregory's case and was also handling the family court investigation. Shelby expressed concerns about a possible conflict of interest resulting from "Jones's support of judicial candidates who may have been targets of the probe" (Tedford 1996).

In January 1995, Jones confirmed that the Justice Department's Office of Professional Responsibility (OPR) was "investigating allegations that her office" had misdirected the three-year probe of the Harris County family courts (Graham, 20 January 1995). This investigation (of the investigation), Jones claimed, was at her request. She insisted that "politics was not a factor in her decision" but she wanted to "lay rumors to rest" (Tedford 1996). The results of this OPR investigation were never made public, but the Justice Department "removed supervision of the investigation from Jones and transferred it to the Washington-based Public Integrity Unit" (Graham, 4 February 1995). Rumors were not laid to rest.

Accusations of partisan politicking dogged Jones's career as U.S. attorney. A former FBI agent charged that her office "dragged its feet in prosecuting dozens of cases" at NASA, which is located in Houston (Carreau and Tedford). She was chastised for suggesting that the FBI institute a policy preventing former agents from talking to the media.[2] She was accused of singling out a Republican judge, Bill Henderson, for prosecution of bankruptcy fraud. And the Henderson case was not the final ordeal. Jones was also charged by an FBI agent with using her post to "protect influential Democrats" in a bribery probe (Tedford 1996).[3] The journalist covering the case wrote, "Whether it's a tale of partisan politics attempting to kill an investigation that could have nailed Democratic big-wigs or a Hooveresque FBI official [Wilson] trying to bring down a powerful female counterpart [Jones], no one yet knows" (ibid.).

Nor will anyone ever know. Jones resigned her position as U.S. attorney in October 1997, left government service, and joined the Compaq Computer Corporation.

Wherever politics intrudes into the judicial process, from the highest levels—the United States Supreme Court, the Justice Department, and the FBI—and downward throughout the system, justice may be compromised. Independence from politics on the part of attorneys and judges is not simply desirable, it is fundamental. But in Houston, where judges are elected and affiliated with political parties and where lawyers are campaign contributors, politics can infect the courthouse. In the years prior to reform in Houston, it surely did, and some claim that it still does, albeit to a lesser degree.

The need to finance expensive elections led to numerous abuses. Judges misused and misappropriated campaign funds. The huge cost of an election campaign increased with each election year,[4] and it was lawyers who were the major contributors to judges' campaigns—a peculiar state of affairs. (Such a practice, which can be construed as an obvious conflict of interest, continues to be permitted, and not only in Houston. The public interest journal *TomPaine.Common Sense* recently noted: "We don't let lawyers in court hand cash to judges about to render a decision. That would be unseemly." But "lawyers *can* give them money in the form of campaign contributions" ["Justice Corrupted"].) In Houston, judges were reported by numerous lawyers, including Randy Burton, not only to have *accepted* but to have *solicited* contributions from lawyers with "pending cases" in their courts (Elliott 1992, 34). It is not inevitable that campaign contributions from lawyers will affect a judge's decision, but the situation does present an opportunity for favoritism and cronyism—exactly what Harris County judges were accused of when they made their now-notorious court appointments.

Yet another serious problem results from Houston's "one-lever" system, in which voting must be on a straight party line: judges can be elected because of their party affiliations, even if they are not the best candidates. In the past, this worked to the advantage of Democrats, but in 1994 (and since) it has worked to the benefit of Republicans. In fact, Linda Motheral, the one Democrat who was unopposed and therefore remained on the bench in 1994, has since switched political parties. In 1998, Motheral explained that she was comfortable with the Republican Party's emphasis on "families and family values" ("Campaign 98"). But whether the switch was based on principles or pragmatism, it probably has saved her judicial career and, fortunately, has kept her on the bench.

Needed reform of the judicial election system had been an ongoing topic of discussion for many years prior to the 1994 election. But afterward, statewide and local newspapers, lawyers' newsletters, and legal journals were flooded with articles. After the 1994 GOP victories purged "all but two Democratic judges from the [state] Supreme Court on down," an editorial in the *Houston Post* entitled "Misjudgment Day" bemoaned the system that they had criticized "time and time again," which was "largely based on party affiliation, straight-ticket voting, or familiar names." Some "proven judges were swept off the benches at the courthouse," along with every black and Hispanic judicial candidate. Among them was highly respected Harris County Family Court Judge Robert Hinojosa. Harris County was left with "the whitest judiciary since the 70s" ("Misjudgment Day"). At the time of this writing, on the tenth anniversary of that election, there are no minorities or Democrats on the family court bench.

The Republican judges elected in 1994 were an improvement over those Democrats who resigned after being challenged by CourtWatch; there is little disagreement about that. I was told by many, including Mary Frances Parker, Phrogge Simons, and Marinelle Timmons, the director of the Victim Assistance Center, that the difference is like night and day—although Timmons corrected herself: "I should say, like darkness into light." But some of the new judges proved to be disappointing. One was Bill Henderson, who was convicted of bankruptcy fraud and subsequently left the bench.[5] Annette Galik, another judge elected in 1994, has had continual problems. Both had been opposed by CourtWatch in the general election.

Annette Galik's judicial career is an interesting illustration of consequences that may result from partisan sweeps, which can carry candidates into elected posts who are relatively inexperienced, as she was, or who lack the qualifications or temperament for the positions. Both Galik and her Democratic rival had been endorsed by CourtWatch in the primaries, but when CourtWatch withdrew its endorsement in the general election, Galik became very angry and accused CourtWatch of partiality toward Democrats. Florence says the record proves otherwise. CourtWatch, whose assessment seems to have been vindicated, simply felt that Galik was not the best candidate.

In spite of CourtWatch's opposition, Galik prevailed over her rival in the Republican landslide. She took her seat on the bench in January 1995 along with two incumbents, Motheral and Montgomery (the reelected Republican incumbent) and the six other newly elected Republican judges. Galik was then appointed administrative judge. In addition to judicial responsibilities, administrative judges also have coordinating responsibilities which are supposed to ensure the smooth operation of the courts. As early as February 1995, however, Galik was embroiled in her first dispute with the other judges. She was chastised over a "unilateral" decision to remodel two of the floors of the courthouse without informing the judges on those floors of the plan (Flynn, 13 May 1995).

Galik offered her resignation as administrative judge (not from the bench) as a result of the remodeling imbroglio, but the judges demurred. It wasn't long though before a more serious issue arose and Galik *was* asked for her "immediate resignation" as administrative judge by five of the family court judges: Dempster, Hellums, Montgomery, Motheral, and Squier (Stinebaker). Montgomery, the legislative liaison for the court, had learned that Galik had requested a change in the residency requirement for assistant judges, ostensibly to appoint an out-of-county friend to the position (Flynn, 13 May 1995). What made it "a hell of an embarrassment," Montgomery said, was that although Galik had said that her fellow judges approved of the change, she actually hadn't consulted any of them (Stinebaker). And Montgomery acknowledged that there were additional incidents that had not been made public. But this was the last straw. Galik resigned as administrative judge in May 1995, a mere five months after she had taken her seat on the bench.

The *Houston Chronicle* endorsed Galik for reelection in 1998. "Despite a somewhat shaky start and some valid criticism about her early performance in office," an editorial claimed, "Galik has grown in stature as a judge" ("Campaign 98"). She was commended for her role in significantly reducing the court's case backlog, for "initiating a pilot program" offering free mediation in child support disputes, and for creating additional attorney-client conference rooms. Galik was reelected, but the next year she was again caught up in a serious problem when she was "issued a public warning" and fined a total of $1,300 for "filing late and incomplete campaign finance disclosures" (Bernstein, "Judge is Fined"). The fine was one of the largest ever imposed by the Texas Ethics Commission. Fortunately for Galik, although information was missing from her campaign report, she had been cleared of the more damning allegation: that she had broken the ban on accepting campaign money from corporations.

A year later, Galik was "formally scolded" by the State Commission on Judicial Conduct for "abusive and offensive" conduct in a child custody case. The scolding, an official public reprimand, is the "second most severe criticism possible" that carries no penalty. The problem stemmed from

Galik's order of the arrest of a seventy-six-year-old great-great-grandmother, after which the woman was made to spend the night in jail and was interrogated without her lawyer present. The woman's attorney later said that Galik had been treated leniently. A judge had been removed from the bench in a similar case elsewhere in Texas (Bernstein 2000).

Annette Galik has been elected, and elected, and elected—in spite of rebukes, reprimands, and consistently poor ratings of her performance on the bench. Of the attorneys polled in the annual Houston Bar Association surveys, between 50 and 60 percent have repeatedly given Galik the lowest or near-lowest ranking. While the surveys are "not scientific," they do provide the public with a glimpse of the performance of the judges they elect (Bernstein 2001).

Prior to the most recent judicial elections in 2002, voters were again reminded that partisan election of judges "poorly serves the public." The power of the Republican Party has made it possible for a "handful of intemperate, partial, or intellectually challenged judges to be elected and returned to the bench as surely as their most respected colleagues." Furthermore, "partisan elections shelter—sometimes foster—incompetence as distinguished judges of the minority party are swept out, often to be replaced by inferior candidates of the political majority" (Elliott 2002). In 2002, Texas Supreme Court Chief Justice Tom Phillips said that "the state must consider changing how it selects judges to restore public confidence and remove politics from the judiciary" (quoted in "Chief Justice Calls for Change"). One can only hope that Phillips, who has been chief justice since 1988, is more successful now than he was ten years ago, when he made the same declaration.[6]

Although election reform was not part of CourtWatch's stated agenda, it was an underlying issue in the movement to reform the family courts. Politics played an indirect role in the payback system of judicial appointments, as with guardians ad litem, an issue that was very much a part of the Court-Watch agenda.

While the Texas Supreme Court Task Force before whom Melanie testified on the issue of ad litem appointments had investigated other districts, most of the ad litem abuses and subsequent attention was directed at Harris County. Diana sent me her copy of the task force report in which she had highlighted findings that were based upon Melanie's 1992 testimony. There was evidence, the task force reported, that some appointees were "unqualified" but received "excessive fees." Moreover, there was "not just the appearance of impropriety," but "actual impropriety," and an "abuse of discretionary authority." In addition, the task force report concluded, there was "forceful evidence" of rewards or incentives for campaign supporters.[7] The report made several recommendations that led to immediate reform; afterward, the Texas Supreme Court mandated "strict disclosure of ad litem and other money-making appointments doled out by judges" to their supporters. The order required the newly elected Harris County judges to "list their court appointments, the amount paid, and the party paying the fee" (*Report of the Supreme Court Task Force,* 14). Diana's marginal note is written in a bright red marker in her bold handwriting: "Yay!"

Although the Supreme Court still hasn't been able to agree upon the best way to handle the broader issue of campaign finance reform, Supreme Court Chief Justice Phillips is to be commended for setting a good example. He announced prior to the 2002 election that he would not accept campaign contributions and would limit his reelection spending to the campaign funds that were already in his account. His stand was significant. Texas is a state "where many judicial races have become bitter, high-dollar political contests, often funded by competing special interests seeking to elect judges sympathetic to their causes." Being a Republican, Phillips was "in a better position than most candidates" to make his point (Villafranca and Robison). Since 1994, Republican judicial candidates have been virtually assured of reelection.

Even after the November 1994 election, Phrogge Simons and her "unlikely band of family court protesters" were reluctant to abandon their protest at the Family Law Center while so many complex issues remained unresolved. They remained at the courthouse until January 1995, when the new judges were seated. Since then, Simons has had some legal entanglements related to two children she was determined to protect from their alleged abusers. She has also been involved with a successful lobbying effort to reduce the age (from fourteen to twelve) that a child can sign an affidavit; that is, request their custodial parent. But for the most part, Simons's life has been quiet. "Low key," she says. She's enjoying her two grandsons, a part-time job, and married life in community about seventy-five miles from Houston.

The two years of protest, "two years of service to my country," she calls it, changed Simons's life. She believes that the protest, the "radical" expression of the reform movement, made a genuine contribution to the reform effort.

Phrogge Simons during the protest at the Family Law Center. Photo courtesy of Mary Frances Parker.

She knows it made a difference to many parents who thanked her for being there—even before the election, the protest put the judges directly in the spotlight and tempered their behavior. For Simons, it was exactly the right thing to do at the right time. "Everything I did before in my life prepared me for this," she says. But the experience has also given her an even more jaundiced view of the way the law functions than she had previously—a view of "another level that exists" out of public view. Once you've seen it, she says, you can't ignore it.

Changing judges, however, isn't the "permanent solution," Simons wisely said. "The system itself needs changing" (quoted in Flynn 1994).[8] And Donna Ringoringo, Simons's predecessor in the protest, also believed the changes in the family courts would be "short-lived at best" (Turner, 20 May 1997). After Ringoringo recovered from her hunger strike, Marinelle Timmons hired her to work at the Victim Assistance Center in Houston. But Ringoringo didn't give up her activism. On May 17, 1997, she was in the eleventh and final day of her solo 160-mile Houston-to-Austin Walk for Justice. She was to meet with officials in Austin the next day at Governor Bush's office to present a petition calling for further court reform. Little more than a block from the hotel where she was to have spent the night, Ringoringo was killed in a hit-and-run accident.[9]

Ringoringo's death was as flamboyant and dramatic as the last years of her life had been; it was precisely her sense of drama that was her greatest asset. Florence "welcomed every crazy thing" Ringoringo did, she said (quoted in Turner, 18 May 1997). Ringoringo was also praised by highly respected Family Court Judge Jim Squier for having made people aware "that protests could have any effect at all." Marinelle Timmons said that Ringoringo's determination was amazing. People were surprised when she hired Ringoringo, Timmons told me, but that was "because they didn't know her." Ringoringo was extremely well organized; she conducted thorough research and knew when someone was trying to exploit her name for an unwarranted case. Timmons believes that Ringoringo's early protests were well founded, since "you only had to sit in family court five minutes to know something was terribly wrong" (Makeig 1997).

Although she was not naïve, Florence had higher expectations for improvements in the family court system than either Simons or Ringoringo. In a commentary she wrote for the *Houston Chronicle* in July 1995, she said there could be a "new era" for the family courts—but only if promises for reform were kept. Some certainly were; many reforms were implemented on the local level. New local rules, Florence said, "made it clear that peace is preferable to war in the divorce arena." Mediation was being encouraged, except in cases where there was good reason for an exception—such as in cases of domestic violence—and free counseling was made available. Judges were sending parents to a facility called the Escape Family Resource Center for a mandated parenting course. The course was developed to help parents "understand and learn to deal with their new family structure," to teach them "how to understand divorce from their children's point of view," and to help the children cope "with parents in separate households" (Escape Family Resource Center).[10]

Because there was often no adequate representation of children during divorce proceedings, Family Court Judge Georgia Dempster instituted another important program. She established a Guardian Ad Litem Task Force that evolved into a nonprofit organization called Children's Friend in Court. It was patterned after CASA (Court Appointed Special Advocates), which provides services for the juvenile courts.[11] Judges or court-appointed ad litems could request a volunteer child advocate who had gone through an intensive training program with Children's Friend in Court. These volunteers do not have legal expertise, but they receive specialized training and have the time that an attorney would not be able to spare to thoroughly investigate circumstances that could inform a custody decision.

Several administrative changes have also made a major difference in the way the Harris County Family Courts functioned. A new system of managing the court docket gave the judges control over lawyers who had used such tactics as discovery rule abuse, unnecessary depositions, multiple hearings, and resetting trial dates to draw out the divorce process. These "games," as Florence calls them, favor the partner who has money and often bankrupt the other. Prior to the changes, lawyers determined the trial dates and it was customary for delays to be granted. The new rules, known as court-driven dockets, were designed to bring cases to trial within one year of filing—or even sooner if the couple would allow the process to be expedited further. Court-determined dockets enable judges to determine the dates for hearings and trials, keeping the process on track through a form sent to the attorney that specifies deadlines. "With that prodding stick, and liberal dismissal of cases languishing in the system," Harris County judges "dramatically reduced the backlog of cases" from six thousand pending at the end of 1994 when they took office to 1,500 at the end of 1996 (Flynn 1994). Bonnie Hellums, who was elected in 1994, said that she "stepped into a full docket." When she "took the bench there were approximately 270 cases that were five years and older." But now, she added, "I don't have anything that's over two years." Predictably, some attorneys were angered at what they described as "draconian measures" to keep the cases moving through the system (Flynn, 20 July 1997). But other attorneys agree that the docket system is being continually refined to make room for greater flexibility, necessary for cases complicated by custody issues.

When the turnover in the 1994 election left only two incumbents on the bench, Linda Motheral and John Montgomery, some visiting judges were called in to help relieve the backlog. (To her credit, for the short time that she acted as administrative judge, Annette Galik played an important role in bringing in the outside judges.) The visiting judges also gave the seven brand-new judges some time to become acclimated to a system in which 32,000 divorce cases were filed annually. Without this help, the new judges' inexperience could soon have led to an even larger backlog in a short time.

Mary Sean O'Reilly was one of the visiting judges brought to Houston "in unprecedented numbers" (ibid.). At that time O'Reilly had been an associate and then a family court judge in Fort Worth for nine years, but since 1994 she hasn't run for reelection. As a Democrat, she doesn't see the point. In 1995–1996, O'Reilly worked as a visiting judge for the Harris County Family Courts full-time, continuing part-time for another year. She turned a conference room into a courtroom, "complete with kitchenette," and with her typical good humor she turned adversity to her advantage. "The leaking faucet is my form of water torture," she said. "You'd be surprised at how many settlements we get from that" (Flynn, 28 November 1995).

Like Florence, O'Reilly believes that the courts can remedy legal problems, but there are no legal answers to family problems. She thinks we have "miles to go" in that area. People "have a TV-drama notion that they will be validated, vindicated." It's more realistic, O'Reilly says, to think of it "as a cattle drive where they round you up, put a 'D' for divorce on your rear, and drop you out the other side." A trained mediator and arbitrator, O'Reilly applauds the consistent use of mediation in the Harris County Family Courts today.

Bonnie Hellums, with some reservations, is a strong advocate of mediation. "I tell couples that it's the one time that they can sit down and custom-design their own situation." If a couple comes into court already having reached an agreement, they aren't sent for mediation. "But if they come in and they would like a three-day trial, I say, 'Oh no, go to mediation first,' and I explain it to them." She says,

If you can mediate it, you can keep control in your own hands. Because invariably, I will make some decisions about things that you're not going to like. I'm not going to know what's really important to you. Once you start getting on the stand and doing all this stuff, there are going to be things that are falling through the cracks. "*I didn't know that china set was real important to you because it*

came from your aunt—and here, I've just given it to her." There's a lot of stuff
that you-all can resolve yourselves.

Mediation does give couples an opportunity to resolve issues outside of the
courts. But the process has changed a great deal since Florence first introduced it in Houston. "What I did was conference mediation," Florence
explains.

Couples sat in the same room with a mediator but without attorneys. Although
they were free to bring their attorneys, no one did; that was an added expense. It
was a lot cheaper and much better than the courts.

Mediation was not ever done in one day. We tried to speed it up but it didn't
often work. Usually three or more sessions were needed to reach an agreement. It
was done over a period of several weeks and sometimes over several months.

One couple hadn't talked to each other for weeks. After a mediation session, I
looked out my office window and there they were, in the parking lot, talking to
each other for over an hour. My success rate was between 75 and 80 percent—
meaning that a couple who reached an agreement didn't go back on it, because
it was truly their agreement.

When attorneys took over mediation, Florence says, a trend toward caucus rather than conference mediation developed. In caucus mediation (also
known as "shuttle" mediation), the disputing parties are in separate rooms
and the mediator goes back and forth between them, trying to negotiate an
agreement. Florence is critical of the process. She agrees that *if* mediation
is recommended in cases involving domestic violence, caucus mediation is
preferable. But for most other cases, she says it's a "one-day, one-shot mediation effort where the parties don't see each other, where they're given a time
deadline, and where they have to reach an agreement by then or they go to
trial. The literature calls it 'muscle mediation.'"[12] Caucus mediation is the
model that is usually practiced in Harris County today.

At a dinner party at Florence's home, where I first met Bonnie Hellums and
Mary Sean O'Reilly, Hellums remembered when caucus mediation was first
implemented. She told us "a session could go on until everyone was so tired
and they hadn't eaten and there was this pressured kind of atmosphere. Later
they would say, 'I was exhausted and I was being held up for food. I would
have agreed to anything. I would have put my kid out on Main Street.'"

Now that attorneys have seen "some of the fallout from that," Hellums said, such as agreements that "fall apart," they end the session by five or six o'clock in the evening. "If it's real close, they'll go to seven. But it's still only a one-day deal."

O'Reilly added, "It's mostly a one-day deal because of the expense," which is about $1,000 to $1,500 for the day's session for each party. Hellums agreed. Just that day there had been a couple in mediation who had three teenage children. The parents hadn't spoken to each other in five years; it was "a true cold war deal," Hellums said. "The lawyers were first-class professionals and were prepared," but it still took seven hours to resolve the issues. This family had an income of about $45,000. The mediation cost each of them $1,500 for that day and they had already spent about $7,000 on unsuccessful mediation sessions. It cost them $20,000 to get a divorce. "With everyone working with a pure heart and diligently, it still cost them $20,000, but if they had to go to trial next week," Hellums said, "they would have spent another $10,000 to $12,000 that they didn't have."

Lawyers liked the caucus model, Florence says. They found that "mediation was easier than practicing law, since there was less paperwork, a much shorter timetable for each case, and this model provided fees up front." Florence thinks that caucus mediation was the model the judges adopted and which is in use in the Harris County courts today because attorneys "had the ear of the judges when the courts finally accepted mediation." The caucus model has also been adopted by mediators who do civil mediation, commercial disputes, or insurance claims. Florence has no quarrel with that; she thinks that it is appropriate for non-family cases where the disputants may never see each other again. "However," she says, "that was not what family mediation was supposed to be about. In my opinion, lawyers have fatally flawed the mediation process by restricting, rather than fostering, communication between parents who are destined to have an ongoing relationship with each other throughout their children's lives."

Philosophically, Hellums agreed with Florence:

In the ideal world I think it ought to be a process like Florence is saying it should be: a couple of weeks or a couple of months. But what's happening also is that the courts are being forced to move things through, to expedite their dockets more quickly so a divorce is less expensive. So it's all these systems and methodologies that collapse in on one another. It has to go so quickly now that there isn't the time. Also, most people bring their attorneys now. So you're trying to coordinate professional people's schedules and the schedules of the litigants.

Hellums is, finally, a pragmatist. "What stuck was what worked," she believes. No, it's not ideal, she admits, "but then, it's better than not; it's better
than what was before."

A lot of things are better than they were before, both in Harris County
and in Hellums's court. She's come a long way from the day in 1995 when
she approached Dean Huckabee at his office for help in making a smooth
transition (she had won his seat). She told me that he refused to speak with
her—and slammed the door. Hellums has had consistently high ratings in
the Houston attorneys' survey. One reason may be that she will not take
campaign contributions from lawyers who practice in her court. In the
Houston Chronicle's 2002 Voter's Guide, Hellums was endorsed for reelection because of a number of successes during her years on the bench.

Her court, Hellums claims with some pride, "has the highest collection
rate of child support" in the county. Because she is very conscious of the
high cost of litigation, she works hard to manage a still-overloaded docket.
Hellums regrets that visiting judges are only utilized about five times per
month; Harris County could still use the relief they give to the sitting
judges.[13] She is a firm supporter of alternative dispute resolution, including
collaborative law. And she is a "cookie cutter" when it comes to ordering
parent education classes. O'Reilly says, "There's a nationwide movement for
parenting classes. It's usually a one-time, four-hour course. Hawaii started
having it in their courts. While the parents are having their instruction, the
children write letters to their parents, they role play a scene, they visit the
courthouse, so it's not scary."[14]

Hellums consistently enforces a ruling in her court that requires ad litem
appointees to have taken the mandated training program, although "not all
judges are as diligent." Her associate judge keeps an up-to-date list of those
who have taken the course. Sometimes, Hellums says, when she challenges
ad litems to verify their credentials, they are shocked. "They look at me like
a deer in the headlights."

Hellums has pursued innovation. In a recent conversation she told me
about her newest project, a "Family Drug Court"; she was just about to
leave for an implementation training session at the University of Nevada in
Reno.[15] The Houston Family Drug Court plan is based upon similar programs elsewhere, such as one in New York. Drug courts, claims New York's
Chief Judge Judith Kaye, direct nonviolent defendants to strictly supervised
drug treatment programs instead of to prison and are helping to halt "the
revolving door of drugs-crime-jail." The model designed for family courts,

it is hoped, will stop the "devastating cycle of drugs–child neglect–foster care" (Kaye, 13). Since it contains elements of treatment and therapy, Hellums describes Houston's federally funded Family Drug Court as a program in "therapeutic jurisprudence." The target population for Harris County is non-custodial parents, usually fathers, who don't pay child support. They will be screened to be sure they are appropriate candidates who can benefit from the supervision of a ten-person team that includes case workers, foster parents, ad litems, and treatment providers.

Kay Kreck, who was the local attorney for the Lee Grant and HBO cases, believes that CourtWatch "made people aware that there can be changes in judgeships." Kreck was particularly impressed with Hellums's court:

There is an incredible difference. She allowed people to ventilate. She took time to sell the decision to them, its strengths and weaknesses with regard to the interest of the child. Eloquent and beautiful.

Previously the attitude was implied, if not stated, "I've got a lot more important things to do." Now it's just the opposite.

Mary Sean O'Reilly agrees. She appreciates the effort that has been made, since 1995, to have family support programs and believes the judges have internalized their understanding of family law dynamics. They have "become acculturated," she says. She thinks, although some disagree with her, that "there is no one who doesn't get it." Consequently, the Harris County Family Courts are "generally better," even if they aren't able to function as O'Reilly would like. She uses the example of mediation to explain her reservations:

Now we have at least this humane step in the process. But it's still in the context of litigation and time frames. You're still a piece of sausage when you get out. So as we change the system, one of the things we need is to have a separate identifiable process, a prelitigation stage. The mediation-type experience—whether it's through a county agency or the private sector—should be in that phase before you ever start the clock ticking in the court system. It's like trying to create a hybrid dog, although we hope it won't take 150 years.

O'Reilly has another issue with the courts about which she is adamant: she believes that judges, not juries, should make decisions in family disputes. She thinks that jury trials in family law cases are an "aberration" (they are unique to Texas and Alabama) and that nothing justifies their expense or the consequent psychological trauma they induce. Her position is that judges are better informed and better suited to render a decision. That may be true if the judge is Mary Sean O'Reilly or Bonnie Hellums or, indeed, most of the judges on the family court bench in Harris County today. But the issue is still contentious among those who remember the tyrannical pre-CourtWatch family courts. It was Mary Frances Parker's request for a jury trial that ultimately liberated her from what she believes to have been the arbitrary and vindictive behavior of Judge Daggett.

Despite all of the improvements in Harris County, O'Reilly points out, family courts continue to suffer from systemic problems that are outside of their control and require legislative revision. Even with broad judicial discretion allowing some latitude, judges are limited by rules of evidence and procedure. The courts do not have sufficient resources to deal with the sheer volume of cases on their dockets. And, O'Reilly believes, judges still fail to grasp that they are "blind to sexism." Gender bias continues to disadvantage women in the courts, attorneys as well as litigants. Finally, O'Reilly thinks, there is still much misunderstanding with regard to allegations of child abuse. She believes that allegations are valid in most cases; her tendency, and her advice, is to "err on the side of caution for the child."

Whatever changes were made in Harris County "were not made by attorneys who put notches in their belts; they were made by those lawyers and judges who rose above the adversary system," says Florence. One such lawyer is Justice for Children's Randy Burton, a severe critic of the family court system. He believes that decisions related to child abuse constitute the most egregious legal mishandling.[16] He is concerned over the lack of coordination and communication among the courts at any time, but particularly when child abuse is alleged. He strongly favors juries, rather than judges, in custody cases and thinks judges, lawyers, and ad litems are still indifferent, intolerant, or ignorant with respect to allegations of sexual abuse of children. Burton says that there still is "failure to order supervised visitation when a parent has been accused of child abuse" because judges have a "complete lack of understanding of the needs and issues of children in a custody context."

Marinelle Timmons, who created and has directed Harris County's Victim Assistance Center since 1986, agrees that this is still a problem, but she places the blame upon the lawyers, not the judges. She believes that lawyers "are not presenting child abuse cases as they should." Consequently, judges may not be aware of a problem. She does, however, allow that judges may at least be tacitly complicit, since she thinks that they are actually relieved when abuse issues are not raised. "The court is afraid of making a mistake," she says.

Timmons believes that lawyers avoid raising abuse issues for a number of reasons. One is that the issues will complicate and drag out proceedings, consequently increasing the cost of already expensive litigation. (Timmons says that lawyers are the ones who may never receive their fees.) Another reason is that such cases are not only complicated but extremely emotional, fraught with difficulties, and unpredictable. Timmons and Judge John Montgomery were in the midst of devising an approach to this problem when he died of cancer in February 1999. They were working on developing a form for a case file that would "give the judges a heads-up," Timmons said. When a case first came to a judge's attention, the form would indicate that it might contain the issue of domestic violence, or substance abuse, or mental health problems, and so on. Judges need this type of information to guide their temporary rulings. The form would also thwart the ability of an attorney to "manipulate" a case in order to "get it through quickly." Timmons thinks it's a good idea that should be revisited.

In addition to this clerical proposal, Timmons has been in contact with Administrative Judge Squier to institute a change related to supervised visitation. She would like to see a policy put in place staggering the "drop off and pick up" of children so that the disputing parents do not come into face-to-face contact, which sometimes erupts into arguments and even violence.

Randy Burton doesn't deny that there have been improvements since 1995, but he says that many are related to the "sea change in the political landscape" which replaced entrenched Democrats with "fresh blood." He fears, however, that since some of the judges have now been on the bench for ten years, "similar patterns to those which gave rise to the reform movement are emerging." Judges, he says, are still guilty of cronyism. Some still "give preferential treatment to certain attorneys in rulings rather than base decisions on the merits of the case and the law." In some of the family courts, "ad litem attorneys and mental health professionals" are still used "to steer evidence in favor of a certain side rather than provide true advocacy for the child or a truly neutral evaluation of the children or the parents." One of Burton's chief concerns is what he refers to as "indifference/intolerance/ignorance with respect to allegations of sexual abuse of children, and a complete lack of understanding of the needs and issues of children in a custody context." And he is particularly irate over the practice of "allowing experts to testify about a scientifically unproven syndrome known as 'Parental Alienation Syndrome,' or PAS, which is used to undermine the credibility of child witnesses."

Burton agrees with everyone I've spoken with that a major flaw in the judicial system is the partisan nature of judicial elections and the favoritism and cronyism that may result from judicial politics. And, he says, there still is a "lack of accountability of the judges to the voters and those whose lives are in their hands to act impartially and prudently." Yet Burton is not in favor of judicial appointments over elections—a "merit" appointment system provides its own opportunities for corruption. There is a compromise proposal, however, being discussed that involves an initial "merit" appointment, followed by subsequent "renewal elections" ("Courting Disaster"). But even with this compromise, the courts would not be taken out of the political system. Furthermore, in a poll conducted in Texas in 2002, a large majority supported the election rather than the appointment of judges, although they did favor *nonpartisan* elections.[17]

A few years after the 1994 election, Florence was preparing an article for the *Texas Law Reporter*. She sent me a draft in which she wrote, "I find myself examining the present situation with a new sense of frustration. We finally have increased use of mediation, we have highly trained Family Court Services staff, we have many new judges in our family courts, we have an Office of Domestic Relations and a Dispute Resolution Center, and good family law attorneys and family mediators. But we still have a basic legal system that works against the best interest of divorcing families."

Myriad recommendations have been made that address Florence's concerns. There have been proposals for special "Impact Courts," such as both the Family Drug Court that Bonnie Hellums is organizing and a Children's Court that was established in El Paso by Judge Patricia Macias in 1995.[18] One proposal that has been energetically promoted by the American Bar Association and other organizations is known as "Unified Family Court." A Unified Family Court combines traditional family and juvenile courts into one entity. It is a comprehensive court with jurisdiction over all family-related legal matters, and it provides other resources, such as social services, as well.[19] Some states have begun to move in that direction.

Another proposal had been made for expanded implementation of "Conciliation Courts," which have been in use in California and elsewhere for some time. The purpose of these courts, the literature tells us, is the preservation, improvement, and protection of family life through the use of marriage, family, and divorce counseling. Although conciliation counseling falls under the umbrella category of Alternative Dispute Resolution, it is not precisely the same as mediation. Mediation and Conciliation Courts arose at different times; conciliation services, which were associated with domestic relations courts, began to grow in the late 1930s,[20] while family mediation did not develop until the 1980s.

Like mediation, conciliation counseling does not always lead to reconciliation, but it does help couples identify their marital problems and consider solutions. As with family mediation, there is no attempt to force reconciliation; the decision to reconcile or not is made by the couples during the counseling session. In cases in which reconciliation does not occur and divorce is inevitable, counseling can still be helpful in working out reasonable arrangements concerning children or resolving other issues related to the divorce process. Conciliation Court counselors do not give legal advice, nor do they interfere with the attorney-client relationship. The family court and both attorneys are notified when a couple begins conciliation counseling; they are notified again when the parties either decide to reconcile or choose to proceed with a divorce.

But, as Randy Burton, Mary Sean O'Reilly, and others have pointed out, all of these schemes still involve courts. Families are still caught up in the legal system, with its many inequities, class and gender biases, and limitations. Family law and the family courts were never designed; they evolved with repeated adjustments and amendments. Florence cites one example: rules of evidence, developed "ages ago for civil and criminal transgressions," are no longer appropriate "in today's family law." Perhaps they never were. But, as today the very notion of family is undergoing constant challenges, it may be the right time for the entire system to be rethought and, possibly, replaced. Florence wonders, "Are lawyers secure enough to work as part of a team of professionals to help restructure our family law system?"

In the 1998 election, in spite of Florence's frustration, or perhaps because of it, she led a final charge to improve Houston's family courts. CourtWatch had "gone its way by then," Florence said, but "the few of us left over from 1994, Melanie and I and about two or three others, were asked by many interested parties to endorse candidates in the Family Court elections." There was particularly strong interest, Florence said, in finding reform candidates who would be willing to run against incumbents Don Ritter, who had been neither opposed nor endorsed by CourtWatch, and Annette Galik.

Florence got in touch with her "closest group in CourtWatch" to see if they would be willing to go through the screening process to determine whether there were reform candidates they could endorse. "But Melanie had gone on to other things," Florence says, and Diana was in law school. Consequently, Florence called on "new people" who agreed to limited involve-ment—not a full-fledged campaign, but a process leading to endorsement. This was a realistic approach, since the group didn't have funds and were unlikely to raise any. Unlike 1994, there didn't seem to be a pressing need; the courts were very different places.

Florence managed to assemble a small group of six, all professional women. Since only three family district courts had contested primary elec-tions, the women issued endorsements for two Democratic judicial candi-dates they thought would be better choices. They supported Bill Connolly, who ran against Annette Galik, and Jacqueline Smith, a relative unknown who ran against Don Ritter. They also endorsed Republican Doug Warne for the seat that had been vacated as a result of Judge Bill Henderson's suspension.

According to at least one journalist, the 1998 election saw "mean cam-paigns," not only in Houston but throughout Texas. Both Republicans and Democrats ran "nasty and ludicrous campaign TV commercials . . . they lied about each other, distorted the truth, and appealed to base instincts," alienating voters and leading to a record low 30 percent turnout at the polls (Bernstein 1998). The Connolly-Galik race was "one of the more hotly con-tested." Connolly raised questions about Galik's campaign contributions; Galik claimed that the allegations were part of a "smear campaign" (Asin 1998).

"We were all shocked," Florence says. The results of the election "really had nothing to do with who was running, it all had to do with politics." In Harris County, the Republican candidates "body slammed" the Democrats. "Governor Bush was very popular and won again by a large margin" and once again the Republican incumbents were carried along with him (Bern-stein 1998). Annette Galik and Don Ritter remained on the bench.

"Our efforts were not widely noted, but all of us got tons of calls before the election from folks who asked us whom to vote for," Florence says. "But the public interest in the problems of the courts was not anywhere near where it was in 1994. It was interesting that the good judges had no opponents in the primary election, few in the regular election, and all of the incumbents were reelected. The reform of the family courts had clearly become a nonissue by 1998. We did what we could, but that was the end of CourtWatch."

Reform of the family courts, Houston notwithstanding, is anything but a nonissue. Divorce, visitation, custody battles, alimony, and child support—

always there is heartbreak. Family courts all over the country continue to struggle with ways to make their systems, those great, lumbering bureaucracies, more responsive to the needs of all parties in domestic disputes. All are victims of the system. Some are innocent, the children first and foremost, some not so. But all are victims, nevertheless.

Children of divorce are affected by the experience for all of their remaining years. And the impact of divorce upon American society is immense. In the introduction to her twenty-five-year study *The Unexpected Legacy of Divorce,* psychologist and researcher Judith Wallerstein reports that there has been an "ever-increasing army of adults raised in divorced families since 1970. At least a million children a year have seen their parents divorce." Furthermore, as of the year 2000, these people represented "a quarter of the adults in this country who have reached their forty-fourth birthday" (Wallerstein, Lewis, and Blakeslee, xxvi). Wallerstein cites additional sobering figures: "Forty percent of all married adults in the 1990s have already been divorced," and she predicts that 45 percent of first marriages and an even higher percentage of second marriages, 60 percent, are likely to end in divorce (ibid., 295).

Florence has a concept that she thinks could change the pain and distress of families, particularly children, going through the trauma of divorce. In the article she wrote for *Texas Law Reporter* Florence concluded, "My goal for family law in the new millennium is the development of a procedure that minimizes the legal aspects of divorce and maximizes the social aspects. This is a concept in the process of development, so I don't pretend to have the answers. At this point, I just want to raise some issues for your consideration."

As Florence is well aware, many of the problems in the family courts will persist until those in power in our legal and judicial systems advocate for political and financial reform and true systemic change. Be that as it may—Florence, Melanie, Diana, Lance Wilks, and the two hundred women who were at the heart of CourtWatch proved that they could make a difference.

Linda Motheral has seen the difference; she is the only judge who was on the bench prior to CourtWatch and who still holds a seat. As Motheral says, "Every single thing in the world has changed" in the Harris County Family Courts.

Epilogue
Loose (Odds and) Ends

"As individuals we reached deeply within to access our inherent potential and power."

— MELANIE HARRELL

Florence Kusnetz introduced me to Diana Compton; Diana suggested I call Melanie Harrell; Melanie gave me Marinelle Timmons's phone number; and Timmons said, "Yes, I can help you get in touch with Mary Frances Parker." It was six degrees of separation, an expression that comes from a play by John Guare in which a character claims that any two people can be connected by a chain of roughly six or fewer intermediaries.[1] Since the notion became popular in the early 1990s, numerous games and experiments have been contrived to test the principle. But I had no idea that I was playing the game. I was trying to reach some of the women whose stories I had been writing for the past several years. I wanted to know how their lives had changed over the last ten years and what they're doing now. I had not spoken with some of them since we first met—some I'd never spoken to at all, although I knew a great deal about them from the public record. Mary Frances Parker was one of those women.

"Why don't you call her?" Marinelle Timmons said when she gave me Parker's phone number. "I'm sure she'll be glad to talk to you." So I did—and she was. We spoke for a couple of hours, and Parker told me what her life is like today, more than a decade after she won back custody of her daughter Meagan from Meagan's father Bob Casterline. "Meagan says he is not a father but a 'biological contributor,'" Parker told me. Casterline has not seen Meagan since he lost his custody suit, the case that was so insufferable, as Diana Compton said, that it "made Houston erupt."

Unfortunately, not all the news from the Parker household today is good, although Mary Frances has a positive nature that has not been diminished by her struggle with the courts. She was left with considerable debt, some of which has not yet been paid off, from court costs (including some of Casterline's court fees that she was required to pay since she had brought the suit) and from ad litem and court-appointed psychologist fees. As a result of the notoriety of the case, and because of her debts, Parker has had difficulty finding work in her field as a claims adjuster. Insurance companies, she explained, are wary of employees who are in debt because they may be susceptible to bribery or manipulation. She did find a job with the Metropolitan Transit Authority, but lost it after two years (coincidentally, after testifying in a gender discrimination case).[2]

When the custody suit sent Parker's life into a tailspin, her former employer at the ABJ Adjusters Insurance Company generously kept up health insurance premium payments for her. (Her employer and colleagues were very supportive, coming to her aid more than once during the ordeal.) But the company had financial problems, and Parker wasn't able to return to her job there. Since her career was interrupted, her income has been sporadic; she hasn't been able to get "stabilized financially." And, in addition to her insecure financial circumstances, Parker still feels emotionally vulnerable and experiences aftereffects of the stress and trauma. At one point, toward the end of the trial, her therapist told her that she was suffering from post-traumatic shock—it is not difficult to understand why. She was subjected to one psychological abuse after another: losing custody of her child; being sent to jail because she was "hysterical," and then "being permitted" to sign herself in to a psychological hospital; dealing with the aftereffects of the abusive treatment by the judicial system; going into extensive debt.

Yet, after all of this, Parker is able to say that she feels "blessed" because Meagan, now sixteen, is a "well-adjusted, normal kid." And Parker believes that her misfortune had a purpose, since it contributed to important changes in the court. She has courage and generosity of spirit, more than many other women might have in her circumstances.

Through Parker, I was able to get in touch with Sandi Hebert, whose case in Dean Huckabee's court was also presented in *America Undercover: Women on Trial*.[3] She recounted the painful story of how she lost custody of her younger son Wayne to her ex-husband. He was a Houston police lieutenant, whom she had accused of sexually abusing the child. "It all happened in one court session," Hebert says, still incredulous. "They ripped him out of my arms," she told me; "they wouldn't even let me say good-bye."

In spite of repeated efforts to reverse Judge Huckabee's decision, Hebert did not see her child for three years; she was not even allowed supervised visits. She sank into a severe depression. "I lost all hope," she says. "I didn't want to do anything, I didn't want to live." When she finally did see Wayne, Hebert was warned not to tell him the reason he was taken from her. She now believes that she was only able to survive her ordeal through the support of her parents, friends, and "by the grace of God."

Hebert was devastated when her ex-husband died a few years ago and Wayne remained with his stepmother. She had hoped the death would have brought some kind of closure to "all the years that were stolen." Now Wayne is twenty years old and on his own. Hebert thinks he is an unhappy young man, but he refuses to talk about the trauma with her. "I guess he's not ready," she says. But Wayne and Sandi are in touch; they see each other every week and talk on the phone.

Hebert is an excellent seventh- and eighth-grade science teacher. In 1991 she was named Teacher of the Year for her school district, and she has been nominated every year since then. Somehow, she not only managed to complete her master's degree during the trying time of her custody fight, but she also won a grant which funded her graduate studies, a blessing since she had lost everything, including her home. Hebert and her older son John moved in with her parents until a few years later when, despite her resistance, they put all of their savings into a new home for her. They gave up travel and "all of the things they might have done" in their retirement years, she says. "We want you to be happy while we're living," they told her.

I doubt if Hebert would say that she is happy. She is not at peace, she says, but she believes that "at least some good came out of our loss." Hebert is a survivor of a system that fortunately no longer exists, in which "the judges thought they were Gods." She says that she "went in naïve, believing justice is truthful." But she now believes that she was betrayed "by the system"—by the courts; by Child Protective Services (which she disparagingly calls Child Punishing Services) for abandoning their support of her case; and by HBO. She believes that HBO thought it would be cheaper to settle with her husband than continue to fight his libel claim against the network.

A brief side note. Aside from Mike Hebert's, the lawsuits generated by Lee Grant's film were not settled until 1998, by which time they had turned into a mini-drama of their own. The suits had been filed in 1993 by Dean Huckabee and Kit Harrison. Huckabee claimed that the film "knowingly and intentionally ignored, misconstrued, and distorted numerous facts" (Piller,

14 January 1993). Kit Harrison, a court-appointed psychologist, charged that the film unfairly portrayed him as "being indifferent to reports of child abuse" (Nissimov).

In 1995, HBO asked a Harris County court to dismiss the suit, claiming that "the materials presented in the program were protected by constitutional guarantees of free speech." The issue was significant, as Randy Burton, one of the defendants in the suit, pointed out. The effect on news media coverage will be damaging, Randy said, "if you can't be critical of the system you think inflicts injustices on people" (Makeig 1995). State District Judge Sharolyn Wood postponed a decision.

A year later, the First Court of Appeals took "the unusual step" of ordering Wood to rule on the defense motion for dismissal. It was inferred that she was biased in favor of the plaintiffs. "A majority [of the judges] found that she had abused her discretion by refusing to rule for the purpose of thwarting an appeal under the law." When Wood "complied by denying the motion" and calling for a trial, HBO requested a pretrial appeal (Nissimov, 28 August 1998). That was in 1996.

In August 1998, the Texas Fourteenth Court of Appeals reversed Wood's ruling that the cases go to trial. The court proclaimed that "Texas has long been committed to free speech," whether or not, as Huckabee claimed, the documentary was a "piece of crap Time Warner put together to make money" (ibid.).

This time, it was Huckabee and Harrison who appealed the court's decision to dismiss the cases, but again, Wood's 1996 ruling that the cases should go to trial was reversed and the cases were thrown out. That was October 1998. The "true-life drama," a journalist wrote, with a cast that featured "HBO, Time Warner Entertainment, high-powered attorneys, and venerable actress-turned-director Lee Grant," was over (Flynn 1996). HBO, Lee Grant, and the other defendants had won. But the plaintiffs had also won, since the film was never shown again.

I first learned about the HBO film at the dinner party where I met Diana Compton, Sean O'Reilly, and Bonnie Hellums. For my sake, the conversation around Florence's table was punctuated with patient explanations of legal terms as they eagerly told me about CourtWatch and the circumstances surrounding the reform movement. But it was yesterday's news to them. Each of these exuberant women had become involved with new and interesting projects.

Bonnie Hellums, who had been reelected twice with her distinctive slogan "Give 'em Hellums," still does just that. She is tough. Her toughness is tempered, however, by her intellect, wit, and thorough understanding of family dynamics. Prior to becoming a judge, Hellums was a marriage and family counselor; prior to that she was a substance abuse counselor. At Rice University she was director of student activities and counseling, and she was the women's counselor at the University of Houston. In 1991 Hellums received Houston's Women on the Move award, a year after Florence was also honored. Hellums still teaches an occasional law course, leads seminars, and participates in panel discussions. She is also on the boards of various civic organizations, such as Child Advocates, Houston Works, the American Leadership Forum, and Houston's Volunteer Lawyers Association.

It's hard to imagine how Hellums finds the time for these activities and is still able to manage her full docket and implement the new drug court for which she's advocated since the mid-nineties. But none of her judicial responsibilities are suffering, apparently. She is consistently rated highly in the Houston attorneys' surveys, and she has been endorsed by the *Houston Chronicle* in each of her reelection campaigns.

What is all the more remarkable is that Hellums is completing a master's degree in judicial studies (she already holds a master's in education and a JD) at the University of Nevada at Reno, which conducts a joint program with the National Judicial College. She has completed the program except for her thesis, which is on gender communication in the courtroom. "Men and women speak very differently, and men and women hear very differently," Hellums says. "In the legal process, as judges, we need to be able to hear in both languages." An observer cannot see without a perspective, Hellums explains, and judges often fail to acknowledge their own perspectives. Sometimes, judges are so unaware of their own biases or ignorance that they make indefensible decisions and statements. She believes this was the case with some of the pre-CourtWatch judges, even those who may have had the best intentions.

Hellums says that she is "very tuned into" gender issues and believes that she pays "close attention to subtext in the courtroom." But one day, when she was hearing a divorce case, the attorney for one of the parties asked: "Why are you getting a divorce?" Bonnie continues the story:

This witness said, "Well, I feel very betrayed because it was my understanding that when we got married, that after three years we would start a family soon. I got the nursery ready, the house is ready, everything is done that needs to be done. But my spouse is climbing up the corporate ladder."

I had to stop and plug this in. It was a man who was talking.

And I looked hard at the wife, and sure enough, she was sitting there very detached and very cool in her business suit. She was going to be vice president of this big company next year and she wasn't about to stop and have children yet.

There are many gender communication issues which arise in the courts. Hellums says, "If you hear a man say that 'she took the kids and I haven't seen them in a year,' but he's not showing any emotion, you think that he's an SOB, he doesn't care. But that's not the case. He's not used to showing his emotion. And you can't just write off either side from where your perspective is." Hellums is impatient. "That's why I want to get this thesis done," she says, "so I can present this at the judicial college, so that I can start to teach judges to hear."

Mary Sean O'Reilly is also interested in gender issues. She was a contributor to the 1994 Gender Bias Task Force of Texas report and is still on the implementing committee of the task force. Though she hadn't been involved with CourtWatch, O'Reilly was well informed about family court–related issues prior to and since the reforms have been instituted in Houston. She was one of the visiting judges brought in to relieve the backlog after the almost total turnover on the bench.

O'Reilly is the second-oldest of eleven children. She always wanted to become a veterinarian and still indulges her love of animals by breeding bull mastiffs, but she followed a very different career trajectory. O'Reilly entered a convent, a very small Belgian-based community called the Sisters of St. Mary of Namur, in 1968. Although she left the order in 1984, "it's still part of my life," she says. In fact, she donates the money she earns dog breeding to the order.

O'Reilly left the convent for reasons not of faith but of gender. Because of the shift toward a more conservative Church after Pope Paul VI came to power, as a woman she was not permitted to hold a position of civil authority. But she was already an attorney—she had earned her law degree at the University of Houston in 1977 while still in the convent, when "there was *no* indication," she says, "that [the conservative shift] was in the cards." She is very interested in seeing "who the next Pope turns out to be" and how the church will change.

O'Reilly's home is still in Fort Worth, where she was raised and to which she returned after law school to work as a legal aid attorney. In 1983 she was appointed an associate judge; she was elected to an open seat on the bench in 1990. As a Democrat, O'Reilly decided not to run for reelection in 1994 although a lot of judges, aware of the change in the political landscape of Texas, were switching parties. She still sits as a visiting judge in Dallas, Houston, and Fort Worth about once a week, but her primary work is in mediation and arbitration. She commutes between the offices of the Conciliation Institute in Houston and Fort Worth.

O'Reilly has a special interest in domestic violence.[4] One serious difficulty, according to the National Domestic Violence Hotline, is that most incidences of family violence—nearly four million women are abused in America each year—continue to go unreported ("Domestic Violence"). There is little that can be done by legal authorities about this pervasive problem if it isn't brought to their attention.[5] Marinelle Timmons of Houston's Victim Assistance Center says that women are forced, finally, to acknowledge the reality when the violence escalates to the children, as it often does. For some, it is the only thing that motivates them to finally seek a protective order. Timmons is correct, however, in believing that children are victims of abuse even if they are not themselves physically abused.

As O'Reilly points out, it is well documented that, like alcoholism, family violence was often kept a family secret. And society as well as the legal system has been complicit in keeping the secret a private, family matter. Domestic violence was also often dismissed or minimized, "treated as a *joke*" or "just a slap in the face," writes law professor Robin West (West, 67). "*That* ignorance is appallingly widespread," even today. "Way too many people," including the women who are the victims of such abuse, West says, continue to believe that a slap on the face is "normal, ordinary, unexceptional, or deserved." It can, in fact, "dislocate a jaw, dislodge teeth, and leave a bruise." Even more troubling, a slap in the face, "when undeterred, when unacknowledged, when hidden, when societally *condoned,* will often *escalate.*" West believes that too many people do not know that a slap on the face is a crime, "that there is in fact *not* a sharp line between a slap on the face and a life-threatening beating—there is only a continuum . . . the only sharp line that matters . . . is between violence and non-violence, not between bad violence and okay violence. No level of violence is acceptable—none should be tolerated" (West, 68).

Testimony given at one task force hearing prior to 1994 indicated that in Harris County "about half of the judges" required three incidents of family violence before they "saw the need to get into a protective order situation" (*Gender Bias Task Force Report*, 67). Today, women no longer have to present evidence that direct physical violence had occurred in order to get a protective order. O'Reilly is "very impressed" with the district attorney's program for family violence in Harris County; she says that they have "a very comprehensive and aggressive department."[6]

O'Reilly agrees that attitudes are slowly changing, but issues raised by the Gender Bias Task Force of Texas "remain relevant." Shelters need better funding. A serious unresolved issue is the need to synchronize criminal statutes and the family code. And many lawyers and judges are still not well trained in the dynamics of domestic violence, either in the psychology of the syndrome, with its "deeply complex pathology," or in the serious, long-term consequences for the abusers and the children. Judges "don't get exposed to the reality of the experience except through psychological reports," O'Reilly says. She thinks their training should include spending time in a shelter and sitting in on group sessions with abused women and children.

It was abused children that brought Diana Compton and Melanie Harrell into both advocacy work and the court reform movement. The women met when they were students in a fashion design program at Houston Community College. Their children were still babies when the Christi Myers news report ignited their outrage. Diana had already been involved with child advocacy groups—Children at Risk and KID-PAC. She found that children's advocacy organizations were "squabbling amongst themselves for grant money and turf positions," and believes that "there could be a tidal wave of change" if, instead, they could "speak in one political voice." Recently Diana rejoined Randy Burton's organization, Justice for Children, with whom she's worked periodically for about ten years. She thinks of Randy, her good friend, as a mentor.

Diana had been a licensed attorney for two years when I met her in 1999. She graduated from the South Texas College of Law intending to practice family law. But "those who can do family law are very special," she says. They must deal with clients in great crisis; it's very emotional. "You need to be very remote, detached, because the parties who are angry and irrational are even more angry in the end." When Diana first began to practice family law, she hadn't yet developed what she calls her "professional exterior." By the time I met her, she had already learned that she didn't have the stomach for family law. Diana's primary work today is as a mediator, but not in family mediation. She works with the Texas Workman's Compensation Board and finds it very satisfying. "Clients get their feelings out, they get heard, and they own the agreement." Although she doubted and agonized over her decision to close her family law practice, she's now convinced that it was the right one. "I've done as much family law as I possibly can do," she says.

Diana still believes that family law is part of a "broken system," but she also agrees that in Houston, the system is functioning much better than before. "Our candidates who eventually were elected have performed their duties with integrity," she says. "I'm sure that some litigants still feel they get a raw deal. But I haven't heard any more allegations about justice being for sale in the Harris County Family Courts."

Mason and Betty, Diana and Melanie's two babies, are now teenagers, and Diana and Melanie are now single moms. The women don't get to see very much of each other these days. They do keep in touch, but their lives have taken different turns. Melanie wrote me that:

After the frenzy of CourtWatch ended, I didn't know what to do with myself. I had often toiled sixty-hour weeks, and the day after the election it was all over. CourtWatch didn't even have an office to dismantle.

I had neglected myself physically during the previous four years, so I decided to try a yoga class. I discovered that I really enjoyed the practice, and as I immersed myself in this spiritual discipline more and more deeply, my priorities, my out-look, indeed my entire character began to shift rapidly and radically.

Melanie was divorced in 1997 (coincidentally, Diana was divorced a year later). She says, however, that she and her husband managed to maintain their friendship throughout the process. "We knew too much to involve ourselves with those courts!" They hired one attorney-mediator and "ironed out all the details" themselves.

Since the divorce, Melanie has been learning the theories and practices of energy work and hypnosis as "vehicles for healing." She is midway through the Naropa University graduate program in transpersonal psychology. This new focus connects with her advocacy work in an interesting way:

To me, there is nothing more exciting than conscious evolution and nothing more tragic than a life wasted because that potential has been blocked, especially if the obstacles are traumas created by child abuse.

I pray that the children CourtWatch helped will overcome their pain and move forward to lead happy, productive lives. Too often we stay stuck in these childhood experiences, and yet there are ways to release them that are not yet recognized by mainstream medicine.

Melanie reflects upon her work with CourtWatch: "As individuals, we reached deeply within to access our inherent potential and power. As a group, we used that power to fight injustice; and we made a little progress, didn't we? Whenever I feel guilty because my contributions to the planet seem so small, I think to myself, 'Oh, yes. CourtWatch.' And then I'm OK."

For Florence Kusnetz, CourtWatch was the final punctuation in an accomplished career. Or so it seemed at the time. Florence is inexhaustible, despite the fact that, as I write, she has already celebrated her seventy-fifth birthday. In the years since CourtWatch she has been able to juggle a daunting travel schedule and some important professional projects in Houston and Israel.

Florence and Howard make an annual trip to Israel to visit Howard's brother and his family in Jerusalem. In the mid-1990s, Florence says, she was contacted by someone in Israel who asked if she could help set up an educational program for parents going through divorce. She helped the family court services staff find information about such programs in the United States and sent materials that they could adapt to their own cultural needs. Over a two-year period she answered questions, guided the staff's efforts, and helped them implement a program of their own.

Another interesting project caught Florence's attention. In Israel, the secular courts have jurisdiction over civil and criminal matters, but the religious courts—the *bet din*—have jurisdiction over marriage and divorce. Jewish divorce laws, including matters of support, custody, and property, are complicated. And since they are based on Orthodox Jewish law, or *halacha,* women tend to be at an extreme disadvantage. Traditionally women were not allowed in court at all—not even as witnesses. The religious courts favor men. "They get away with abuses," Florence says, because in Orthodox Judaism "all the rabbis are men; women still don't have parity in a lot of areas in religious law."

The proposal for women's advocates in the religious courts in Israel, an effort to address this problem, was already in progress when Florence learned about it. She was able to advise the principals involved, both "the female attorney who helped create the program and the rabbi who eventually instituted it." The proposed program was designed to prepare women to be advocates for other women who were going through divorce proceedings in the religious courts—to speak for them, to explain what was happening. The potential advocates were not attorneys—female attorneys would not be allowed. They were women who would play a role similar to ad litems. The advocates were to take a certifying exam proving that they understood the complexities of the law, and then the chief rabbi would approve certification. It was a radical proposal for a very traditional court system in which women have no voice. The program has since become ongoing, and for the first time since Jewish marital laws were written down, "women [are] in courts with status."

Some are convinced that this could not have happened without divine intervention. Florence tells why:

The reality hit when the first group of women was ready to be certified. As someone said, they probably went along with the idea because they thought the women couldn't do it; that they weren't capable or that they wouldn't be able to complete such a demanding program with all of their other responsibilities.

The rabbi was just about to sign the first certificate when he realized that there were several more underneath. When he saw that, a woman told me sarcastically, "he got a cramp in his right arm and couldn't sign."

When the rabbi didn't sign the certificate, the issue almost went to the Israeli Supreme Court for a ruling, since gender discrimination is technically unconstitutional. The rabbis, however, "were afraid of a written precedent that established gender equality; they didn't want things to go that far." Finally, after three weeks had passed, the miracle occurred: "All of a sudden," Florence says, "the rabbi's arm got better."

Florence is currently involved with a project closer to home. After she won the Women on the Move award, she was invited to become a member of Texas Executive Women (TEW). Their Mentoring Project is something she is very excited about. For many years the organization has sponsored a program for "at-risk" middle-school and high-school girls. Some of the girls are from "seriously dysfunctional" or homeless families, according to Florence.

The Mentoring Project women work with school counselors to identify students who need a role model or mentor to encourage them to finish school and pursue careers. "The program has been very, very successful," Florence says. In the past she worked with the group that had originally set up the program, and she participated in field trips to workplaces that would give the girls ideas of possible careers. More recently, Florence joined a monthly TEW program that sponsors visits at the high school in her neighborhood. Forty-five girls attended the first meeting, "a very effective getting-to-know-each-other session." The next step will be to administer aptitude tests that may help the girls "find their direction" (TEW pays all the costs). In past years, the number of girls who went on to college, Florence says, "was phenomenal" considering their disadvantages. "This is my major area of volunteer work," Florence says. "I get tremendous rewards from working with this group."

Florence's social consciousness has not diminished; neither has her commitment to *tikkun olam,* the repair and improvement of the world. And whether or not they know it, by continuing their important work the other women who have been prominent in these pages are also obeying the Talmudic admonition: "It is not incumbent upon you to finish the job, yet neither are you free to give it up."

At that memorable dinner party, Bonnie Hellums told a story that is attributed to the poet Rilke:

One day, he observed a woman moving oddly along an ocean shore. At first, Rilke thought she was dancing. But as he moved closer, he saw that the woman was throwing starfish back into the sea.

"What are you doing?" the poet asked. The dancing woman replied, "The tide is low, and unless I put these starfish back into the water they will die."

"There are millions of miles of beach and thousands of starfish," Rilke said. "You can't possibly make a difference." With that, the dancing woman leaned forward, picked up another starfish, and threw it into the ocean. "It makes a difference for that one," she said.

Notes on Gender Socialization

The liberal agenda of the 1960s counterculture period—the era of President Johnson's "Great Society"—promoted equality as a value in American society. But values, we know, can't be mandated. Consequently, Congress enacted anti-discrimination measures, such as those outlined in Title IX, that programs receiving federal funds were required to follow. The ultimate goal was to achieve equal opportunity for all those who had been historically discriminated against in education, employment, and business—racial minorities, women, and others. As a result, many barriers began to fall. Since that time there has been a slow but persistent increase in the number of women entering not only law but other professions, "social associations, higher educational institutions, and legislatures" that had previously been male-dominated (Levit, 6). (Men, on the other hand, have not entered feminized professions in large numbers. Lower pay is the main reason, even though men make more money than their female counterparts for the same work. Female nurses, for example, earn only 95 percent of the amount earned by male nurses with equivalent education and training [Levit, 61].)

The fact that women were making significant gains in professions such as law, medicine, and politics supported the claim—the first argument feminists used to attack sexism—that men and women were basically the same but had been assigned different roles in society. Women were brought up to develop different attitudes, value things differently, and behave differently from men. But if boys and girls were raised in the same way, the argument went, the differences would disappear.

In the debate over nature vs. nurture, the pendulum was poised high on the nurture side. It was *only* socialization, it was claimed, that made men and women behave differently—*only!* In 1974 the PBS program *Nova* broadcast a show called "The Pinks and the Blues." The clothes and hair-styles may have changed over the past thirty years, but recent research on gender shows that much of the behavior caught by the *Nova* cameras is still being exhibited today. There are increasing exceptions to the rule, but little girls are still, literally, wearing pink. I have two young friends who recently had female babies and, except for a few pair of jeans, every gift of clothing was either white or pink. I have never seen a little boy dressed in pink; it is taboo, he would be ridiculed. No parent would dare to put a little boy in such a situation.

Even families that are philosophically committed to gender equity often unwittingly reinforce gender stereotypes. Children are taught their sex roles from birth.[1] There are very few fathers who bring little footballs to their newborn baby girls in the hospital. Parents also tacitly approve or disapprove of particular behaviors differently in their male and female children. "Specific tasks are assigned to members of each sex, and various social activities—from housework to sports to occupations—are considered principally the domain of one sex but not the other. Crossing traditional gender lines is viewed as a violation of cultural norms" (Levit, 62). Recently a little boy refused a lollipop that I offered him, the kind that has a face and sugary features. He said it was a "girl" lollipop. His mother, a modern, informed, well-educated woman, protested that all the boys in the nursery school he attends are highly aware of boy things and girl things—she didn't believe she had anything to do with his sensitivity. Perhaps she didn't. But it is difficult to believe that the boy doesn't receive gender messages when his mother dresses her little girl like a doll in the most typically "feminine," frilly, and lacy outfits.

We've seen great changes since the 1970s, but Americans, like the rest of the world's population, continue to live in a highly gendered society. In spite of decades of consciousness-raising by feminists, and in spite of substantial changes, the vast majority of boys and girls in this country are still being socialized to conform to different norms and develop different attitudes and values. Girls are given much greater latitude than boys to express their emotions, both negative and positive. But girls also learn passivity, submissiveness, and interdependence.

Most boys, on the other hand, are socialized to value rationality over

emotion and to act aggressively, competitively, and independently. A semi-
nal study conducted in the 1950s looked at gender socialization in parent-
child interaction. It demonstrated how intolerant parents were when their
little boys cried, even those as young as two and three years of age. Boys
were told that they needed to be tough and strong and suppress their feelings.[2] More recent studies confirm the persistence of this almost reflexive
response. (Oddly, there is greater tolerance of girls being "tomboys" than
of boys being "sissies"—an example of the greater leeway given to female
behavior.) As boys mature, American society continues to make conflicting
demands upon them by asking them "to move away from historical roles of
masculinity; yet cultural expectations of men remain tied to traditional defi-
nitions." Men are "still judged according to a set of stereotypically masculine
expectations, including rugged individualism, independence, competitiveness, physical prowess, and emotional toughness" (Levit, 39.)[3] Those who
have a strong enough will to break free of these expectations have proven
that "men can connect to other human life. Men can nurture life. Men can
mother. Obviously, men can care and love and support and affirm life. Just
as obviously, however, most men don't" (Smith, 528).

Over the past thirty years, a vast amount of data on gender differen-
tiation has been compiled by researchers—from biochemists to cognitive
psychologists to historians to linguists. Almost every possible avenue is
being explored to account for the enduring and pervasive differences in the
behavior, attitudes, and values of males and females. Some differences may
ultimately prove to be innate or due to hormonal and other influences upon
fetal development—we are no longer confidently claiming that behavioral differences are due *only* to socialization. We may learn that not only is
our gender determined biologically, but there may be biologically "gender-
specific tendencies" (Levit, 29).

Acknowledging that men and women have differences, however, doesn't
mean that we have to accept the simplistic idea that biology is destiny, that
gender differences are "inherent or inalterable" (Chamallas, 26). We are
steadily gaining a better understanding of the complex relationship between
nature and nurture. Yet even as we become more open to the idea that there
are biologically determined differences between men and women, we can
claim with even more assurance that sex roles are constructed in social settings; these two broad determinants, biology and society, interact in a multitude of ways. As social norms change, so does behavior. Recent evidence
of this, sadly, is the increasing number of female juvenile offenders, "an

indication of growing social acceptance of girls and women demonstrating aggressive behaviors," which is "gradually ceasing to appear unnatural" (Levit, 26).[4]

The family is still the primary socializing institution in American society. Basic attitudes are shaped within the family as boys and girls observe the behavior of parents and other significant adults and receive direct instruction, i.e., rewards, for acceptable behavior and punishment for undesirable behavior. As women become more aggressive and men are encouraged to become more nurturing, we are seeing changes in parenting behavior that will inevitably change the way sons and daughters view themselves and construct their future roles as parents.

Schooling also plays an important role in socialization. Schools have two primary functions: an academic purpose, and a socializing function. Some educational theorists think, in fact, that academics are the least important part of schooling. More important, they say, is the teaching of social norms. Indeed, a primary reason for the huge growth in home schooling in recent years, particularly among religious conservatives, is to remove children from the influence of the public schools and enable families to reclaim the prerogative of socialization.

The two functions of schooling are not neatly separated; they are intertwined and often in conflict with each other. For schools to successfully fulfill their academic function, students must be academically prepared not only for the present but also for the foreseeable future; they should be exposed to the newest ideas, concepts, and technologies. New knowledge often requires developing new attitudes and values. The academic aspect of schooling is progressive—students inevitably become agents of change—while the socialization function is conservative, helping to ensure the continuation of the culture's norms, values, and existing attitudes. These clashing expectations lead to a state of tension between change and stability, transition and conservation. This is one of the reasons that education, as a social institution, is always in conflict with itself, and the conflict is just as relevant for schools of higher education and professional institutions as it is for public schools.

In the early days of American public schooling, in the mid-nineteenth century, Irish Catholics and others who were not Anglo-Saxon Protestants began arriving on our shores in large numbers. It was this country's first period of intense immigration. A major justification for the development of free public schooling was, in fact, that it would serve the purpose of "Americanizing," that is, socializing immigrant children. Reformers such as Horace Mann openly acknowledged that it would be in the schools that immigrant children would be taught acceptable social behaviors and develop American attitudes and values, including individual self-reliance, responsibility, and competitiveness. These attitudes were expected to translate into a motivated and competent citizenry that would be able to function in a democratic society as well as supply the growing needs of American industry with a reliable workforce. Later, the socializing function became, and has remained, implicit; it has come to be known as the "hidden curriculum" (Vallance). The content of the hidden curriculum changes as a society's norms change, but its function remains constant: to socialize children with the attitudes, values, and behaviors that are generally acceptable to the society in which it is based. The hidden curriculum is exemplified by comments on children's report cards on such topics as getting along well with others, completing work, working neatly, being well prepared, and even getting to school on time.

Reinforcing gender norms is also a function of the hidden curriculum. With regard to gender equity, much work still needs to be done at all levels of schooling in America, including professional schools. Teachers, starting with day care and continuing through the primary and secondary school years, continue to tolerate and encourage different classroom behaviors on the part of boys and girls. Teachers still tend to assign different classroom roles to boys and girls. Who, for example, is most likely to be called upon to set up the audiovisual equipment or help move the classroom furniture?

Many teachers did not learn and, consequently, do not use methodologies that have been acknowledged to create a fairer classroom climate for girls. One example is the discouragement of "calling out," which boys tend to do more readily than girls. (Why? Perhaps girls learn to follow the rules more closely. Perhaps boys don't wait to be sure they have the right answer because they have learned to be better risk takers.) One practice that helps girls participate more in classroom discussion is called "wait time." Wait time involves allowing a few seconds, as little as two or three, to pass after posing a question and before accepting an answer. Teachers can also encourage girls' participation through the use of cooperative education methodologies such as group work and non-competitive games. These strategies are often grouped under the heading of "feminist pedagogy"—an unfortunate designation, since most are simply good teaching practices that can benefit all students. (These points are surprisingly relevant in examining newer law school methodologies and clinical teaching strategies.)

Many teachers practicing today were not taught how to avoid gender bias or encourage equitable treatment in the classroom, but even so, the situation has been improving over the past several decades. Most teacher education programs now include courses related to gender issues and multiculturalism. (It is unfortunate, however, that once a teacher is behind the closed door of his or her classroom, the need to cover mandated course content or to address the curriculum to standardized testing, among other pressing demands, often forces a retreat to traditional methodologies.) Both classroom practices and curriculum materials are improving. Previously, those who selected the texts used in schools—often lay committees rather than professional educators—were not consistently aware of or sympathetic to these issues. Pressure upon publishers from feminist groups has made a significant difference in this area.[5]

The teaching of math and science is of particular interest. Math has been called the "critical filter" because math avoidance and anxiety, although far less so than previously, still keeps many females out of some high-powered fields.[6] Teacher preparation programs do not uniformly provide instruction in methods to help girls achieve in math and science. In fact, many subtle teaching practices actively work against this achievement, reinforcing girls' lack of confidence in these areas, resulting in less success, which, in turn, reinforces negative assumptions. If we begin with the assumption that girls have less aptitude for math, we have a lowered expectation that they will be able to do the work and thus we treat them differently from the boys in their math classes. For example, studies have shown that teachers tend to assist girls more with problem solving, suggesting possible solutions, while they encourage the boys to work out the problems for themselves. Consequently, girls don't acquire the same problem-solving skills as boys, which serves to reinforce the original negative assumption—and the cycle repeats itself.

While schools constitute our formal educational system, there is another educational system in America today that is informal, but pervasive and extremely powerful—and problematic with regard to sex roles. It is broadcast media, and particularly television. On television, issues have to be easily resolved within half-hour or hour time slots, so both plots and characters are simplified, superficial, and stereotypical. For the most part, "gender stereotypes are [still] embedded in the images children see" (Levit, 39). Women—

in the same shows that present them in nontraditional roles such as attorneys and judges—are usually glamorous (they have been since Veronica Hamel's first serious portrayal of a female attorney in *Hill Street Blues*), and the profession itself is romanticized. Women remain stereotypically feminine, distracted by their emotionalism. Emily Jane Goodman, a New York State Supreme Court justice, claims that there are numerous examples of female attorneys and judges in law-based series such as *The Practice, Judging Amy, Ally McBeal,* and *Family Law,* but the legal settings are simply "bookends to support mini-plots of seduction, sexual harassment, and abuse of power, while at the same time discrediting the idea of women having power and authority" (Goodman, 47).[7] Programs on networks that are targeted toward youth, such as MTV, are especially offensive and often sexist. This may be a result of the still male-dominated TV industry. "For the third consecutive year," the Directors Guild of America reported on the employment of women and minorities, "white men directed more than 80 percent of 860 episodes" in prime time ("Television Hiring Practices").

However, that said, shows that feature women attorneys, such as *Ally McBeal* and *The Practice,* may have helped bring about change by adding to the "push guiding more women to the law school door" (Froom). Shows highlighting women in other professions, inadequate as many of them are in reshaping gender stereotypes, may serve a similar function.

Justice for Children and Child Protective Services

Randy Burton is the founder and director of the national child advocacy organization Justice for Children (JFC), which he began in May of 1987. Surprisingly, in his past life this gentle and soft-spoken man was chief prosecutor for the Harris County District Attorney's Office in their Family Offenses Section. Since then he has devoted the better part of his legal career to documenting cases of child abuse.

Justice for Children is a nonprofit organization of volunteers concerned about children's rights and protection from abuse. Its national headquarters is in Houston, but there are regional offices in Washington, D.C., and Scottsdale, Arizona. Burton says that JFC handles about six thousand calls a year from all fifty states; the problems that are presented are "identical." The organization's mission is "to raise the consciousness of our society about the failure of our governmental agencies to protect victims of child abuse, to provide legal advocacy for abused children, and to develop and implement, on a collaborative basis where possible, a full range of solutions that enhance the quality of life for these children."[1] JFC won the American Bar Association's Public Service Award in 2001 for its exemplary Houston Young Lawyers Association Attorney Training Program.

Child abuse, Burton says, is a huge problem, and a major obstacle in dealing well with child abuse cases is Child Protective Services (CPS), the very agency that is meant to protect children. For many years—before *Women on Trial,* before the round-the-clock protest at the Family Law Center, before CourtWatch—Houston had a serious child abuse problem. In 1986 alone, thirty-six children reportedly died of abuse or neglect. By 1991 the number had escalated to 103, although only one parent was convicted of charges.

A series of articles in the *Houston Post* examining the role that CPS played in this catastrophe claimed that the agency was hampered in its efforts to protect children by several major obstacles. Fundamentally, Harris County's CPS was "stretched to the limit and beyond," (Gangelhoff).[2] Its funding was inadequate to deal with a huge and growing caseload, and CPS was given an impossible, inherently contradictory mandate. The agency couldn't maintain its commitment to protect children and at the same time meet its charge to keep the family intact since, most often, children had to be protected from abusers *within* their families, and that meant placing the children in foster care, at least temporarily. Since the agency couldn't both keep the family intact and effectively protect children from abuse, they often chose to hold "family preservation higher than the welfare of a child"—the wrong choice (Burton 1993).

CPS also suffered from a lack of law enforcement training or authority. Despite scanty qualifications in this area, once a case was reported to CPS (as it usually was, rather than to local police authorities), caseworkers resisted turning investigations over to the police. But child abuse is a crime that requires investigation by experienced professionals no less than any other crime, and failing to treat it as such was a "throwback to the notion that family violence is a 'family problem' and not a police matter" (Burton 1993). Burton wrote a scathing indictment of CPS, which was used as the basis for an award-winning series in the *Houston Post* in May 1987. He documented eleven particularly repugnant cases of abuse. He is no less critical of the agency today.

For those interested in learning more, Burton recommends reading *Adjudicating Allegations of Child Sexual Abuse When Custody Is in Dispute* (September 1996), a publication of the State Justice Institute, a project that was jointly sponsored by the NOW Legal Defense and Education Fund and the National Association of Women Judges. Randy Burton also wrote the following:

Terrorism Is Nothing New to America's Abused Child
Terrorism comes in many forms. While the September 11th attack on the United States is surely the most horrific attack against innocent Americans in our history, an assault against our country's children of comparable proportions has been occurring silently for years.

Each year roughly 1,300 children are murdered at the hands of their parents. Another million children, it is conservatively estimated, are confirmed by Child Protective Services (CPS) each year as victims of child abuse and neglect. Tragically, CPS closes 72 percent of these validated cases of abuse without providing any protective services whatsoever. It is a small wonder, then, that roughly half of all the child homicides in the United States were previously known by local CPS and that many of the children who are returned to dangerous homes (or never removed to begin with) continually recycle through the system, revictimized time and again by their parent abusers. When a child is left in a "home" with their abusive parents by CPS, it is like incarcerating them with their offender. They cannot escape. The persons that they would normally turn to for protection are, unfortunately, the same persons that are torturing them. And, our government is a passive co-conspirator.

So why would conscious decisions be made to send little children back into these hellish environments? The answer is a little-known concept that drives virtually all CPS and court decisions pertaining to the custody of abused children known as "family preservation." Family preservation can be traced back to the earliest roots of our child-welfare establishment, where it was stated that it is "better to save the home from the child than to save the child from the home." This well-intentioned policy has been the goal of all CPS decision making for a century and, since 1980, has been the focus of federal funding for local CPS organizations.

Justice for Children has long held that it is this policy that is directly responsible for unnecessary suffering for millions of our nation's children. Family preservation is a throwback to the notion that child abuse is a "family problem," not a crime, and should be handled by the family. The system argues that because the child "loves" his or her parents, rehabilitating the family is better than breaking it up. This attitude fails to recognize that children love their parents unconditionally, regardless of their flaws and regardless of abuse. Such love is no different than that found in the domestic violence situation in which the battered spouse stays in an abusive relationship because she loves her abuser.

One aspect of this analogy is critically different, however. In the child abuse scenario, the rights of the abuser are seen by CPS as superior to those of the victimized and blameless child. Were the victim to be a woman, it would be unthinkable for society to force the battered victim to live with her batterer or the rape victim to live with her rapist. This would be as crazy as turning our society over to terrorists. For the child victim who cannot escape and in some instances has not even learned to talk, the unthinkable is the norm.

In 1997, the federal funding legislation was rewritten with the help of Justice for Children. Under the Adoption and Safe Families Act (ASFA), federal funds will support family preservation only where the home is safe. As a matter of law, the new priority of CPS is the protection of the child, not the preservation of the family. Sadly, successful implementation of this law has been difficult due to the entrenched family preservation bias in state laws and policies, CPS training curricula, and the attitudes of caseworkers and administrators.

Any continued resistance to the ASFA should be shattered by a recently published study on the results of family preservation. Already under attack from child advocacy organizations such as Justice for Children and public policy makers, this six-year definitive study by the renowned Kempe Children's Center in Denver compared outcomes for children who were reunified with their biological families after placement in foster care with children who were not reunified. The results are compelling. Compared with youth who were not reunified, reunified children "showed more self-destructive behavior, substance use, risk behaviors, arrests, lower grades, total behavior problems, and lower total competence." More importantly, the study notes that children themselves "thought that it was in their best interest [to be placed in foster care] and reported that things would have gotten worse at home without . . . intervention."

On September 9, two days before the terrorist attack, the *Washington Post* published a landmark four-part series entitled "The District's Lost Children: A Decade of Deadly Mistakes." The lead story in that Sunday's *Post* described how "critical errors in the City's [child protective] network were found in 40 child fatalities . . . Confidential files show a wide pattern of official neglect." Let's hope that with this problem so magnified in Congress's own back yard, government will finally address the issue which most of the rest of the country has already faced: the existing system has failed our children.

Domestic Violence and Mediation

In the past, domestic violence was a closely guarded family secret. When the violence escalated—as it inevitably did—and could no longer be kept in the family closet, the police had to be summoned, but they were usually reluctant to intercede. Such attitudes are grounded in the history of domestic violence and cultural beliefs which, we know, resist change.

Numerous studies have shown that officers who responded to a family violence call, even when the abuse was obvious, did not usually make an arrest unless the victim signed an arrest warrant.[1] Exceptions occurred when the abuser had been drinking or was disrespectful to the police. Police officers thought of family violence as a private matter best dealt with within the home. In addition, blame for the violence was often placed on the victim rather than on the abuser. Often, officers underestimated the degree of violence, believing that most incidents of family violence involved nothing more than a slap or a push—a myth that continue to persist.

Attitudes have also been conditioned by "countless misconceptions about domestic violence," myths which are tied not only to views about family privacy but also to common stereotypes, particularly those related to gender role, race, and social class. Among them are the following:[2]

Myth: Women usually provoke the violence. Fact: Women may be more persistent about discussing an issue, which may provoke an argument. But when the argument becomes violent, it becomes illegal. Nothing justifies physical abuse; it is a criminal act.

Myth: Women are the only victims and men are the only abusers. Fact: Women can abuse, but men are the perpetrators 90 percent of the time. Furthermore, 70 percent of the men who abuse women also tend to abuse children. In 2002, the U.S. Department of Health and Human Services estimated that almost one million children were beaten by family members (Pear 2004).[3] Family violence touches all relationships; elder abuse is a phenomenon that is also becoming widespread.

Myth: Children are not aware of what's going on. Fact: Children are very perceptive; they have been effective in providing witness testimony. Children also suffer in another way, because domestic violence is the primary cause of homelessness in the United States.

Myth: Battered women who remain in violent relationships do so because they're masochistic. Fact: Most women who remain in abusive relationships do so for a number of well-founded reasons, including fear of disrupting the children or permanently losing custody and fear that the abuser will hunt them down and kill them.[4] Women may be totally dependent on their intimate partners financially, and psychologically they may be bonded to these partners through their shared trauma and complex coping mechanisms.

Myth: Family violence is a problem only in the lower socioeconomic classes. Fact: Family violence is a pervasive problem that occurs in all social classes, religions, races, and ethnic groups. The problem is more visible in the lower class because it is more frequently reported there.

Myth: If she leaves, it is over. Fact: This is an unfortunate and dangerous belief. The most perilous time for a woman is when she tries to leave. Violence often increases after a woman leaves, and this is when most deadly encounters within couples occur. Therefore, it is not in the woman's interest to leave without an appropriate safety plan.

Despite the persistence of these and other myths, within the law the situation has changed dramatically since the early 1970s. At that time, feminists began describing the nature and extent of domestic violence, in part through victims' narratives. They also identified patterns of abusive behavior that are still useful. In a recent women's health advisory, the Mayo Clinic Department of Family Medicine referred to just such patterns of abuse, including being jealous and possessive; being nice, then irrational and upset; throwing and breaking things; making humiliating comments such as name calling; threatening or intimidating the children; isolating the intimate partner from family and friends; controlling the money; blaming the partner for all of the problems; locking him or her out or in; hitting or forcible sex ("Domestic Violence").

Feminist writers also defined and elaborated upon a concept, first used by psychologist Lenore Walker in her 1980 book *The Battered Woman,* that has come to be known as the "battered woman's syndrome." It refers to the long-term effects of violence, which make the victim feel both that she cannot control what is happening and that resistance or escape is impossible. The concept of battered woman's syndrome has helped judges and juries understand why a victim does not simply solve the problem by leaving (Chamallas, 257).

In the 1970s, as feminists gathered statistics on the incidence and destructiveness of family violence, allegations of its magnitude were supported with shocking data. Twenty years later, in 1994, the numbers were still appalling. According to Violence Against Women, a survey conducted by the U.S. Department of Justice, half a million assaults were reported yearly to federal officials. But even that large number, it was believed, represented a fraction of the assaults, which were estimated to be between two and four million. Another example of under-reportage was the number of sexual assaults: only 132,000 were reported, while the estimated number was 1.2 million. In 1994, four women were killed by intimate partners in this country *each day*! What made that figure even more egregious was that in most cases of family violence fatality there was a documented history of physical abuse. In addition, pregnant women who reported having been battered required twice the health care needs and costs. Countless numbers of children witnessed these violent acts and were four times as likely to become juvenile offenders than children who had not witnessed violence.

Sadly, domestic violence data have hardly changed. It is estimated that four million women in the United States suffer abuse from their intimate partners or ex-partners each year ("Domestic Violence"); 60 percent are abused when they are pregnant and are often, if inconceivably, beaten in the stomach.[5] According to a recent FBI report, family violence is the single major cause of injury to women.

The Texas data are also discouraging.[6] Texas alone reported almost 200,000 incidents of family violence in 2001. The worst news was that Texas figures for women killed tends to be higher than the national average (in 1997 it was 7 percent higher); about six hundred women were murdered by intimate male partners in the five-year period from 1997 to 2001. Currently, domestic violence accounts for nearly half of all police calls in Texas. An even more surprising finding provided by the Texas Department of Human Services is that in 2000, more than 615 officers were assaulted during the course of a family violence incident. Officers are cautioned that incidences of family violence can be one of the most dangerous situations they encounter.

In 1994, the Gender Bias Task Force of Texas made a number of recommendations similar to those made by other such studies that had been conducted throughout the country. The Texas task force was especially concerned about training for judges, attorneys, and other law enforcement personnel so that they would understand the "dynamics of domestic violence" as well as the "options available for the disposition of cases" (*Gender Bias Task Force Report*, 9).[7] The task force found that the Texas justice system did not protect women. Orders of protection were not adequately enforced, victims of domestic violence had difficulty obtaining legal assistance, and when they did, they faced "discriminatory attitudes" throughout the legal hierarchy, from police officers to judges (*Gender Bias Task Force Report*, 5). The task force found that problems arose from the perception on the part of some of the judiciary and law enforcement officials that domestic violence was not as serious as other criminal acts. These officials were also inclined to believe that women lied about their experiences, and that they themselves provoked the violence. One judge was quoted as asking a battered woman, "What did you do to cause him to hit you?" (*Gender Bias Task Force Report*, 76).

Since that time, the Texas Commission on Law Enforcement optimistically reports that "family courts have undergone major institutional reforms, enhanced their technology, implemented automated case tracking systems, protected the victim's confidentiality rights, and have made the offender more accountable. Some courts are providing 24-hour service for issuing protective orders, as well as providing pro bono attorneys and other resources. Research indicates that victims are being assisted and their legal rights are being protected through the enforcement of court orders [orders of protection]" ("Family Violence," Appendix C).

In 1994, the National Organization for Women, the NOW Legal Defense and Education Fund, and other organizations finally secured passage of the Violence Against Women Act, which provided a $1.8 billion budget to address issues of family violence. This was a major breakthrough. The act has allowed federal and state agencies to work collaboratively through innovative programs, hotlines, a crime victims rights and compensation program, a sex offender registration and notification system, and statutes protecting family violence victims. One of the major changes is that warrantless arrests are possible when the police officer sees probably cause, even if the victim does not wish to prosecute.

The American Bar Association advocates that all law students should be taught to screen for domestic violence and to conduct safety planning with victims of domestic violence. Equally important is that police officers are trained in how to deal with domestic violence complaints. The ABA also advises the general public that domestic violence is now a crime in all states, although each state's laws are a little different *(Know Your Rights)*.

Domestic violence can be handled in three types of courts. In criminal court, the state will prosecute the abuser for crimes including abuse of an intimate partner, violation of a protective order, elder abuse, murder, rape, and property destruction. If someone calls reporting an incidence of domestic violence, the police will go to the scene and, if necessary, make an arrest. In civil court, victims might address the violation of an order of protection or sue for monetary damages. In family or divorce court, domestic violence could directly affect divorce proceedings and factor into determining custody or visitation.

In Harris County, family courts can issue protective orders valid for up to two years, but if the order is violated, Judge Bonnie Hellums says, the court has no power to apply criminal sanctions. Rather, the District Attorney's Office will file charges in criminal court. Harris County's Assistant District Attorney in the Family Crimes Law Division, Beth Baron, says that more than two thousand protective orders were filed by her office in 2003. Others, but far fewer, are filed by private attorneys.

Victims of domestic violence in Harris County can come to the District Attorney's Office for assistance—they do not have to file a complaint, and there is no cost. Following an interview with a caseworker, they may be advised to file for an order of protection or to go to the police. They may be referred to counseling or for legal assistance.[8] Judge Hellums has been instrumental in applying for federal grant money to set up a single physical facility in Harris County in which all services can be offered in the future— perhaps in the family courthouse.

One of the recommendations made by the Gender Bias Task Force of Texas in 1994 was caution in the use of mediation for solving disputes in families that have a history of violence. Since that time, mandatory mediation has been abandoned in most states for cases that involve domestic violence. In fact, an American Bar Association publication for attorneys states that as a general rule attorneys should resist mediation in cases involving domestic violence and those in which criminal charges have been filed ("Teaching Domestic Violence Law"). The ABA (and many others) offer a number of reasons for this standpoint. They cite the significant imbalance of power between the victim and abuser; an abuser may see mediation as an opportunity to continue his control and manipulation of the victim. They claim that the victim can reveal very little in a mediation session without fear of retaliation. And the mediation session itself provides an opportunity for such retaliation, since the abuser knows exactly where the victim will be at a given time. The safety of the victim is critical.

Because mediators could not ignore such predicaments, special training programs are now available and, in some states, required for mediators to become certified. Mediators can learn techniques to balance the power between abuser and victim, or they can have a support person for the victim take part in the session. Since mediation can be dangerous for the victim because the disputing parties will have to meet face-to-face, a safety plan has to be thought out prior to any mediation session. Caucus or shuttle mediation, in which the parties are not in the same room, can sometimes take the place of conference mediation. Advocates believe that, given those types of precautions, mediation is still the best option for settling domestic disputes.

Both Assistant District Attorney Baron and Judge Hellums adamantly disagree. Hellums maintains that it is the obligation of the judge to see to it that the victim is protected. In her court, all cautionary measures are taken—if necessary, an order of protection is issued; Hellums may order anger management therapy; she makes sure that the exchange of children is carried out safely; she orders supervised visitation, and so on.

Not all judges, however, are Bonnie Hellums. It is precisely because of judges who were less informed, less caring, and even overtly biased, that family mediation was promoted in the first place. Alternatives to litigation were sought because the judicial system failed "to adequately address" the needs of "these very same women" who are being cautioned against mediation today (John, 10).

There is still no guarantee that the courts are a better alternative for domestic dispute resolution. Women are as financially disadvantaged in the courts as they were ten years ago; men still usually have greater resources and can afford better counsel. Some critics believe that "the courts further victimize women who have been in an abusive relationship" in a number of ways (John, 9). The legal system has been shown to "increase hostility between the parties." Advocates for mediation claim that *automatically* excluding mediation in domestic violence cases denies a victim what can be "a very worthwhile alternative to the battleground of the courtroom" ("Mediation in Cases").

Clearly, both sides in this debate present powerful arguments to support their points of view. Evaluating each case requires taking into account individual and idiosyncratic circumstances, among which are not only the circumstances of the case but the strengths and weaknesses of the court system and the quality and availability of dispute resolution alternatives. The American Bar Association does not rule out mediation altogether in families in which there has been evidence of domestic violence. Recommending mediation, they claim, depends upon a number of factors: whether the mediator is trained in domestic violence issues; whether the victim can have an advocate present; the victim's attitude toward the process; whether security measures are in place where the mediation sessions would occur and whether the victim would be safe when leaving; and whether caucus or shuttle mediation is available *(Representing Victims)*. Theirs is probably the most reasonable position.

CourtWatch Protocol and Board Members

Candidate's Statement of Commitment

TO: All Candidates for Harris County Family Courts
RE: Consistent Campaign Positions for Candidates and CourtWatch

Is there anything on this list you cannot commit to?

1. I will campaign for improvements to the operation of the family law courts.

2. If not elected, I will continue to work for improvements in the courts.

3. I will make all court appointments based on the appointee's background, training, and experience related to the issues of the case.

4. I favor continuing education about child abuse and domestic violence for family law attorneys and Judges.

5. I will support a court-connected mediation program.

6. I will use low cost programs and non-attorney volunteers when available and appropriate for a case.

7. I will limit campaign contributions from attorneys who practice in family courts.

8. I will not raise campaign funds unless I have an opponent or I need to retire campaign debts.

Facsimile of Questionnaire for Family Court Judicial Candidates

COURTWATCH   A Committee For Family Court Reform

Questionnaire For Family Court Judicial Candidates

SECTION I. - BACKGROUND INFORMATION

NAME_____ Position Sought_____

Address: Office:_____   Phone:_____

              City: _____   Zip: _____

              Home:_____   Phone:_____

              City: _____   Zip: _____

AGE:_____   MARITAL STATUS:_____   CHILDREN:_____

LAW SCHOOL: _____   YEAR: _____

UNDERGRADUATE & OTHER DEGREES (School, major, year)_____

_____

HONORS:_____

DATE LICENSED IN TEXAS: _____   OTHER STATES: _____

COURTS BEFORE WHICH YOU ARE LICENSED TO PRACTICE: _____

CERTIFICATIONS: _____   YEAR:_____

NUMBER OF YEARS IN PRACTICE: _____

A.   Describe your law practice generally: areas, concentrations, firm affiliations, etc. _____

_____

_____

B.   Briefly describe your judicial experience, if any: _____

_____

C.   TRIALS AND APPEALS (As an attorney)

Number of civil cases tried: Jury: 0___1-5___ 6-25____ 26-50____ 51+____   Non-Jury: 0___1-5___ 6-25____ 26-50____ 51+____

Number of civil cases appealed to Court of Appeals: 0___1-5___ 6-25____ 26-50____ 51+____

Number of cases appealed to Supreme Court: 0___1-5___ 6-25____ 26-50____ 51+____

Number of criminal cases tried: Jury: 0___1-5___ 6-25____ 26-50____ 51+____   Non-Jury: 0___1-5___ 6-25____ 26-50____ 51+____

Number of criminal cases appealed to Court of Appeals: 0___1-5___ 6-25____ 26-50____ 51+____

Number of cases appealed to Court of Criminal Appeals: 0 ___1-5___ 6-25____ 26-50____ 51+____

How many of the above cases were family law cases? _____   How many juvenile law cases? _____

D: TRIALS AND APPEALS (As judge)

Number of civil cases tried: Jury: 0___1-5___ 6-25____ 26-50____ 51+____   Non-Jury: 0___1-5___ 6-25____ 26-50____ 51+____

Number of civil case decisions appealed to Court of Appeals: 0___1-5___ 6-25____ 26-50____ 51+____

Number of case decisions appealed to Supreme Court: 0___1-5___ 6-25____ 26-50____ 51+____

Number of criminal cases tried: Jury: 0___1-5___ 6-25____ 26-50____ 51+____   Non-Jury: 0___1-5___ 6-25____ 26-50____ 51+____

Number of criminal case decisions appealed to Court of Appeals: 0___1-5___ 6-25____ 26-50____ 51+____

Number of case decisions appealed to Court of Criminal Appeals: 0___1-5___ 6-25____ 26-50____ 51+____

How many of the above cases were family law cases? _____   How many juvenile law cases? _____

Have you ever been the subject of a Writ of Mandamus?_____If yes, how many times?_____

260

E: Present political party affiliation: _____

Past political party affiliations: _____

F: Have you previously held or run for any public office? _____ If so, identify the office and political party through which such office was sought or obtained: _____

G: List political campaigns in which you have actively participated: _____

H: Have any complaints been filed against you with any agency, committee, commission, or court in this, or any other state? _____ If so, explain: _____

I: Has any professional disciplinary action been taken against you by any agency, committee, commission, or court in this, or any other state? _____ If so, explain: _____

J: Are there any past or pending civil suits or judgments against you? _____ If so, explain: _____

K: Are there any convictions or pending criminal charges against you? _____ If so, explain: _____

L: Describe your qualifications for this position: _____

M: What activities have you been involved in which demonstrate your support for children and families under the law? _____

N: To which organizations do you belong, or have you belonged, or have you contributed money? _____

O: What volunteer work have you done and in what charitable activities have you participated? _____

LEGAL PERSPECTIVES

Children's Issues

1.   If criminal child abuse charges have been filed against a party in your court, would you be willing to consult with the criminal court personnel handling the case?

2.   What do you consider to be the best evidence in child abuse cases?

3.   What laws should be changed in order to provide maximum safety for children?

4.   What new laws are needed to provide maximum safety for children?

5.   What changes should be made in the Court for which you are running?

Court Appointments

1.   What specialized credentials or training will you require of:

      a. Attorneys ad litem?

      b. Mental health professionals?

      c. Personnel who prepare social studies?

      d. Receivers

2.   Will you require your court-appointed persons to submit itemized statements justifying the fees they request?

3.   Will you establish a fee schedule for court-appointed persons and a method to assess these fees according to the relative abilities of the parties to pay them?

4.   Do you favor a continuing educational requirement for court-appointed persons?

5.   What qualifications would you require for attorneys ad litem?

6.   What selection process would you favor for appointments of:

      a. attorneys ad litem?

      b. mental health experts?

7.   Would you appoint guardians ad litem (non attorneys) to represent the children in your court based on their expertise on the issue before the court?

8.   How would you monitor your attorneys ad litem to assure they are complying with your expectations?

262

Would you require attorneys ad litem to meet the children they represent prior to any court appearance?

10. Would you require your attorneys ad litem to talk to the children they represent about their needs, their wishes, and why they feel as they do?

11. Would you honor a parent's request that the attorney ad litem speak to their child prior to representing the child in court?

Part C. - General

1. As a family court judge, who would be your constituency - The families in court?   The voters?   The children in your court?   The attorneys?   Please state your vision of whom you will be serving.

2. What do you believe is the most appropriate way to select judges (elected, appointed, term limits, etc.)?

3. Should children be treated as competent to testify in legal proceedings?

4. The Family Code speaks of "relative qualifications" of the parents. What do you consider to be the three most important qualifications of a parent?

5. Do you believe that due process requires that children be allowed to participate in a meaningful way in legal actions which involve their family status?

6 Discuss the balance between "the best interests of the child" and the black letter law.

7. Would you favor a court-connected divorce mediation program?

8. In the absence of a court-connected program, would you refer cases to private mediators?
If yes, how would you decide which cases go to mediation?

9. Are there any issues you feel are inappropriate for mediation?

10. Would you be open to examining and instituting reform measures that have been proved successful in other jurisdictions in order to: a. Expedite the work of the court?
     b. Bring a higher level of satisfaction to litigants?
     c. Reduce the costs of litigation?
     d. Change the present deleterious image and climate of family courts?
     e. Use the Family Court Services personnel in new, expanded roles?

III. - YOUR AGENDA FOR VICTORY   263
What are the major issues in your campaign?

2.   Please attach lists of your contributors, your steering committee, or a representative sample of your supporters.

3.   Have you set a limit on campaign contributions?   Will you?

4.   Will you accept contributions from professionals who are likely to appear in your court?

5.   Have you sought endorsements for your candidacy?   If yes, from whom?

6.   Have you received endorsements for your candidacy?   If yes, from whom?

7.   Are you willing to campaign on issues of court reform?

8.   What will distinguish you from the incumbents/other candidates seeking victory in the family courts?

9.   State law now mandates judicial training related to the problems of family violence, sexual assault, and child abuse. How do you plan to comply with that requirement?

10.   Please provide campaign literature for the committee to review.

11.   Please provide copies of every report your Treasurer filed with the Texas Ethics Commission.

12.   Why should CourtWatch endorse you?

* * * * * * * *

Before May 31,1994 please mail five copies of this completed questionnaire and all documents requested to:

COURTWATCH,   P.O. Box 570005,   Houston, TX   77257-0005.   An interview will be scheduled after receipt of your material.

CourtWatch Executive and Advisory Boards
EXECUTIVE BOARD

Florence M. Kusnetz, JD, Director
Melanie Harrell, CPA, Treasurer
Susie Alverson
Ellen Brodsky Gaber, CPA
Mary Gollin, JD
Sandra Shafto
Lance E. Wilks

ADVISORY BOARD (AS OF MARCH 1994)

Laury Adams
Joan Alexander
Alma A. Allen, EdD
Elaine J. Altschuler
Carolyn H. Ashe, EdD
Susan S. Askanase
Jeff Baker
Pam Baker
Ira J. Black
Gloria Bluestone
Valinda Bolton
Richard A. Bormet, JD
Davna Brook
Hon. Kevin Brady
Sylvia Robertson Brauer, JD
Alexis Dowling Britton
Robert L. Byrd, JD
Rogene Gee Calvert
Harold E. Caplan, MD
Shirley Caplan
Dorothy A. Cato, MD
Ellen R. Cohen
Hon. Paul Colbert
Rev. Elbert C. Curvey
Shelly Cyprus

Pat Dangerfield
Beth Everts
Raquel I. Fernandez
Diva Garza
Harry Gee Jr., JD
Don West Graul, JD
Jackie M. Greer
Dolores "Lolita" Guerrero
Rev. Dr. M. Douglas Harper
Charles E. Harrell, JD
Gilbert Herrera
Kari Herrera
Michael A. Hiller, JD
Carol Hoffman, CPA
Leonard S. Hoffman, MD
Ellen Howard
Glenda Joe
Karl M. Johnson, CPA
Lisa S. Jones
Gayle E. Kamen
Marcia Katz
Stanley Katz
Ann Kaufman
Rebecca T. Kirkland, MD
Jeanne Lee Klein

Jeffrey A. Lehmann, JD
Alfred E. Leiser, MD
Susan Lieberman
Sherry Lowry
Linda K. May
Rev. Dr. J. Pittman McGehee
Dixie Melillo, MD
Sherry M. Merfish
Hon. Cathy Mincberg
William P. Moore, MD
Lou Beth Nemzin
William K. Nemzin
Doris J. O'Connor
Maureen Peltier, JD
Carole A. Pinkett
Gordon Quan, JD
Rabbi Joseph Radinsky
R. Alan Rudy

G. Kelton Ro-Trock, DPH
Larry J. Sachnowitz
J. Victor Samuels
Rev. Robert I. Schaibly
Hon. Sue Schechter
Richard Schechter, MD
Moses H. Schimmel
Sandra R. Schimmel
Rabbi Jack Segal
Prof. Eugene I. Smith
Elizabeth R. Stewart, PhD
Cassandra R. Thomas
John P. Vincent, PhD
El-Matha Wilder
Sam Williamson, MD
Lee J. Winderman, PhD
James Winfrey
Sally Winfrey

Attorneys for Negotiated Resolution and Collaborative Family Law

In collaborative law, each of the parties in a family dispute—over issues such as divorce, custody, and property—resolve their conflicts via attorneys using cooperative strategies rather than adversarial techniques and litigation. For current information about collaborative law, go to www .collaborativelaw.org.

The following are policies and procedures that were developed for Attorneys for Negotiated Resolution, the Houston organization for collaborative family law created by Florence Kusnetz and Maureen Peltier in 1991.

POLICIES

1. Our goal is to contain and manage family conflict, protect children, and reduce the probability of post-divorce litigation.

2. No unilateral action will be taken unless reasonable efforts are made to notify the other attorney of events which may affect his or her client. Special efforts will be made to contact the other attorney before setting any date that affects the other party.

3. A pre-settlement conference will be given serious early consideration in order to educate both parties on the following issues: a) emotional impact of divorce on children and adults; b) court procedures and what they mean (e.g. filing, temporary injunctions, sworn inventories); c) financial matters (e.g. need for the bills to be paid, court costs, attorney's fees); d) Family Code provisions on custody, child support, spousal support, and periods of possession; e) issues of confidentiality.

4. Avoid taking positions on issues before discussion is held on the above information. We believe in "No conflict before its time."

5. Use standard forms to maximize consistent language and understanding of material.

6. Full disclosure and sharing of all relevant documents will be made by both parties within a specified time frame.

PROCEDURES

EDUCATION

Legal issues: Explain what filing means, when answers are filed, what court is like, the risks and benefits of contested litigation, tell clients about ADR.

Emotional issues: Discuss how to reduce hostility, need for good communication, timing (who is ready for divorce and who is not), separation of spousal roles and parental roles.

Children's issues: Stress the need to protect children from being used by either parent, the effect of conflict on children, what behavioral changes may occur, encourage the use of professional help in developing plans for shared time with the children.

Financial issues: Work on plans to keep payments current, protect credit, separate bank accounts and credit cards, explain need for detailed inventory of assets and liabilities and for documentation, define what is required to be disclosed, explain what happens if assets are hidden, discuss how businesses are valued. Advise clients of how to handle early financial issues without court action, e.g. temporary support for spouse and children, moving expenses, attorney fees, court fees.

Filing in court: If filing, file minimal pleadings. If representing the Respondent, file answer or cross-petition as appropriate. Reach agreement on whether mutual temporary injunctions are justified by the concerns of the parties.

DISCOVERY

Mandatory: Last three years' tax returns, current pay stubs and income information, third-party documents for each asset and liability including retirement funds, valuations on real property, pensions, businesses, and professional practices, disclosure and tracing of any separate property.

Optional: Cancelled checks, credit card records, depositions.
Documents: To be updated upon request.
Goal: To prepare an inventory that each party can verify.

NEGOTIATIONS

Generate all options and alternatives that are possible.

Examine the needs and interests of both parties.

Keep positions flexible as long as possible.

Give the parties ample time to consider the alternatives before proposals are made.

Identify all areas of agreement.

Identify areas of disagreement and confine dispute to those.

Separate the dispute from its emotional baggage.

Do reality testing on the proposals of each.

Search for new options that may change the proposals.

HANDLING IMPASSE

Use outside resources: Mediators, psychologists, accountants, tax attorneys, business brokers, appraisers, financial planners, etc.

Court conferences: Bilateral informal meetings with the court master or judge on how they would apply the law to certain fact issues.

NON-COMPLIANCE WITH AGREEMENTS OR COURT ORDERS

If by client: Make clients aware that their actions are likely to lead to adversary proceedings. Discuss the additional costs involved.

If by attorney: Call or meet opposing counsel to determine if ANR policies are to continue or not. If not possible, give notice that ANR policies are suspended.

FINAL DOCUMENTS

Use evenhanded language. Submit drafts for review. Write the decree to be enforceable by both parties. Share costs of document preparation or split tasks. Have both parties appear at the final hearing. If appropriate, design a ritual closure to this procedure.

Original prepared by Florence M. Kusnetz, JD, Houston, TX

Case Histories

During her professional career, Florence Kusnetz dealt with many of the problems which plague family law practitioners and the family courts. In this appendix Florence describes several particularly illustrative case histories. The cases are factual but the names have been changed.

Paul and Jane

Paul and Jane were acquaintances of mine, a middle-aged couple with two grown children. They had grown apart but were not at all hostile to each other. When Paul decided he wanted a divorce, they decided to seek a divorce mediator rather than an attorney. It was a wise choice.

Paul was a successful man who owned many oil and gas leases. Jane had been a teacher but had not worked for many years. When they came to me for help I could see that the biggest hurdle would be the great imbalance of power that existed. My kind of mediation has always been conducted in conference style, where the mediator meets with both parties in the same room.

Seeing them together confirmed that Jane did not understand much about the marital assets. We spent a session or two with Paul trying to educate his wife about their holdings. At first Jane exhibited real interest, but when the balance sheets and legal documents were put before her, her eyes glazed over and she was lost. At one session, she got such a bad headache we had to cancel our meeting. I suggested that she take some time to familiarize herself with the subject matter. I asked if there was anyone she could talk to who could help her understand the nature of this property.

She said she had an uncle who was an attorney in New York and would ask if he could help. We decided to postpone our meetings for two weeks until Jane was ready.

We set up our next mediation session, and when Jane came in she was carrying a stack of books and a briefcase. She had a completely new attitude. She said that her uncle had suggested someone in our town who could advise her, someone she could trust to protect her interests. She had met with that person and he had taught her what she needed to know to understand and evaluate oil and gas leases. It was no big mystery, only a different form of property yielding a different form of income. She had done her homework and came in fully prepared to talk about property division.

After that session things went smoothly, with Jane fully participating in the negotiations. She had truly been empowered to recognize and bargain in her own self-interest. The mediation concluded with a signed printed document that covered every aspect of their divorce. They then consulted their own attorneys, and the divorce proceeded as an uncontested matter in court.

I could only imagine what might have happened if they had sought legal help instead of a mediator. When there is a gross imbalance of power in a divorce, you usually end up with a very expensive proceeding because the weaker party's attorney becomes a warrior for his client. This erodes the possibility of peaceful negotiations, because the imbalance is transferred to the attorneys. What usually happens then is that the weaker party goes to the most powerful attorney he or she can get, and the battle is joined. If the attorneys know that the couple has money there is often no incentive to settle the case before trial, and the costs escalate. I have had couples come to me for mediation after they got in that position, saying that they had no idea how the case got so hostile when they were not hostile to begin with. In this case, Paul and Jane got their divorce and remained civil to each other, which benefited not only them, but also their grown children.

Barbara and George

For the last few years of their marriage, Barbara and George had been experiencing tension and estrangement. George worked for an oil company and traveled often. Barbara's family lived nearby and she spent a great deal of time with them when George was away. They started to drift apart. The only love they shared was their son, Tommy, who was four years old.

When George got a job assignment to move to Venezuela for two years, they both saw this as an opportunity for a fresh start on their life together. The job was very stressful, however, and Barbara could see that it was taking a harsh toll on George and on their marriage. She started talking about going home. George was torn between his work and his marriage. He blamed Barbara for not adjusting to their new surroundings. He berated her for her dependence on her family. His behavior became increasingly erratic. Finally, Barbara could cope with it no longer and left for home with Tommy.

There were long-distance calls and letters, but George and Barbara failed to find common ground. In fact, they became increasingly hostile toward one another, and Barbara decided that she would seek a divorce. The divorce was filed and the necessary documents sent to George, who hired an attorney to represent him. George's attorney and I were working out the specifics of custody arrangements for Tommy when I was informed that George had a business trip in the United States and was taking an additional day to come home for a visit with Tommy. Barbara was very apprehensive about seeing George but had no objection to letting him visit with his son. The opposing counsel and I worked out an arrangement for an all-day visit at the home of Barbara's brother, since he and George had always had a friendly relationship.

The day of the visit, Barbara's brother and Tommy drove to the airport to pick up George. It was a very happy reunion, and they started back to the brother's home. George had brought a large bag of gifts for Tommy. Father and son were in the back seat of the car, unwrapping the presents, when George took a gun out of the bag and shot and killed his son. He then put the gun to his head and killed himself.

We learned later that George had been planning this act for some time. He had changed his life insurance policies, naming his parents as beneficiaries. He had also signed a new will disposing of all his possessions. He made sure that Barbara would get nothing, and since he took Tommy with him, that his son would need nothing.

Family violence has many different faces. This one was uglier than most.

Alice and Will

Alice married Will over her parents' objections. Perhaps they saw beyond his bluster and braggadocio to something more sinister, but Alice was swept off her feet by this college football player, whose large stature and good looks outweighed her parents' concerns. After they married they moved away from her hometown and had a son. Will was successful in completely alienating Alice from her parents.

Alice soon learned that Will had both a public persona and a private one. He became abusive at home, and when angry he often lashed out at Alice. The beatings became worse. Alice had no one to turn to for help, because she couldn't bear to face her parents and admit that they were right in warning her away from Will. She endured the physical abuse until one day Will struck her while she held their baby. The baby fell out of her arms but was not hurt. It was then that Alice realized that her child was also at risk. Alice sought a divorce and Will, who was then working on a doctoral degree in psychology, had neither the resources nor the time to contest the divorce.

Two years later, when Will was a professor at the local university, Alice sought a modification of child support. The original amount was set when Will was a student and had been very low. Alice had a middle-management job and supported the family, but now their child suddenly had extra medical needs and Alice had difficulty providing for him. She came to me to handle the modification of child support. She told me their background and that Will was still very angry. She did not know how he would react to a request for more money.

Will hired an attorney who bore out the old adage that everyone gets the lawyer they deserve. John W. was a brusque, antagonistic, and unprofessional opponent. His strategy was to stonewall and force every effort and every communication to go through the court, which caused Alice's case to become long and costly. I finally set a hearing on the child support modification to bring the court's attention to Will's deliberate failure to supply the information I was entitled to receive. On the day of the hearing Alice was served with a motion to modify custody and a motion to join the issues of child support and custody together. Clearly it was a delay tactic, since the issue of child support is relatively simple compared to the modification of custody, which is a very lengthy and expensive legal procedure.

In another court I might have depended on the judge's common sense to see through this maneuver to delay the child support modification. But in the court where Alice's case was being heard there was a political appointee who had been appointed to fill a vacancy until the next election. This man was so poorly prepared to be a judge that he literally hid in his chambers for most of the day while his appointed associate judge handled most matters. The associate judge saw no injustice in combining the two claims and promptly did so.

It soon became evident that Will was out to bankrupt Alice through legal maneuvering. He scheduled multiple depositions, and his attorney saw that each was long and expensive. My only choice was to seek sanctions in court knowing my chances were poor with a weak and ineffective judge. An attorney ad litem was appointed for the child, as the law provides, but he was a golfing buddy of the judge who was not interested in the merits of the case. His fees, determined by the judge and apportioned to the parties, were way beyond Alice's ability to pay them. I wondered where Will was getting the money for all the depositions and his own lawyer's fees.

The case finally came to trial, and I was not at all sure that the court would not be taken in by Will's public persona. He denied any allegations of abuse. He developed grandiose plans for how he would educate the child and how he could provide a better life for him. Alice knew he was lying, since he had never shown much interest in the child's welfare.

I searched for a way to bolster her story of what Will was really like. Will had once told Alice of a woman he had an affair with while they were married. He also told her of a fight he had with one of his graduate students. Since we couldn't afford an investigator, I decided to try to find these people myself. I did find the student and he admitted that Will had gotten angry with him in class and slammed him against a wall, but he was afraid of Will and refused to be a witness. Then I tracked down the woman, who told me that Will had physically abused her on more than one occasion. But she would not testify in court because her ex-husband might learn of the affair and try to get custody of their child. I asked her to consider what might happen if Will actually got custody of his son and raised him in his own image. Is this what she would wish for any child? I promised I would do all I could to protect her. She cried and said she couldn't live with herself if she didn't help a child escape from Will's influence.

By the time Alice's case came to trial, the judge had been voted out and a new, inexperienced family court judge was on the bench. We went to trial and the testimony from Will and from the attorney ad litem was damaging. They tried to convince the court that Alice was lying, since no woman would have stayed with someone who was repeatedly physically abusive. There was no doubt that Alice was a good and loving parent. They just didn't believe anything she said about Will's violent behavior. Fortunately, my witness came in and without once looking at Will, shaking with fear, she told what she knew about Will's behavior. She begged the court not to entrust a child to his care. All the while she was in the witness chair, Will glared at her as if he would kill her if he could, and this was not missed by the judge. She was excused and allowed to leave the courthouse.

The modification of custody was denied and the issue of child support was set for another date. But it was never heard. Will left the university, left town, and was not heard from again. The whole thing had been a game with him. He manipulated his attorney and the court. He caused Alice to go broke and worry herself sick at the thought of losing her son.

About two months after Will's disappearance I got a call from his attorney asking if I knew where Will might be—he owed him thousands of dollars in fees. Even worse, the attorney was stuck with the costs of the many depositions he took and would have to pay over two thousand dollars of his own money to the court reporter.

Alice owed me a lot of money when the trial was over too. We agreed that we were both victims of a system that was broken and subject to abuse by those who were out to do harm. This case had nothing to do with protecting legal rights or seeking justice. It was a family problem with personal and financial issues. Courts should not be the only place where solutions to these problems are found.

Alice and I worked out a payment schedule where she could pay off her debt without interest for as long as she needed. After a year, Alice got married and moved out of state. She owed me $6,000 when she left. She still does.

Lily and Carl

Lily and Carl had been separated for six months when the unthinkable happened. Carl took Danny, their seven-year-old son, for a weekend visit and then disappeared with him. Carl had no family in town and no job. Lily was frantic because she had no idea where to look for her child.

Neither parent had filed for divorce, so there were no court orders covering parental responsibility or custody. It was not a case of kidnapping since each parent had equal rights to the child. Lily didn't know where to turn.

Lily came to see me. I explained that the law offered her no way to get a court order to reclaim the child, even if she knew where he was now living. I thought that Carl would probably establish residency in another state. He would file for divorce there and undoubtedly seek custody. And he would ask the court to order Lily to pay child support. Of course, if he did that, she would know their whereabouts and could countersue, but that might take a very long time and be very costly. Lily was unwilling to wait and asked what her alternatives were.

Somewhere in law school I had a professor who explained the doctrine of "self-help." It was a last resort when disputes fell between the lines of the black-letter law in the statute books. There are plenty of examples of this practice. The wife who cleans out the bank accounts before filing for divorce is indulging in "self-help." The husband who pays an attorney an enormous retainer fee with the understanding that any overage will be "returned" after the divorce is also helping himself to assets that are there for the taking at that time.

These are the games people play in the effort for self-preservation. In Lily's case, however, there was more than money at stake. Here was a mother who had always been her son's primary caretaker who had lost her child. She was willing to do anything legal to get him back. I told Lily to ask the people at her child's school and those in her church to contact her immediately if any inquiry or information came in about Danny.

In August of that year, during school registration, Danny's school got a request from a school in Denver for a transfer of his records. I told her to let them send the records and to get the name of the school.

Lily and I carefully orchestrated the following scenario: Lily would fly to Denver one morning and take a taxi from the airport to Danny's new school. She would tell the driver she was picking her son up from school for a doctor's appointment. In her large purse she would have a brown paper bag filled with a school lunch. When she got to the school she would show identification and tell the office that she had to give Danny his lunch and instructions for after school. When she saw Danny she would ask to talk to him in the hall for a moment. If they got that far, she would take the boy out to the waiting cab and leave. If there was time, I told her to change cabs at a convenient stop so the same driver would not take her back to the airport. She would have two tickets for the return trip. I told her all the things that might go wrong, but she was more than willing to take the chance.

Lily chose the day and off she went. I was a nervous wreck. I sat by the phone and prayed that she would be successful. When her call came, I could tell by her voice that all was well. She sounded ecstatic and relieved at the same time. The plan had been a success. The only unexpected event was Danny's reaction when he saw his mother enter the classroom. Lily quickly realized that his response was going to be emotional and quickly placed her finger on her lips to indicate that silence was called for. He got the signal and acted appropriately and followed her out to the hall. She was so glad to be home with her child, I didn't have the heart to tell her that she had to go to court immediately to get an emergency temporary order giving her full custody of Danny. It was the only way to prevent the child from being a football in the fight between his parents.

Lily filed for divorce and temporary orders the next day. We didn't even have to serve papers on Carl. He did not want to fight for custody. The provisions they worked out were fair for both parents and were approved by the court.

This case serves to illustrate one of the lessons learned in the practice of family law. Things are not always what they seem. A parent separates a child from the other parent for reasons that may seem loving and protective. But when challenged, that parent examines whether it was love for the child or wanting to hurt the other parent, or sometimes just wanting to avoid the payment of child support, that was the motivation for the action taken. In a perfect world all parents would be screened for truthfulness, good moral character, and honorable intentions. No one promised children perfect parents, but common sense warrants that children be protected from devious parents with selfish agendas.

Notes

Introduction

1. Because I refer to and quote the founders of CourtWatch (Florence Kusnetz, Diana Compton, and Melanie Harrell) repeatedly throughout the text, I have not cited each reference. They are taken from telephone conversations and written communication (letters, e-mail, notes from personal files, etc.) which each of the women has had the opportunity to peruse and approve. Unless otherwise noted, quotes from Randy Burton, Judge Bonnie Hellums, Kay Kreck, Sandi Hebert, Judge Linda Motheral, Judge Mary Sean O'Reilly, Mary Frances Parker, Maureen Peltier, Phrogge Simons, and Marinelle Timmons are also taken from personal interviews and personal communication. See References.

Before CourtWatch

1. Houston has also been home to medical pioneers such as Denton Cooley and Michael DeBakey. The Texas Medical Center is the largest medical campus in the world, the site of more heart surgeries than any hospital in the world; the first successful artificial heart transplant was performed there in 2001.

2. Family and divorce mediation will be discussed further in Chapters 4 and 5.

3. An article in the *New York Times* on June 15, 2001, discusses this ongoing and persistent problem ("States Taking Steps to Rein In Excesses of Judicial Politicking"). The article calls for an end to the elective system, saying that it is not only time-consuming but is becoming ever more aggressive and expensive.

4. According to numerous attorneys, law professors, and other legal experts such as Linda Greenhouse of the *New York Times,* those decisions could be characterized as having been political since they were a departure from the prior philosophical position of the Court.

5. George Katseras, a good friend, is a judge in Athens, Greece. He was astonished when he learned that judges here run for office. Although the court system in Greece has its own problems, to be sure, judges are appointed on the basis of an examination system, much like other civil servants.

6. See Appendix D for more information on Justice for Children.

7. This is another of the persistent problems in the judicial system nationwide, not in Houston alone. A November 2002 editorial in the *New York Times,* "New York's Farcical Judicial Elections," complained that voters are asked to approve candidates but

in reality the decision is made "by political insiders." They control who "gets to run on the Democratic Party line, thereby ensuring their elections."

8. The American Law Institute has had a major influence upon the development of American legal practices since it was founded in 1923. In November of 2002, the prestigious organization, composed of eminent lawyers, judges, and legal scholars, concluded an extensive study of family law practices. One of its chief concerns has to do with judicial discretion in divorce proceedings; the report recommends major changes in family law that would make judicial decisions more consistent and predictable (Pear 2002).

9. See *Gender Bias Task Force Report.*

10. See the Alice and Will case study in Appendix F.

11. See *Gender Bias Task Force Report.*

12. Recent census figures show that the median income for married couples with children is $60,168, although when both parents work full-time it is $72,773. The median income for single fathers is $32,427; for divorced mothers it is $24,363 (Hacker 2002, 64).

13. See Appendix B, Justice for Children and Child Protective Services.

14. In custody cases in Texas it is possible for either party to request a jury trial. There is a minimal court fee for doing so. But there are a number of reasons why women tend to avoid jury trials. They can be very long and drawn out, thereby increasing an already expensive process; some attorneys trust judges rather than juries to make informed and objective decisions; and data show that women tend to lose custody in contested cases. See Levit, page 20.

Florence

1. The word is derived from the Hebrew word for Germany, *Ashkenaz.* The other major Jewish group, the Sephardim, are from the Mediterranean lands and southern Europe. See Louis Menasche's article in Ilana Abramovitch and Sean Galvin's *Jews of Brooklyn.*

2. But even at its very worst, when the poor neighborhood suffered grievously during the Depression, Brownsville was not the sad community that it is today. It is one of the most destitute in all of New York City. See Greg Donaldson's book *The Ville.*

3. For a more detailed discussion of life in Brownsville see Ford, *The Girls* and "Nice Jewish Girls"; Sorin, *The Nurturing Neighborhood;* and Landesman, *Brownsville.* Additional references can be found in Abramovitch and Galvin.

4. See Joselit's interesting discussion of the various meanings of "eating out" in *The Wonders of America.*

5. See Gerald Sorin's book *Irving Howe* for a discussion of City College in this era.

6. For more on this subject see Ford, *The Girls.*

7. Elaine Tyler May's book is a thorough and convincing discussion of the relationship between the "cult of domesticity" and Cold War ideology.

According to Coontz, data show that the "traditional" family of the 1950s was a new phenomenon, a historical anomaly. She wrote that the fifties were qualitatively different, a reversal in fact, from any other period in American history.

8. See Kaledin, *Mothers and More: American Women in the 1950's.*

9. See Sachs and Wilson, Chapter II.

10. While Stanford's law program was developing, Emma Gillett and Ellen Spencer Mussey were opening the legal profession to women in D.C. at American University. In 1896, they founded the Washington College of Law. But law school admissions for women remained extremely low through most of the twentieth century.

11. The data on female law school enrollments are interesting: in 1963, 3.8 percent; 1966, 4.3 percent; 1970, 8.5 percent; 1973, 15.8 percent; 1975, 22.9 percent; 1976, 25.5 percent (Sachs and Wilson, 232).

12. See Appendix A for a fuller discussion of the "dilemma of difference."

13. There is a basic contradiction in the law, which is that while it is meant to defend against injustice, because it is based upon precedent, it may actually perpetuate the injustice. Western law, as CUNY Professor Patricia Smith points out, "does not invite innovation or self-examination." The application of the rule of a prior case to a present case perpetuates the precedent, or the status quo (Smith, 212). *Stare decisis,* the rule of following precedent, is, therefore, inherently conservative.

Gender Bias and the Law

1. American society is not different from other societies on this point, except in degree—not to say that degree is irrelevant. For example, no one would argue that an American woman's claim that she is still disadvantaged is in any way equivalent to the same claim by a woman living in the Muslim world. The degree of difference is a world of difference. But because women throughout the world share many similar traits, the argument that our behavior is biologically determined is extremely seductive.

2. See Appendix A, Notes on Gender Socialization, for a more fully developed discussion of this issue.

3. Discussed further in Appendix A.

4. Guinier is better known outside of the legal profession for having been nominated for attorney general by President Clinton, who subsequently withdrew her candidacy.

5. An article on women in law schools in *South Carolina Lawyers Weekly* quoted one young woman who echoed Florence's remarks. In 2001, this woman consulted her advisor; she "was struggling with whether to withdraw." Her advisor said that the student "really hated it and said she wanted to cry every day she goes to class." This is not an isolated incident. Although many law schools have made great strides in dealing with female students, it is still such a serious problem that dozens of symposia, workshops, and the like have sprouted up all over the country to discuss the issues of gender bias in law schools. See the extensive bibliography in the Association of American Law Schools' "Getting Unstuck . . . Without Coming Unglued."

6. See Guinier, page 3.

7. A study of law students at the University of Pennsylvania conducted from 1990–1993 found that "women underwent more stress, received lower grades, and earned less honors than their male classmates." See Mangan.

8. Objectivity, an issue that is particularly relevant to family law, will be discussed in detail in Chapter 4.

9. However, these courses are often simply added to, not integrated into, the traditional curriculum. They are similar to what has come to be known in women's studies, derisively, as "add women and stir" courses (see Minnich). An example is a course on women writers rather than courses that include and integrate the work of women writers. The alternative calls for major curriculum transformation, and in fact some law schools are proud to announce that they have been doing just that, most notably the Washington College of Law at American University, Stanford Law School, Washington University in St. Louis Law School, Duke University School of Law, and the University of Kansas Law School.

10. Supreme Court Justice Sandra Day O'Connor doesn't believe that her decisions differ significantly from those of her male colleagues, although one study claims that she employs what would be called a feminine, contextual approach. See Hutchinson.

11. Until the time of the American Civil War, Harvard was one of the few law schools in the country. At that time it was more common for students to "read law" in a lawyer's office and to receive guidance

in return for clerical services. Applicants were granted admission to the bar when they passed an oral examination (even today variations of this alternate route exist, although the examination is much more difficult). As law became a formal field of study, that is, as legal scholarship evolved, it was centered in the developing university systems. Harvard and its dynamic president, Charles Eliot, led the way.

12. Another problem with the emphasis on the Socratic method is that current law practice has many more facets today. In fact, in some fields, lawyers rarely enter a courtroom.

13. Interestingly, she also found that "gender disparities are more apparent in the elite schools regardless of the gender of the professor" (Guinier, 12).

14. I think labeling it "feminist" pedagogy is a mistake. It does the principles upon which it is based a disservice and diminishes its stature.

15. See "Campuses Still Chilly for Nontraditional Student."

Ethical Dilemmas
1. In *ABA Watch*, August 1996, there is a discussion of a 1995 ABA report in which they refer to the "Sisyphus Factor." The report concluded that discrimination against women in the legal profession was a "rampant and enduring problem."

2. Bowman cites numerous references, such as *Curriculum Vitae (Feminae); Clara Shortridge Foltz: Constitution Maker* (she was the first woman lawyer in California); *America's First Woman Lawyer: The Biography of Myra Bradwell; The Invisible Bar* (which traces the history of women lawyers in America from 1638 to the present); and *Excluded Voices.*

3. The *Mishnah,* the commentary on Talmudic law, specified women's rights with regard to when sex was legitimate, but also set a recommended norm for its frequency, that is, how often a man should have intercourse with his wife. It depended upon his occupation. Men who were independent should do so daily; laborers, twice a week; drivers, once a week; camel drivers, once a month; and sailors, once every six months (Shepherd, 40).

4. In 1920, the New York Conciliation Court was founded by Louis Richman (a lawyer) and Samuel Buchler. Its purpose was to deal with matters of special Jewish concern that might be incomprehensible to non-Jewish judges. These included moderating agreements between individuals and their synagogues, handling messy disputes between Jews to keep them out of public civil proceedings, making peace between disputants, and dispensing justice. Most of the arguments were carried on in Yiddish (Scarf, 53).

5. See Appendix C, Domestic Violence and Mediation.

6. Baer notes that by the 1990s, patriarchal family law had quietly and steadily been invalidated. Although some states retained some of these laws, within a ten-year period the Supreme Court made them effectively "dead letter" through decisions in landmark cases such as *Reed v. Reed; Stanton v. Stanton; Orr v. Orr;* and *Kirchberg v. Feenstra,* which "declared that the Constitution prohibited laws based on the notion that the husband was head of the household" (Baer, 126–127).

7. Discussed in Orenstein.

8. Stage theories describe human development as proceeding through a hierarchical series of steps, in sequential and ascending order, that is, from a simpler to a more complex level. Kohlberg's theory of moral development is based upon and corresponds to Jean Piaget's theory of intellectual development.

9. Piaget, too, initially developed his theory of cognitive or intellectual development from exclusively male subjects.

10. See Rhode, "No-Problem Problem," 176–77 and note 27.

11. According to Smith, Margaret Jan Radin offers this pragmatic view.

12. To complicate matters further, not only does family law include a broad scope of cases in ever-increasing numbers, but several cases involving the same family might be heard in different courts at the same time. Using the hypothetical example of a drug-abusing parent with adolescent children, there might be a case dealing with illegal drug use in criminal court, child custody in family court, problems related to the children in juvenile court, and so on. Family law didn't start out this way. Like an old city, it grew into a complicated maze without a plan.

13. At that time, if Florence had designed a certification process for family lawyers, the required knowledge and skills would have included child development, family dynamics, and communication and negotiation skills. Today she would add mediation training to this list.

14. See Appendix C, Domestic Violence and Mediation.

15. The first national organization was the Family Mediation Association, which later became the Academy of Family Mediators. Florence served on its board from 1988 to 1992.

Florence, Melanie, and Diana

1. See Appendix C, Domestic Violence and Mediation.

2. The amended process that is in use in Houston today is known as caucus or shuttle mediation. It is discussed further in Chapter 7.

3. Gayle Cooper was appointed to the newly created position.

4. For an example, see the case of Lily and Carl in Appendix F.

5. Stuart Webb's organization, located in Minnesota, is still active. The Web site is www.collaborativelaw.org.

6. An extreme example of the truth of this claim is the case of Barbara and George outlined in Appendix F, in which there was no warning of the potential for lethal violence.

7. For ANR Policies and Procedures, see Appendix E.

8. Gillece cites Harrell's report to the task force.

9. The attorney had publicly acknowledged what was being inferred. The more common response was given by Michael Wood, who had served as an ad litem, that "campaign contributions did not sway judges' decisions in court" (Greene, 16 May 1992). An interesting sidenote is that Michael Wood was married to State District Judge Sharolyn Wood, who was later reprimanded with regard to the suits against HBO.

10. I tried to contact Jolene Reynolds and Lee Grant for comment, but neither responded. The information about *Women on Trial* is taken from the recollections of individuals involved, as well as from the public record, primarily newspaper and other written sources.

11. The abuse of judicial discretion was of sufficient concern that the State Commission on Judicial Conduct was looking into complaints about how child sexual abuse cases were being handled in divorce courts, not only in Houston but throughout Texas.

12. Dinah Bailey's account is cited in *America Undercover: Women on Trial.*

The Election of 1994

1. One striking finding of the Gender Bias Task Force of Texas was that there was a significant gap in the perceptions of men and women concerning the extent and direction of bias. Females surveyed were much more likely than men to perceive that bias does exist, but the task force found that both men and women experienced discriminatory or inequitable treatment.

2. See Connelly, page 1. In Houston, family court judges had been solely male for twenty years.

3. In 1995, of divorces filed in one year in four states, Connecticut, Virginia, Mon-

tana and Oregon, two-thirds were filed by women. In Tierney.

4. The Paul and Jane case history in Appendix F illustrates this point.

5. A recommendation was made by the Gender Bias Task Force for what has been called "rehabilitative alimony" or "spousal maintenance." This is a sum that is paid by one spouse, usually the husband, for a limited period to allow the unemployed spouse to get training that would allow him or her to become economically independent.

6. A study of 46,000 divorce cases by Margaret F. Brinig and Douglas Allen, both economists at the University of Iowa, reported that the partner who expects to get custody is most likely to file for divorce. This factor "swamps all other variables" (Tierney). In states where shared custody is the presumptive norm, divorce rates are lower. Also, in shared custody, fathers are less likely to renege on child-support payments.

However, most children remain with their mothers. Depending on the state, maternal custody ranges from a low of about 70 percent to a more common high of about 90 percent. (See Baer page 144, Levit page 120, and Levit footnotes 92 and 93 on page 271.)

In her book *The Gender Line,* law professor Nancy Levit examines gender biases in the law that disadvantage both men and women. Research, she claims, suggests that many attorneys advise fathers not even to request custody (Levit, 120). The lawyers continue to give this advice despite a "general trend" in recent years toward allowing the parent who has custody to move (even out of state if it were thought to be in the best interests of the child), which could deprive fathers of regular visits with their children ("Mothers with Custody"). As in all matters related to domestic disputes, however, the issue of custody is very complex. Levit says, "While the empirical evidence is decidedly mixed, the cumulative evidence seems to indicate that gender

biases run in both directions under different circumstances" (Levit, 119).

7. See the case of Alice and Will in Appendix F.

8. Wallerstein followed a group of children in a longitudinal study for ten to fifteen years. Her recently updated study (the children are now in their forties) will be discussed briefly in Chapter 7.

9. The idea of "Unified Family Courts" is one of the ABA's recommendations that could correct such fragmentation.

10. See Appendix D for a complete list of the names of executive and advisory board members.

11. CourtWatch was a grassroots movement of middle-class women, not of poor women, who are most abused by the system.

12. Family courts are part of the civil court system, and in many parts of the country they are not separate from the general civil courts. In 1976, Houston established a separate family court, which was housed in the newly built Family Law Center the following year.

13. The four judges were due to retire when their terms ended in December 1994; Elliott would remain a controversial figure until almost the very last moment. In the midst of a sensational divorce and custody suit that was being battled out between Kenny and Vicky Bingham, the case was transferred to Elliott's court. During the course of the contentious litigation, accusations resurfaced that had been made against Elliott by Jon Lindsay, a political opponent in an election campaign, twenty years earlier. Lindsay, who defeated Elliott in 1974, had charged him with taking free European trips courtesy of "a political ally who wanted county funds deposited in certain banks." Elliott denied the allegations as "half-truths" and "dirty tricks." More relevant to the Bingham case, however, were assertions of "judicial cronyism and insider justice." Vicky appealed to have Elliott removed from the case since he was

said to have connections with both Kenny Bingham's family and with its "politically well-connected army of lawyers" (Ratcliffe). But to no avail; her appeal was turned down by Judge Daggett.

Houston

1. See "A Shameful Betrayal," and Karotkin.

2. See Tedford 1994, and "No Muzzle."

3. John Peavey Jr., the judge who first allowed the use of mediation in the courthouse, was one of those who resigned as a result of this investigation. He was one of the Democrats who had lost his seat on the bench in the November election. Subsequently, he was appointed to the Houston City Council.

4. *TomPaine.Common Sense* claims that the costs continue to grow—exponentially, it seems. By 2000, candidates raised $45.6 million in court elections, double the amount raised in 1994 ("Justice Corrupted").

5. Associate Judge Doug Warne, who took Henderson's seat, has received the highest ratings in Houston Bar Association surveys.

6. Texas is far from being alone in dealing with the issue of judicial election reform. In spite of influential proponents such as Phillips, more than a dozen states including Wisconsin, Pennsylvania, North Carolina, and Michigan have had a difficult time in their efforts to limit the role of politics in their judicial systems. See Glaberson 2000.

7. A few months after Melanie testified, task force chairman Judge Mark Davidson told her that it was her report that changed the minds of three members of the twenty-person task force.

8. Phrogge Simons was ultimately given the opportunity to make specific charges of corruption before a grand jury. But the allegations were dismissed. See Liebrum.

9. Walk for Justice committee co-chairperson Ann Webb told a reporter that Ringoringo had said that she had received death threats and that "if she got killed not to believe that it was an accident." Webb believes "it was deliberate," but the police found no evidence of foul play. See Turner, "Victim Activist."

Phrogge Simons also believes Donna's death was not an accident. Even if it were, she thinks that the effort to indict the driver was very lax (Telephone interview).

10. Escape also offers other support programs—for grandparents and other relatives, for example, who are raising children due to the absence of the child's biological parents.

11. CASA is a program that was designed for juvenile courts by a national organization called Child Advocates. The Houston Web site is http://www.childadvocates.org.

12. According to Florence, the caucus mediation process was devised by a Dallas lawyer named Steve Brutsche, who started an organization called the Attorney-Mediator Institute.

13. In a recent phone conversation, Judge Linda Motheral told me the same thing. Harris County judges have an enormous and constantly growing workload. Motheral told me that two additional judgeships were recently created, but the county assigned the judges to the civil courts. That the family courts were disregarded was very disappointing since, if you look at the numbers, it's clear theirs is the greater need.

14. The Hawaii program, developed by former Maui Judge Doug McNish, is known as Kids First and is required for all children at the First Circuit Family Court in Honolulu.

15. The University of Nevada at Reno offers a program in judicial studies and sponsors seminars in many related areas.

16. See Appendix B for a discussion of Justice for Children's efforts to address issues related to child abuse.

17. In a recent example of the pitfalls of political appointments, the American Bar Association has cited a number of concerns over New York Judge Dora Irizarry's judicial temperament. As a state judge she was described as "rude to lawyers who appeared before her, sometimes screaming and throwing an object in at least one case." The ABA rated her "unqualified." Despite this, New York Governor Pataki endorsed Irizarry's nomination to be a federal district court judge in Brooklyn. An editorial in the *New York Times* claims that this is political spoils, a repayment for her difficult and disappointing campaign in 2002 against New York's popular attorney general Eliot Spitzer ("Pataki's Controversial Federal Judge").

18. In March 2003, the El Paso Commission for Women (see State of Texas House of Representatives H.R. 484) inducted Judge Macias into its Hall of Fame for "countless hours spent educating the community on the effects of child abuse and neglect." Judge Macias is credited with "greatly improving the lives of countless Texas youth by establishing El Paso's Children's Court." One indication of its success is that the adoption rate for foster children increased by 300 percent.

19. See *Symposium on Unified Family Courts.*

20. In 1963 the Conciliation Courts affiliated as the Association of Family and Conciliation Courts, an international organization concerned with providing family counseling as a complement to judicial procedures. The Association of Family and Conciliation Courts has a Web site (http://www.afccnet.org) with links to other organizations, literature and videos, information on conferences, etc.

Epilogue

1. "Six degrees" grew out of work conducted by the social psychologist Stanley Milgram in the 1960s. Milgram decided to investigate the so-called "small-world problem": the theory that everyone on the planet is connected by just a handful of people. In Milgram's experiment, a few hundred people from Boston and Omaha attempted to get a letter to a target, a complete stranger in Boston. But they could only send the letter to a personal friend whom they thought was somehow closer to the target than they were. When Milgram looked at the letters that reached the target, he found that they had changed hands only about six times.

2. Mary Frances has a suit pending against MTA that is being handled pro bono; the attorney thinks she lost her job as a consequence of her testimony.

3. See Chapter 5 for details. The following is taken from a telephone interview.

4. See the Association of Family and Conciliation Courts' publication "Domestic Violence Visitation Risk Assessment."

5. There are also many other reasons that cases, Florence says, "fall between the cracks." For a different example, see the case of Lily and Carl in Appendix F.

6. See more on this in Appendix C.

Appendix A. Notes on Gender Socialization

1. The terms "sex" and "gender" have been assigned different nuances, although gender seems to be the term in more current usage. In this essay I generally use the two interchangeably.

2. See Hartley.

3. For men, according to Virginal Valian at the CUNY Graduate Center, these expectations often work to their advantage. For women, however, the reverse is often true. (See Valian, 9–10.)

4. There are also increasing numbers of women on death row each year. On the other hand, women still account for only 6.6 percent of state prison inmates. And while the female prison population more than doubled between 1990 and 2001, men's incarceration rate is still fifteen times higher than women's. In addition, over 70 percent of women in prison have been convicted

of nonviolent crimes, mostly drug offenses, a rate that is almost the inverse for men. Further, as of data compiled in 2001, the lifetime chances of a person going to prison are 9 percent for men and 1.1 percent for women. See *Incarcerated Women in the United States,* "Women in Prison Project," and Gilliard and Beck.

Female aggression, referred to as "relational aggression," appears to be a growing problem among young adolescents. It takes the form of nonviolent but cruel behaviors, including ostracism. There is debate about whether the problem has always existed and is only now being labeled, or whether, like the increase in female inmates, it is a new phenomenon. See Talbot.

5. According to Diane Ravitch's newest book *The Language Police,* a critique of the textbook industry, there have been some unintended negative consequences due to pressure from both liberals and conservatives. She believes that the content of texts has been compromised by political correctness.

6. See Tobias's *Breaking the Science Barrier, Overcoming Math Anxiety, The Hidden Curriculum,* and *Rethinking Science as a Career.*

Although more women are receiving degrees in science, some studies show that women in science drop out "at every stage of their career in greater proportions than men," for reasons that are poorly understood. Women have been making gains in areas "long considered relatively unfriendly to women." Some scientists say that the "the iceberg is beginning to break up but there's still a lot of ice there" (Angier). Also see David Sadker's article "Answering the Backlash: Gender Games."

7. Goodman reports that on one episode of *Judging Amy,* a show about a single-mom judge who is easily bossed around by her own mother, Amy proves that she has her "priorities straight." She says to her daughter, "This judge thing is cool but the best job I am ever going to have is being your mom."

Appendix B. Justice for Children and Child Protective Services

1. The Justice for Children Web site is http://www.jfcadvocacy.org. The address of their national headquarters is 2600 Southwest Freeway, Suite 806, Houston, Texas, 77098.

2. The following articles also appeared, but the *Houston Post* is out of print and the dates are unavailable: "Even Caseworker Couldn't Save Tot," second in the series, and "Child Protective Services' Dual Roles Can Conflict," last in the series.

Appendix C. Domestic Violence and Mediation

1. Unless otherwise noted, the following is taken from the course called "Family Violence" that is offered online for police officers. See References.

2. Paraphrased from Chapter 1 of "Family Violence."

3. Federal standards for the safety and well-being of children have been violated by a number of states. Some states will be sanctioned with financial penalties if they don't correct the deficiencies in their child welfare systems. A penalty of $3.5 million has been estimated for the state of Texas.

4. Children have been removed from their mother's custody under the rationale that because the child witnessed the violence, then the mother is responsible for failing to protect him or her from danger. See Sengupta.

5. Cited in the online "Family Violence" course mentioned above.

6. The following, reported by the Texas Department of Human Services, is cited in "Family Violence," Chapter 1, page 7, and Chapter 5, pages 1 and 5.

7. See *Gender Bias Task Force of Texas Final Report* recommendations related to domestic violence, numbers 8–25.

8. The address of the District Attorney's Office in Houston is 1210 Franklin, Second Floor, Suite 2160. The phone number is 713-755-5892.

References

Interviews by the Author

My primary sources for information about CourtWatch and the events surrounding the court reform movement were individuals who were eyewitnesses. Foremost among those who were present and involved in the events are Florence Kusnetz, Diana Compton, and Melanie Harrell.

Florence Kusnetz: We have been in contact since I began researching the story of CourtWatch. My first interviews with Florence were by telephone on 1 October 1995 and 22 March 1996. For approximately five days in December 1999 and for several days in March 2001, I interviewed her extensively in person. We also have had innumerable telephone conversations and have exchanged information and material via mail and e-mail. She has provided me with primary sources consisting of CourtWatch archival material, newspaper clippings and articles, and personal accounts.

Diana Compton: Personal interview, 9 December 1999. Telephone interview, 1 July 2003. Diana has also recounted events and responded to questions via written correspondence; she provided me with material from her personal files as well. We have also been in periodic contact via e-mail.

Melanie Harrell: Telephone interviews, 23 April 2003, 7 July 2003. In written correspondence, Melanie has recounted events, responded to questions, and provided me with material from her personal files. We have been in periodic contact via e-mail.

In addition:

Baron, Beth. Telephone interview, 30 April 2004.

Bosker, Brett. Telephone interview, 9 June 2003.

Burton, Randy. Telephone interviews, 29 March 2003, 4 July 2003, 12 August 2003. In addition, we communicated via mail and e-mail and he provided me with material from his personal files.

Hebert, Sandi. Telephone interview, 4 November 2003.

Hellums, Bonnie. Personal interview, 9 December 1999. Telephone interviews, 12 August 2003, 30 April 2004.

Kreck, Kay. Telephone interview, 10 December 1999.

Motheral, Linda. Personal interview, 10 December 1999. Telephone interview, 14 October 2003.

O'Reilly, Mary Sean. Personal interview, 9 December 1999. Telephone interview, 13 August 2003.

Parker, Mary Frances. Telephone interview, 14 October 2003.

Peltier, Maureen. Telephone interview, 9 June 2003. In addition, she provided me with material related to Attorneys for Negotiated Resolution and collaborative law.

Simons, Phrogge. Telephone interview, 11 November 2003.

Timmons, Marinelle. Telephone interview, 12 October 2003.

Williamson, Claudia. Personal interview, 9 December 1999.

Publications

ABA *Watch*. August 1996. Washington, DC: The Federalist Society for Law and Public Policy Studies. http://www.fed-soc.org/Publications/ABAwatch/abawatch.htm.

"About Women in Law." 21 October 1996. In *Women in Law at the University of Kansas School of Law*. Lawrence, KS: University of Kansas School of Law.

Abramovitch, Ilana, and Sean Galvin, eds. 2002. *Jews of Brooklyn*. Hanover, NH: New England University Press.

"Advice for Women on Choosing a Law School." 1999. New York: *The Princeton Review*. Excerpted from *Best Law Schools,* by Ian Van Tuyl. New York: Random House.

America Undercover: Women on Trial. 1992. Joseph Feury Productions, with Time Warner Cable/HBO. Lee Grant, Director.

Angier, Natalie. 2003. "No Parity Yet, but Science Academy Gains More
    Women." *New York Times,* 6 May, F2.

Asin, Stefanie. 1993. "Family Court Judges Targeted." *Houston Chronicle,*
    9 November, A15.

———. 1998. "Election 98: Republicans Win All Family Court Judgeships."
    Houston Chronicle, 4 November, A32.

Babb, Barbara A. 1998. "Where We Stand: An Analysis of America's Family
    Law Adjudicatory Systems and the Mandate to Establish Unified Fam-
    ily Courts." *Family Law Quarterly* 32 (Spring): 31–65.

Baer, Judith A. 1991. *Women in American Law: The Struggle toward Equality
    from the New Deal to the Present.* New York: Holmes & Meier.

Baker, Adrienne. 1993. *The Jewish Woman in Contemporary Society: Transi-
    tions and Traditions.* New York: New York University Press.

Ballard, Mark, and Richard Connelly. 1994. "Logjam Breaks, but Houston
    Family Courts May Not Change." *Texas Lawyer* (28 February): 1, 30–31.

Bard, Jennifer S. 2003. "Unjust Rules for Insanity." *New York Times,*
    13 March, A25.

Barnard, Jesse. 1981. "Women's Educational Needs." In *The Modern American
    College,* edited by Arthur Chickering, 104. San Francisco: Jossey, Bass.

Barth, Linda. 1993. "Divorce—Houston Style." *Houston Metropolitan*
    (June): 28.

Bernstein, Alan. 1994. "Judge Elections Debated Anew." *Houston Chronicle,*
    10 November, A1.

———. 1994. "Judge Is Fined $1300 for Violation of Rules on Campaign
    Reports." *Houston Chronicle,* 10 November, A1.

———. 1998. "Mean Texas Elections Put Hammerlock on Candidates and
    Voters." *Houston Chronicle,* 8 November, A38.

———. 2000. "District Judge Scolded by State Judicial Panel." *Houston
    Chronicle,* 23 September, A33.

———. 2001. "Several New Judges Fare Well in Survey of Houston Law-
    yers." *Houston Chronicle,* 12 July, A23.

———. 2002. "Judicial Restraint: Family Court Judge Banned from Stay-
    ing with Oilman When His Daughter Is Around." *Houston Chronicle,*
    1 August, A29.

Blumenthal, Ralph. 2003. "After Bitter Fight, Texas Senate Redraws Con-
    gressional Districts." *New York Times,* 13 October, A1.

Bowman, Cynthia G. 1999. "Women and the Legal Profession." In *Femi-
    nist Jurisprudence, Women and the Law: Critical Essays, Research Agenda,*

and Bibliography, edited by Betty Taylor, Sharon Rush, and Robert J.
Munro, 625–643. Littleton, CO: Fred B. Rothman & Co.

Brinig, Margaret F., and Douglas Allen. 2000. "These Boots Are Made for
Walking: Why Most Divorce Filers Are Women." *American Law and
Economics Review* 2: 126–169.

Bronner, Ethan. 2001. "Posner v. Dershowitz." *New York Times Book Review,*
15 July, 11.

Burton, Randy. 1992. "Court Critique Correct." *Houston Chronicle,*
30 December, A11.

———. 1993. "Children Abused by Parents, Agency's Social Philosophy."
San Antonio Express-News, 24 April, C4.

"Campaign 98: Family Courts." 1998. *Houston Chronicle,* 17 October, A30.

"Campuses Still Chilly for Nontraditional Student." 1990. In *On Campus
with Women.* Washington, DC: Association of American Colleges.

Carreau, Mark, and Deborah Tedford. 1994. "Ex-agent Says NASA Sting
Stalled." *Houston Chronicle,* 15 May, A1.

Cates, Sheryl. 2004. "Making Connections to End Domestic Violence."
New York Times, 6 May, A35.

"Celebrating a Century of Women at Stanford Law School." Palo Alto, CA:
Stanford Law School, Office of Alumni Relations and Development.

Chamallas, Martha. 1999. *Introduction to Feminist Legal Theory.* Gaithers-
burg, NY: Aspen Law & Business.

Chickering, Arthur, ed. 1981. *The Modern American College.* San Francisco:
Jossey, Bass.

"Chief Justice Calls for Change in Judicial Selection System." 2002. *Houston
Chronicle,* 25 November, A20.

Child Advocates. http://www.cadvocates.org.

Children and Divorce. 1992. Tucson, AZ: Association of Family and Conciliation Courts, The Family Center of the Conciliation Court.

Connelly, Richard. 1994. "Shaking Up Texas's Male Judiciary." *Texas Lawyer*
(25 April): 30.

"Contempt of Court." 1993. *Houston Chronicle,* 14 November, 2A.

Coontz, Stephanie. 1992. *The Way We Never Were: American Families and
the Nostalgia Trap.* New York: Basic Books.

"Courting Disaster: Partisan Elections Almost Guarantee Some Poor
Judges." 2001. *Houston Chronicle,* 27 July, A34.

Dayton, Kim. 1995, 1996. "Feminist Theory: Select Bibliography." Lawrence, KS: Wheat Law Library, University of Kansas School of Law.

Diehl, Kemper. 1993. "Legislator's Reform Bill Targets Financing for Judicial Campaigns." *San Antonio Express-News,* 28 March, 2L.

Dillon, Sam. 2003. "First Woman Is Appointed as Dean of Harvard Law." *New York Times,* 4 April, A18.

———. 2003. "School Violence Data under a Cloud in Houston." *New York Times,* 7 November, A1.

Dinnerstein, Myra. 1992. *Women between Two Worlds: Midlife Reflections on Work and Family.* Philadelphia: Temple University Press.

"Domestic Violence." Newsletter, April 2004. Rochester, MN: *Mayo Clinic Women's HealthSource.*

Domestic Violence Handbook. 2000. Bloomfield Hills, MI: Oakland County Coordinating Council Against Domestic Violence. http://www.domesticviolence.org.

"Domestic Violence Visitation and Risk Assessment." October 1994. Madison, WI: Association of Family and Conciliation Courts.

Donaldson, Greg. 1993. *The Ville: Cops and Kids in Urban America.* New York: Ticknor & Fields.

Duenwald, Mary. 2002. "2 Portraits of Children of Divorce: Rosy and Dark." *New York Times,* 26 March, F6.

Elder, Robert, Jr. 1993. "Ad Litem Reforms Approved." *Texas Lawyer* (15 November): 1, 22.

Elliott, Janet. 1992. "Court's Task Forces Shape Vast Reforms." *Texas Lawyer* (22 June): 34+.

———. 1994. "After Gender Bias Study, Now Comes the Hard Part." *Texas Lawyer* (4 April): 40.

———. 2002. "Ethics Rules Revised for Candidates." *Houston Chronicle,* 23 August, A34.

Escape Family Resource Center. http://www.escapefrc.org.

"Family Court Judges." 1994. *Houston Chronicle,* 30 October, 18.

"Family Violence." Part of 576-hour online course for police officers. Chapters 1–7, Appendices A–E. Austin: Texas Commission on Law Enforcement Officer Standards and Education.

Fein, Richard. 1986. *The Dance of Leah: Discovering Yiddish in America.* Cranberry, NJ: Associated University Presses.

Feldstein, Dan. 1992. "Fasting, Protest Aim at Legal System Shakeup." *Houston Post,* 2 December, A18.

"Finding More Room for Ethics in Divorces." 1990. *Wall Street Journal,* 27 September.

Fineman, Martha Albertson, and Nancy Sweet Thomasden, eds. 1991. *At the Boundaries of Law: Feminism and Legal Theory*. New York: Routledge.

Fitzgerald, Wendy A. 1999. "Women, Children, and Family Obligations: An Introduction to Feminist Jurisprudence." In *Feminist Jurisprudence, Women and the Law: Critical Essays, Research Agenda, and Bibliography*, edited by Betty Taylor, Sharon Rush, and Robert J. Munro, 431–466. Littleton, CO: Fred B. Rothman & Co.

Flynn, George. 1994. "Family Court Siege Enters a New Phase." *Houston Chronicle*, 20 November, A37.

———. 1995. "Squier Named Family Courts' Administrative Judge." *Houston Chronicle*, 13 May, A40.

———. 1995. "Family Court's Visiting Judges Draw Praise—and Criticism." *Houston Chronicle*, 28 November, A1.

———. 1996. "Appeals Court Ruling Stalls Trial of HBO Documentary Case." *Houston Chronicle*, 8 January, A9.

———. 1997. "Courts Put Divorce on the Fast Track." *Houston Chronicle*, 20 July, A29.

———. 1997. "Judge Faces Jail, Fine over Child Support." *Houston Chronicle*, 19 November, A26.

———. 1997. "Poll Gives Judgments on Judges." *Houston Chronicle*, 21 November, A37.

Ford, Carole Bell. 2000. *The Girls: Jewish Women of Brownsville, Brooklyn, 1940–1995*. Albany, NY: State University of New York Press.

———. 2002. "Nice Jewish Girls." In *Jews of Brooklyn*, edited by Ilana Abramovitch and Sean Galvin, 129–136. Hanover, NH: New England University Press.

Froom, Gregory. 2001. "Law School Sees Steady Rise in Applications from Women." *South Carolina Lawyers Weekly*, 22 October. http://www.sclawyersweekly.com.

Gangelhoff, Bonnie. 1987. "Children Who Die: A System Failure." *Houston Post*, 3 May, 22A.

Garvin, David A. 2003. "Making the Case: Professional Education for the World of Practice." *Harvard Magazine* 106 (September–October): 56–62.

Gender Bias Task Force of Texas Final Report. February 1994. Work Copy. Austin: State Bar of Texas, Department of Research and Analysis.

"Getting Unstuck . . . without Coming Unglued." 1999. Bibliography of the Association of American Law Schools' 1999 Workshop for Women in Legal Education. http://www.aals.org/wle99/biblio.html.

Gilbert, Julie. 1985. "Judge Advocates Divorce Mediation." *Houston Post,* 20 October, A1.

Gillece, Bernadette. 1993. "Blind Injustice: Courts of No Resort." *Houston Press,* 3 June, 12–17.

Gilliard, Darrell K., and Allen J. Beck. August 1997. "Prison and Jail Inmates at Midyear 1997." Washington, DC: Bureau of Justice Statistics Publications, Department of Justice.

Gilligan, Carol. 1982. *In a Different Voice: Psychological Theory and Women's Development.* Cambridge: Harvard University Press.

———. 1986. "On *In a Different Voice:* An Interdisciplinary Forum." *Signs: Journal of Women in Culture and Society* 11 (Winter): 304–333.

Glaberson, William. 2000. "A Bipartisan Effort to Remove Politics from Judicial Races." *New York Times,* 28 October, A18.

———. 2001. "States Taking Steps to Rein In Excesses of Judicial Politicking." *New York Times,* 15 June, A1.

Goodman, Emily Jane. 1999. "Seducers, Harassers and Wimps in Black Robes." *New York Times,* 19 December, 47.

Graham, Marty. 1994. "FBI Conducting Investigation of Family Courts." *Houston Post,* 5 March, A23.

———. 1994. "Family Court Activists Help Assure Change." *Houston Post,* 7 April, A23.

———. 1995. "Justice Dept. Joins Probe of County Family Courts." *Houston Post,* 20 January, A1.

———. 1995. "Jones' Contribution to PAC Questioned in Family Law Probe." *Houston Post,* 4 February, A26.

Grandolfo, Jane. 1990. "Critics Say Houston Far Behind in Mediating Marital Breakups." *Houston Post,* 14 October, A1.

Graycar, Regina. 1990. *Dissenting Opinions: Feminist Explorations in Law and Society.* Sydney, Australia: Allen & Unwin.

Greenberg, Blu. 1981. *On Women and Judaism: A View from Tradition.* Philadelphia: Jewish Publication Society of America.

Greene, Andrea. 1992. "Law Panel Gets Comments, Ideas on Attorneys for Kids." *Houston Chronicle,* 16 May, 11.

———. 1992. "Hunger Protest at Family Law Center Draws National Attention." *Houston Chronicle,* 29 December, A11.

———. 1992. "Spat Erupts between Law Center Protesters, Lawyers." *Houston Chronicle,* 30 December, A25.

———. 1994. "Court Protester Turns Banned Cots into Sign." *Houston Chronicle,* 18 March, A27.

Greenhouse, Linda. 2003. "Justices, 6-3, Legalize Gay Sexual Conduct in Sweeping Reversal of Court's '86 Ruling." *New York Times,* 27 June, A1.

Gross, Jane. 2004. "Amiable Unhitching, with a Prod." *New York Times,* 20 May, F1.

Guinier, Lani, Michelle Fine, and Jane Balin. 1997. *Becoming Gentlemen: Women, Law School and Institutional Change.* Boston: Beacon Press.

Hacker, Andrew. 2000. "The Case against Kids." *New York Review of Books* (30 November): 12.

———. 2002. "How Are Women Doing?" *New York Review of Books* (11 April): 63–66.

Harper, Jane. 1993. "Motheral Gets Family Court Post." *Houston Post,* 2 January, A25.

———. 1993. "Family Court Judge Sues HBO for Libel." *Houston Post,* 14 January, A28.

Hartley, Ruth Edith. 1972. *Sociality in Preadolescent Boys.* New York: Teachers College Press.

Harvey, Brett. 1993. *The Fifties: A Women's Oral History.* New York: Harper Collins.

Hebert, Bob. 2002. "Deciding Who Will Live." *New York Times,* 18 March, A25.

Helton, Anne Stewart. 1989. "Citizen Watchdogs Needed in Our Family Court System." *Houston Post,* 4 December, 1.

Hensel, Bill, Jr. 1992. "Witnesses Say Family Courts Need Reform." *Houston Post,* 6 March, A21.

———. 1992. "Supreme Court Task Force to Look at Abuses in Appointing Attorneys." *Houston Post,* 30 April, A33.

Hetherington, Mavis, with John Kelly. 2002. *For Better or Worse: Divorce Reconsidered.* New York: Norton.

Hodges, Ann. 1992. "HBO Documentary Takes Shocking Look at Local Courts." *Houston Chronicle,* 27 October, 1.

Hofstadter, Richard, and Hardy C. DeWitt. 1952. *The Development and Scope of Higher Education in the United States.* New York: Columbia University Press.

Hull, Mary, and Amy Boardman. 1994. "Few District Incumbents Axed: But Five Houston 'Outsiders' Won Family Court Races." *Texas Lawyer* (14 March): 13.

Hutchinson, Dennis J. 2003. "The Majesty of the Law." *New York Times Book Review,* 29 June, 22.

"Inadmissible." 1992. *Texas Lawyer* (11 May): endnotes, 47.

Incarcerated Women in the United States: Facts and Figures. 2002. New York: Correctional Association of New York, Women in Prison Project.

"In the Loop: No Way to Run Court's Business at Family Law Center." 1991. *Houston Chronicle,* 29 August, A28.

John, Rodney. April 2001. "Mediation and Domestic Violence: An Inquiry." http://www.ontariomediation.ca.

Jones, Kathryn. 2003. "What's Doing in Houston." *New York Times,* 2 March, 13.

Joselit, Jenna Weissman. 1995. *The Wonders of America: Reinventing Jewish Culture, 1880–1950.* New York: Hill and Wang.

"Justice Corrupted." 2002. Advertisement from TomPaine.Common Sense. Printed in *New York Times,* 20 February, A21.

Kaledin, Eugenia. 1984. *Mothers and More: American Women in the 1950's.* Boston: Twayne Publishers.

Kaplan, David. 1989. "Using Visitation as a Weapon after Divorce." *Houston Post,* 13 January, D1.

Karkabi, Barbara. 1996. "A Black History Month Biography: Barbara Jordan Was One of the First Black Women To Make a Name in Politics." *Houston Chronicle,* 10 February, 1.

Karotkin, Lisa. 1993. "A Lender and a Borrower Be?" *Houston Press,* 12 August, 9.

Kaye, Judith. 1999. "Making the Case for Hands-On Courts." *Newsweek* (11 October): 13.

Kazin, Alfred. 1951. *A Walker in the City.* New York: Harcourt Brace.

Kennedy, Tom. 1993. "Women Could Fill More Political Seats, Benches." *Houston Post,* 20 November, A27.

Kennerley, Mitchell. 1912. *The Laws of American Divorce, by a Lawyer.* New York: Mitchell Kennerley.

Know Your Rights. 2001. American Bar Association. Chicago: Division for Public Education.

Kusnetz, Florence. 1986. "Divorce Mediation: Help for Families in Crisis." *Texas Bar Journal* (February), draft copy.

———. 1996. "The Challenge of Family Law in Today's World." *Texas Law Reporter* (February), draft copy.

Kusnetz, Florence, and Melanie Harrell. 1994. "Rid Harris County Family Courts of Cronyism." *Houston Chronicle,* 27 January, A21.

———. 1994. "To The Editor: CourtWatch Has Spent on Campaigns." *Houston Chronicle,* 14 March.

Landesman, Alter F. 1971. *Brownsville: The Birth, Development and Passing of a Jewish Community in New York.* New York: Bloch Publishing Company.

"Law School: Still a Man's World!" 1989. *On Campus with Women* (Summer): 1.

"Law Schools Hostile toward Women Profs?" 1989. *On Campus with Women* (Summer): 2.

Ledgard, Laurie. 1992. "Family Violence Training Law Ignored." *Houston Post,* 19 September, A23.

———. 1993. "Task Force Targets Court Corruption." *Houston Post* 16 March, A1.

Lenhart, Jennifer. 1994. "Family Law System Is Ripe for Reform, Critics Assert." *Houston Chronicle,* 16 January, C1.

Levit, Nancy. 1998. *The Gender Line: Men, Women and the Law.* New York: New York University Press.

Liebrum, Jennifer. 1995. "Family Courts Case Yields No Indictment." *Houston Chronicle,* 24 January, A12.

Linkin, Barbara. 1993. "Judge Previously Accused of Wrongdoing." *Houston Post,* 11 March, A27.

Linkin, Barbara, and Bill Hensel Jr. 1993. "Times Changing for Family, Probate Courts." *Houston Post,* 10 July, A12.

Luque, Sulipsa. 1993. "Convicted Judge Bids Staff Goodbye." *Houston Post,* 10 July, A1.

———. 1993. "Corruption Unit Now High-Profile." *Houston Post,* 8 August, A27.

MacKinnon, Catharine A. 1993. "Toward Feminist Jurisprudence." In *Feminist Jurisprudence,* edited by Patricia Smith, 610–619. New York: Oxford University Press.

Mackson, Oliver. 2003. "Family Court: A Big, Messy Picture throughout the State." *Times Herald-Record,* 16 June, 4.

Madden, Laurie. 1994. "Bipartisan Organization Promotes Family Court Reform." *The Newspaper,* 2 March, A1.

Makeig, John. 1994. "Turnover Will Alter Family Judge Makeup." *Houston Chronicle,* 18 September, 1.

———. 1995. "End of HBO Suit Sought: Network Lawyer to Argue Issue of Free Speech." *Houston Chronicle,* 23 February, A23.

———. 1997. "Ringoringo's Long Crusade Impacted Family Law Courts." *Houston Chronicle,* 20 May, A16.

Mangan, Katherine S. 1997. "Lani Guinier Starts Campaign to Curb Use of the Socratic Method." *Chronicle of Higher Education,* 11 April, A12.

Manson, Patricia. 1991. "Lawyers' Group Prefers Negotiation over Confrontation." *Houston Post,* 7 July, A1.

———. 1993. "*Women on Trial* Harsh Indictment of Family Courts." *Houston Post,* 14 November, A11.

Marshall, Thom. 1994. "Protestor Sleeps under the Stars." *Houston Chronicle,* 15 April, A25.

Mashburn, Amy R., and Janice T. Martin. 1999. "The Three Faces of Eve: Difference, Dominance, and Beyond." In *Feminist Jurisprudence, Women and the Law: Critical Essays, Research Agenda, and Bibliography,* edited by Betty Taylor, Sharon Rush, and Robert J. Munro, 187–199. Littleton, CO: Fred B. Rothman & Co.

May, Elaine Tyler. 1988. *Homeward Bound: American Families in the Cold War Era.* New York: Basic Books.

McCall, Nathan. 1995. *It Makes Me Wanna Holler: A Young Black Man in America.* New York: Vintage Books.

"Mediation and Domestic Violence." Illinois Coalition Against Domestic Violence. http://www.ilcadv.org/legal/mediation_n_DV.htm.

"Mediation in Cases involving Domestic Violence." Georgia Commission on Dispute Resolution. http://www.ganet.org/gadr.

Menasche, Louis. 2002. "Sephardic in Williamsburg." In *Jews of Brooklyn,* edited by Ilana Abramovitch and Sean Galvin, 115–119. Hanover, NH: New England University Press.

Merryman, John Henry. 1969. *The Civil Law Tradition: An Introduction to the Legal Systems of Western Europe and Latin America.* Palo Alto, CA: Stanford University Press.

Minnich, Elizabeth Kamarck. 1990. *Transforming Knowledge.* Philadelphia: Temple University Press.

Minow, Martha. 1993. "Justice Engendered." In *Feminist Jurisprudence,* edited by Patricia Smith, 217–241. New York: Oxford University Press.

"Misjudgment Day." 1994. *Houston Post,* 10 November, A36.

Moen, Phyllis. 1992. *Women's Two Roles: A Contemporary Dilemma.* New York: Auburn House.

Moore, Deborah Dash. 1981. *At Home in America: Second Generation New York Jews.* New York: Columbia University Press.

Morales, Dan. 1993. "Why Texas Needs New System of Electing State District Judges." *Houston Post,* 5 February. Reprinted by Mediation Associates of Houston.

"Mothers with Custody Can *Always* Move Out-of-State." 1996. *Lawyers Weekly US* (3 June): 10.

Moussaieff, Jeffrey. 1984. *The Assault on Truth: Freud's Suppression of the Seduction Theory.* New York: Farrar Straus and Giroux.

Naffine, Ngaire. 1990. *Law & the Sexes: Explorations in Feminist Jurisprudence.* Sydney, Australia: Allen & Unwin.

"New President Named at Penn." 2004. *New York Times,* 23 January, A20.

"New York's Farcical Judicial Elections." 2002. *New York Times,* 2 November, A16.

New York Times Education Supplement. 7 April 1996.

Nichols, Bruce. 1993. "Judiciary under Siege." *Dallas Morning News,* 17 January, A1.

Nissimov, Ron. 1998. "State Appellate Court Throws Out Defamation Suit of Former Judge: Unfair Treatment of Women Described in HBO Documentary." *Houston Chronicle,* 28 August, 37.

———. 1998. "Another Court Throws Out Suit in HBO Case." *Houston Chronicle,* 9 October, 38.

"No Muzzle: Retired Public Officials Also Have Right to Free Speech." 1994. *Houston Chronicle,* 12 October, C10.

O'Reilly, Mary Sean. 1994. In *Gender Bias Task Force of Texas Final Report,* 8, 105. Austin: State Bar of Texas, Department of Research and Analysis.

Orenstein, Aviva. 1999. "Feminism and Evidence." In *Feminist Jurisprudence, Women and the Law: Critical Essays, Research Agenda, and Bibliography,* edited by Betty Taylor, Sharon Rush, and Robert J. Munro, 507–538. Littleton, CO: Fred B. Rothman & Co.

Pack, William. 1993. "Judge Accused of Fraud in Divorce Case." *Houston Post,* 7 October, A20.

"Pataki's Controversial Federal Judge." 2003. *New York Times,* 15 October, A18.

Patner, Andrew, and Wayne E. Green. 1983. "Matrimonial Attorneys Spar in Chicago." *Wall Street Journal,* 8 August, Legal Beat section.

Patterson, Randall. 2002. "Houston Does Not Believe in Tears." *New York Times Magazine,* 9 June, 82.

Peabody, Zanto. 2002. "Election 2002: Family Courts." *Houston Chronicle,* 6 November, A30.

Pear, Robert. 2002. "Legal Group Urges States to Update Their Family Law," *New York Times,* 30 November, A1.

———. 2004. "U.S. Finds Fault in All 50 States' Child Welfare Programs, and Penalties May Follow." *New York Times,* 26 April, A16.

Piller, Ruth. 1991. "Rapist Drops Bid Seeking Custody of Girl." *Houston Chronicle,* 3 July, A29.

———. 1991. "Family Courts Pose Financial Burden in Divorce Cases." *Houston Chronicle,* 25 August, A8.

———. 1991. "Struggle for Justice: Harris County Family Courts, An Imperfect System." *Houston Chronicle,* 25 August, 1.

———. 1991. "Courts Trigger Support Groups: Cases Are Unlike, but Participants Have Much in Common." *Houston Chronicle,* 26 August, A11.

———. 1993. "Judge Claims He Was Libeled As He Files Suit against HBO." *Houston Chronicle,* 14 January, A18.

Rafferty, D. M. 1993. "Now the Public Knows." *Houston Chronicle,* 22 January, A25.

Ramsey, Ross, John Makeig, and Kathy Walt. 1994. "Campaign '94." *Houston Chronicle,* 8 October, A31.

Ratcliffe, R. G. 1995. "Political Big Guns Influence Custody Case." *Houston Chronicle,* 13 August, 1.

Ravitch, Diane. 2003. *The Language Police: How Pressure Groups Restrict What Students Learn.* New York: Alfred A. Knopf.

"Remember the Children." 1990. *Houston Chronicle,* 15 February, A22.

Report of the Supreme Court Task Force to Examine Appointments by the Judiciary. January 1993. Austin: Supreme Court of the State of Texas.

Representing Victims of Domestic Violence. 2001. American Bar Association. Chicago: Division for Public Education.

Rhode, Deborah L. 1999. "The No-Problem Problem: Feminist Challenges and Cultural Change." In *Feminist Jurisprudence, Women and the Law: Critical Essays, Research Agenda, and Bibliography,* edited by Betty Taylor, Sharon Rush, and Robert J. Munro, 121–184. Littleton, CO: Fred B. Rothman & Co.

———. 2000. *In the Interests of Justice: Reforming the Legal Profession.* New York: Oxford University Press.

Rodriguez, Lori. 1994. "CourtWatch Is Embroiled in Dispute." *Houston Chronicle,* 5 November, A29.

Ruse, Michael. 2003. "Nature via Nurture." Review of *Genes, Experience, and What Makes Us Human,* by Matt Ridley. *New York Times Book Review,* 20 July, 11.

Sachs, Albie, and Joan Hoff Wilson. 1978. *Sexism and the Law.* Edited by

C. M. Campbell and P. N. P. Wiles. Oxford: Martin Robertson and Co. Ltd.

Sadker, David. 2000. "Answering the Backlash: Gender Games." *Washington Post,* 30 July. http://www.sadkerorg/gendergames.htm.

Sadker, Myra, and David Sadker. 1995. *Failing at Fairness.* New York: Touchstone.

Sapiro, Virginia. 1990. *Women in American Society.* Mountain View, CA: Mayfield Publishing Co.

Sayler, Robert N. 1988. "Rambo Litigation." *ABA Journal* (1 March): 78.

Scales, Ann C. 1993. "The Emergence of Feminist Jurisprudence: An Essay." In *Feminist Jurisprudence,* edited by Patricia Smith, 94–107. New York: Oxford University Press.

Scarf, Mimi. 1988. *Battered Jewish Wives: Case Studies in the Response to Rage.* Queenston, Ontario: The Edwin Mellen Press.

Schemo, Diana Jean. 2003. "Questions on Data Cloud Luster of Houston Schools." *New York Times,* 7 November, A1.

Schwartz, Matt. 1993. "PAC Aims to Oust 5 Family Courts Judges." *Houston Post,* 9 November, A1.

———. 1993. "Judge Bill Elliott Won't Run Again for Family Courts." *Houston Post,* 8 December, A15.

———. 1994. "Judicial Protesters Reject Compromise." *Houston Post,* 16 March, A21.

Sengupta, Somini. 2000. "Tough Justice: Taking a Child When One Parent Is Battered." *New York Times,* 8 July, A1, B2.

"Sexual Assault Statistics." 2001. Houston Area Women's Center. http://www.hawc.org/statistics.htm.

Shalleck, Ann. 1999. "Feminist Theory and Feminist Method: Transforming the Experience of the Classroom." *Journal of Gender, Social Policy & the Law* 7: 229.

"A Shameful Betrayal." 1993. *Houston Post,* 10 July, A26.

Shepherd, Naomi. 1993. *A Price below Rubies: Jewish Women as Rebels and Radicals.* Cambridge, MA: Harvard University Press.

Smith, Patricia. 1993. *Feminist Jurisprudence.* New York: Oxford University Press.

Sorin, Gerald. 1990. *The Nurturing Neighborhood: The Brownsville Boys Club and Jewish Community in Urban America, 1940–1990.* New York: New York University Press.

———. 2002. *Irving Howe: A Life of Passionate Dissent.* New York: New York University Press.

Sowers, Leslie. 1990. "Unheard Voices: Children, Abuse and the Courts." *Houston Chronicle,* 11 November, Lifestyle section, 1.

State of Texas House of Representatives. 2003. House Resolution (H. R.) 484. 78th Texas Legislature. Austin, 17 March.

"States Taking Steps to Rein in Excesses of Judicial Politicking." 2001. *New York Times,* 15 June, A1.

Stinebaker, Joe. 1995. "Family Court Judges Ask Galik to Resign." *Houston Chronicle,* 8 April, A29.

Surface, Jo Ann. 2001. "Personal Interview with Florence M. Kusnetz, Mediation Pioneer." Unpublished essay.

Swartz, Mimi. 2001. "Season's Greetings from Houston, the Bipolar City." *New York Times,* 25 December, A27.

Symposium on Unified Family Courts. 1998. Special issue of *Family Law Quarterly* 32 (Spring).

Talbot, Margaret. 2002. "Girls Just Want to Be Mean." *New York Times Magazine,* 4 February, 24.

Taylor, Betty, Sharon Rush, and Robert J. Munro. *Feminist Jurisprudence, Women and the Law: Critical Essays, Research Agenda, and Bibliography.* Littleton, CO: Fred B. Rothman & Co., 1999.

Teachey, Linda. 1993. "Hunger Striker Goes to Hospital." *Houston Chronicle,* 10 January, A21.

"Teaching Domestic Violence Law." American Bar Association Commission on Domestic Violence. http://www.abanet.org/domviol/teaching.html.

Tedford, Deborah. 1994. "FBI Urged To Set Media Policy." *Houston Chronicle,* 8 October, A29.

———. 1996. "Everyone Involved Stung by FBI Sting: Jones Is Accused of Playing Politics." *Houston Chronicle,* 3 June, A1.

———. 1997. "District Judge Convicted of Bankruptcy Fraud." *Houston Chronicle,* 7 November, A31.

Tedford, Deborah, and Joe Stinebaker. 1997. "Judge Finds No Political Motive in Henderson Case." *Houston Chronicle,* 8 November, A32.

"Television Hiring Practices." 2003. *New York Times,* 30 June, E2.

"13% of Lawyers in Bar Rated Judges." 2001. *Houston Chronicle,* 15 July, A37.

Thoennes, Nancy, Peter Salem, and Jessica Pearson. 1994. *Mediation and Domestic Violence: Current Policies and Practices.* Madison, WI: Association of Family and Conciliation Courts.

Tierney, John. 2000. "A New Look at Realities of Divorce." *New York Times,* 11 July, B1.

Tobias, Sheila. 1978. *Overcoming Math Anxiety.* New York: W. W. Norton.

Tobias, Sheila, with Daryl E. Chubin and Kevin Aylesworth. 1995. *Rethinking Science as a Career.* Tucson, AZ: Research Corp.

Tobias, Sheila, and J. Rafael. 1997. *The Hidden Curriculum: Faculty Made Tests in Science.* New York: Plenum Press.

Tobias, Sheila, and Carl T. Tomijuka. 1992. *Breaking the Science Barrier: How to Explore and Understand the Sciences.* Princeton, NJ: The College Board.

Turner, Allan. 1997. "Victim Activist Sees Cause Worth the Walk." *Houston Chronicle,* 18 May, A40.

———. 1997. "Activist Dies on Trek to Austin." *Houston Chronicle,* 20 May, A8.

United States Department of Justice, Office of Justice Programs. 2002. *Criminal Offenders Statistics.* Washington, DC: Bureau of Justice Statistics, Department of Justice.

Valian, Virginia. 1999. "Roundtable: The Cognitive Bases of Gender Bias." *Brooklyn Law Review* (April): 65.

Vallance, Elizabeth. 1973–1974. "Hiding the Hidden Curriculum." *Curriculum Theory Network* 4: 5–20.

Van Gelder, Lawrence. 2003. "Arts Briefing: Television Hiring Practices." *New York Times,* 30 June, E2.

Van Natta, Don, Jr. 2002. "Circling the Wagons: White House Spends a Long Day Trying to Distance Bush from Enron Questions." *New York Times,* 11 January, A1.

Villafranca, Armando, and Clay Robison. 2002. "Chief Justice Rejecting Campaign Contributions." *Houston Chronicle,* 13 July, A37.

"Violence against Women in the United States." National Organization for Women. http://www.now.org/issues/violence/stats.html.

Walker, Lenore. 1980. *The Battered Woman.* New York: Harper.

Wallerstein, Judith, Julia Lewis, and Sandra Blakeslee. 2000. *The Unexpected Legacy of Divorce.* New York: Hyperion.

Wattenberg, Ben. 1995. "A Conversation with Catherine MacKinnon." *Think Tank,* PBS, 7 July. http://www.pbs.org/thinktank/show_215.html.

West, Robin. 1999. "Law, Literature, and Feminism." In *Feminist Jurisprudence, Women and the Law: Critical Essays, Research Agenda, and Bibliography,* edited by Betty Taylor, Sharon Rush, and Robert J. Munro, 41–76. Littleton, CO: Fred B. Rothman & Co.

Williams, Joan C. 1999. "The Sameness/Difference (or Equality/Difference) Debate." In *Feminist Jurisprudence, Women and the Law: Critical Essays,*

Research Agenda, and Bibliography, edited by Betty Taylor, Sharon Rush, and Robert J. Munro, 23–38. Littleton, CO: Fred B. Rothman & Co.

Winner, Karen. 1996. *Divorced from Justice: The Abuse of Women and Children by Divorce Lawyers and Judges.* New York: Harper Collins.

"Women and the Law: Women in the Justice System." 1996. In *Elusive Equality: The Experiences of Women in Legal Education.* Washington, DC: American Bar Association, Commission on Women in the Profession.

"Women in Prison Project Fact Sheet." March 2002. Correctional Association of New York. http://www.correctionalassociation.org.

"Women on the Move." 1990. *Houston Post,* 4 November, E1.

"Women's and Gender Studies." American University, Washington College of Law. http://www.wcl.american.edu/gender/womenlaw.cfm

Yardley, Jim. 2000. "Houston Smarting Economically from Smog." *New York Times,* 24 September, 24.

———. 2001. "Death Penalty Sought for Mother in Drownings of Children." *New York Times,* 9 August, A12.

Zimmerman, Alvin L. 1992. "Criticism Is Not Fair." *Houston Chronicle,* 28 December, 13.

Zuniga, Jo Ann. 1993. "Lawsuit Says Court Involved in Bribe Plan." *Houston Chronicle,* 7 October, A26.

Index